THE
EXTREME AGED
IN
AMERICA

THE EXTREME AGED IN AMERICA

A Portrait of an Expanding Population ——————————

IRA ROSENWAIKE

with the assistance of

BARBARA LOGUE

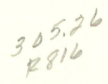

CONTRIBUTIONS TO THE STUDY OF AGING, NUMBER 3

——————————————————————

GREENWOOD PRESS
WESTPORT, CONNECTICUT · LONDON, ENGLAND

Library of Congress Cataloging in Publication Data

Rosenwaike, Ira, 1936–
    The extreme aged in America.

    (Contributions to the study of aging, ISSN 0732-085X;
no. 3)
    Bibliography: p.
    Includes index.
    1. Aged—United States—Statistics. 2. Aged—United
States. I. Logue, Barbara. II. Title. III. Series.
HB1545.R67 1985   305.2′6′0973   85-8014
ISBN 0-313-24857-5 (lib. bdg. : alk. paper)

Library of Congress Catalog Card Number: 85-8014
ISBN: 0-313-24857-5
ISSN: 0732-085X

First published in 1985

Greenwood Press
A division of Congressional Information Service, Inc.
88 Post Road West, Westport, Connecticut 06881

Printed in the United States of America

The paper used in this book complies with the
Permanent Paper Standard issued by the National
Information Standards Organization (Z39.48-1984).

10 9 8 7 6 5 4 3 2 1

Contents

Figures

Tables

Preface

The rapid expansion in the numbers and proportion of older people in the U.S. population has received increasing attention since mid-century. The first major demographic study of the elderly population in America, Henry Sheldon's "The Older Population of the United States," was published in 1958. One of a series of monographs based on 1950 census data, this landmark study helped to establish the elderly as a population appropriate for demographic research. Since that time the number of writers in diverse disciplines who have concerned themselves with the elderly has multiplied manyfold. Gerontologists, sociologists, economists, medical and mental health researchers and others have increasingly become interested in studying this growing subpopulation and scholarly publications have proliferated.

Biologically there is no reason for defining the elderly population in terms of a particular age. Unlike the mutual adolescent experience of puberty, old age does not involve a shared physical threshold. But since many persons retire at age 65 and become eligible for social security, pensions, Medicare and other programs, this age has commonly come to denote the beginning of "old age." While the mere act of reaching age 65 may initiate a major change in life style because of retirement, it does not of itself signify a new period of undifferentiated life experience that will continue until death.

The tendency to group all persons over age 65 into a homogeneous mass is especially detrimental when statisticians and health researchers report their data in this manner. As Eisdorfer noted:

It is unlikely that we would compare all persons during the initial phase of life, e.g., age 0–20 as if they were a unitary mass, yet we persistently do this for persons between ages 65 and 85 as if that two decade spread were irrelevant. Indeed, there is much data to suggest that this is not a valid assumption and that specific age past 65 remains an important consideration with increasing variability occurring with age (1975, p.99).

Within the past two decades, due to the steady growth and increased study of the elderly population, social scientists have come to realize that there are distinct subpopulations among those 65 and over. The segment of the older population that has grown most rapidly and, which differs markedly from the elderly in general, is the very oldest group— those 85 years and older. It is this portion of the aged population that has been chosen for detailed study in this book.

Just as the reasons for defining the "elderly" population as age 65 and above are somewhat arbitrary, so too are the reasons for designating persons of any particular age as the "extreme aged." The population 85 years and over is so identified here primarily due to its recent treatment by the statistical system. The U.S. Bureau of the Census, for example, in its censuses from 1940 on, has used the population 85 years and over as the oldest group for which statistics on certain characteristics (e.g., marital status, living arrangements) have been generated. Similarly, the National Center for Health Statistics, in its annual publications, uses the population 85 years and over as the oldest age group for which death rates are shown. Given these statistical conventions, age 85 has been chosen in this text as the point of entry into extreme old age.

The extreme aged population in the United States has expanded at a truly remarkable rate. Between 1940 and 1960 this population grew from 365,000 to 929,000, a gain of 155 percent. By 1980 the 85 and over group had climbed to 2,240,000, an increase of fully 141 percent above that of 1960. This more than sixfold gain in less than four decades was substantially greater than that of the total elderly population (65 years and over), which climbed by two and one-half times, from 9.0 million to 25.5 million, over the same period. The extreme aged population has thus attained a size which justifies its investigation as a distinct subgroup of the elderly population. But in spite of the current and, more significantly, the future importance of the very aged in

American society, data on the magnitude, characteristics and projected growth of this population remain undeveloped and underexploited.

The justification for a detailed investigation of the demography of the extreme aged is firmly grounded in socioeconomic realities. It is expected that by the year 2000 the extreme aged population may well number about five million and this group is proportionately the most frequent user of the health care system. Social and health planners must begin now to prepare for the expanded services that this growing population will require. Yet relatively little detailed information on the extreme aged is available and some of the published figures are marred by error. Moreover, in recent history, projections of the growth of this subpopulation have been less than satisfactory. For these many reasons, in the face of a rapidly expanding population, it is evident that a reference source for demographic information on the population aged 85 and over will meet many needs and serve as a valuable tool for researchers and planners in gerontology.

Acknowledgments

In the preparation and writing of this book, we have been ably assisted by a knowledgeable team of collaborators, consultants, editors and technical personnel.

We are particularly indebted to Douglas Ewbank who wrote Chapter 10 in collaboration with Ira Rosenwaike; Holger Stub for his collaboration with Barbara Logue on Chapters 5 and 7; and Judith Kinman for her contributions (with other members of the collaborating team) to Chapter 8.The remaining chapters were principally written by the book's authors: Chapters 1, 2, 3, 4, 9, and 12, by Ira Rosenwaike; Chapters 6, 11, and 13 by Barbara Logue.

We gratefully acknowledge the assistance of Janusz M. Szyrmer for his skillful programming assistance, as well as help from Cliff Miller and Stephen Taber in programming; Kathy Kelley-Luedtke and William J. Lynch, Jr., for the preparation of the graphics for the book; Edith Kligman for her major contributions in the organization and revision of the text; William Wortman and Eileen Lynch for their valuable editorial assistance and advice.

Samuel Preston, Philip Sagi, and Richard Suzman provided invaluable advice and guidance.

Above all, we are grateful for and wish to acknowledge the support of the National Institute on Aging in funding the research grant "Demography of the Extreme Aged" (5–R01-AG–03128) that made this book possible.

Ira Rosenwaike
Barbara Logue

THE
EXTREME AGED
IN
AMERICA

1 Population Expansion

The demographic analysis of population subgroups among the elderly is a relatively new phenomenon. Recent statistics indicate that older persons 75 years and over, and especially those 85 years and over, constitute the most rapidly growing proportion of the population in the majority of urbanized industrial countries. Within the American population the extreme aged have increased by over 50 percent in each decade since 1940 (Figure 1.1). As Table 1.1 indicates, this spectacular rate of growth is a new phenomenon, not observed earlier in the twentieth century. Beattie (1976, p. 639) has stated that "it is among those in the advanced stages of life that the greatest proportionate increase is occurring and where the demand on health and social services is the greatest."

Although the proportion of the American population that was 85 years and above experienced continual increase before 1940, the gains from decade to decade were relatively modest; between 1900 and 1940 the proportion in the total population rose from 0.16 to 0.28 percent. By 1980, however, the proportion of extreme aged had climbed to 0.99 percent—approximately one percent of the American people. Table 1.1 indicates that at every intercensal period in the twentieth century the percentage increase among those 85 years and over exceeded that for the total population. Prior to 1930, the rate of growth of the extreme aged never reached twice that of the total population. But each census since then has revealed proportionate gains among the extreme aged from three to five times those for the population of all ages.

TABLE 1.1: GROWTH OF THE TOTAL POPULATION AND OF THE POPULATION 85 YEARS OLD
AND OVER: 1900 TO 1980

(in thousands)

Census year	Total population all ages	Population 85 years and over	85 and over as percent of total	Percent increase from preceding census	
				Total population	Population 85 years and over
1900	75,995	122	0.16	-	-
1910	91,972	167	0.18	21.0	36.7
1920	105,711	210	0.20	14.9	26.2
1930	122,775	272	0.22	16.1	29.4
1940	131,669	365	0.28	7.2	34.0
1950	150,697	577	0.38	14.5	58.2
1960	179,323	929	0.52	19.0	61.1
1970	203,302	1,409	0.69	13.4	51.7
1980	226,546	2,240	0.99	11.4	59.0

Sources: U.S. Bureau of the Census, 1933: Volume II, Chapter 10, Table 7;
1953a: Table 38; 1982a: Table 4; 1983a: Table 45.

FIGURE 1.1: POPULATION AGED 85 YEARS AND OVER: 1900 - 1980

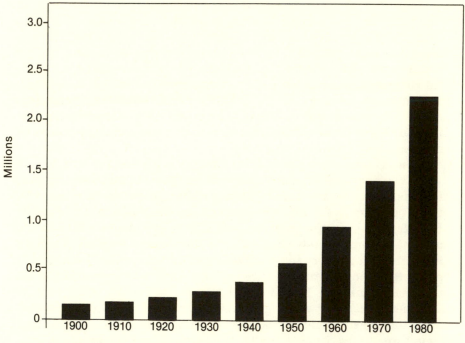

Source: Table 1.2.

TABLE 1.2: GROWTH OF THE ELDERLY POPULATION IN SELECTED AGE CATEGORIES: 1900 TO 1980

Census year	Number of persons (in thousands)			Age group as percent of U.S. total population			Percent increase from preceding census		
	65+	75+	85+	65+	75+	85+	65+	75+	85+
1900	3,080	899	122	4.1	1.2	0.16	-	-	-
1910	3,950	1,156	167	4.3	1.3	0.18	28.2	39.3	36.9
1920	4,933	1,470	210	4.7	1.4	0.20	24.9	27.2	25.7
1930	6,634	1,913	272	5.4	1.6	0.22	34.5	30.1	29.5
1940	9,019	2,643	365	6.8	2.0	0.28	36.0	38.2	34.2
1950	12,270	3,855	577	8.1	2.6	0.38	36.0	45.9	58.1
1960	16,560	5,563	929	9.2	3.1	0.52	35.0	44.3	61.0
1970	19,980	7,533	1,409	9.8	3.7	0.69	20.7	35.4	51.7
1980	25,544	9,969	2,240	11.3	4.4	0.99	27.8	32.3	59.0

Sources: See sources for Table 1.1.

Is this spectacular growth of the extreme aged unique to the age group (85 and over) or does it simply parallel the overall twentieth century increase in numbers and proportions of aged persons in the United States? Table 1.2 attempts to answer this question, with interesting results showing the change in the size of the population 65 and over, 75 and over and 85 and over from 1900 to 1980.

In 1900 there were 3,080,000 persons aged 65 years and older in the U.S., and only 122,000 or 4.0 percent were over age 85. Between 1900 and 1940 virtually no increase occurred in the proportion of elderly who were 85 and over. In 1940, as in 1900, 4.0 percent of those 65 years of age and over were 85 and over; among males 3.5 percent of the elderly were 85 years and above in both years, among females, 4.5 percent were 85 and over at both censuses. By 1940 the population 85 years and over had tripled from 122,000 in 1900 to 365,000.

Between 1940 and 1980 the total elderly population (those 65 and above) increased from 9.0 million to 25.5 million, and the extreme aged had increased from 365,000 to 2,240,000, reflecting a remarkable change in the population of older Americans. With each decade after 1940 an increasing proportion of the population 65 years and over were enumerated at the extreme old ages. Between 1940 and 1980 the share of the elderly who were 85 years and over more than doubled, advancing from 4.0 percent to 8.8 percent as their numbers increased by almost 1.9 million. Among elderly males the percent increased from 3.5 to 6.6 percent during this period; among elderly females, the extreme aged increased from 4.5 percent to fully 10.2 percent.

The data in Table 1.3 make it apparent that a new trend in the age structure of the elderly population began in the 1940s and has continued since; the elderly population in the extreme ages was expanding rapidly, and the proportion in the extreme ages was swiftly increasing from decade to decade.

Changes in the numbers and proportions of the elderly at any given date are the result of the population's demographic experience in preceding years. The numbers in the elderly age group depend on the number of persons born into a given cohort, its mortality experience over the years and the impact of net migration. The proportions in different age groups within the elderly population reflect that cohort's fertility and mortality experience relative to preceding and subsequent cohorts, and the impact of net migration. In general, declining fertility results in an older population age structure, declining mortality can result in a younger age structure if infant and child mortality is reduced relative to adult and aged mortality, and the migration effect depends on the age and numbers of the migrants.

The multifold increase in the proportion of persons 85 years and over results from three separate factors. First and probably best known is the extensive decline in fertility in the century before World War II. The birth rate during the 1930s, for example, was less than half that in the late nineteenth century. As individuals in earlier birth cohorts age, the elderly become an increasingly larger share of the total population because of the smaller numbers in the new generations. Hermalin examined the impact of mortality, fertility and migration on the expansion of the elderly population and concluded that the major demographic force was the impact of declining fertility. "Declining fertility, rather than declining mortality thus emerges as the major factor in the aging of the United States population in the first part of this century" (Hermalin, 1966, p. 452).

A second factor accounting for part of the relative growth of the

TABLE 1.3: POPULATION 65 YEARS OLD AND OVER AND 85 YEARS OLD AND OVER, BY SEX: 1900 TO 1980

(in thousands)

Census year	Both sexes			Male			Female		
	65 and over	85 and over		65 and over	85 and over		65 and over	85 and over	
		Number	Percent of persons 65+		Number	Percent of persons 65+		Number	Percent of persons 65+
1900	3,080	122	4.0	1,555	54	3.5	1,525	68	4.5
1910	3,950	167	4.2	1,986	75	3.8	1,964	92	4.7
1920	4,933	210	4.3	2,483	91	3.7	2,450	119	4.9
1930	6,634	272	4.1	3,325	117	3.5	3,309	155	4.7
1940	9,019	365	4.0	4,406	157	3.5	4,613	208	4.5
1950	12,270	577	4.7	5,797	237	4.1	6,473	340	5.3
1960	16,560	929	5.6	7,503	362	4.8	9,056	567	6.3
1970	19,980	1,409	7.0	8,369	489	5.8	11,610	919	7.9
1980	25,549	2,240	8.8	10,305	682	6.6	15,245	1,558	10.2

Sources: See sources for Table 1.1.

population 85 and above is past immigration trends. The great migrant streams took place between the Civil War era and the beginning of the Great Depression, 1861–1930, during which time the total number of immigrants entering the United States exceeded 32 million (Taeuber and Taeuber, 1971). The average migrant was a young adult, most frequently between the ages of 18 to 35 years. By 1940 and after a large part of the survivors of this vast stream who arrived before World War I had reached the age group 85 years and over. During the 1920s, Congress drastically restricted immigration, and net migration fell dramatically and remained at a low level until the 1960s. By the late 1970s, as a result of a more liberalized immigration policy, the number of newcomers to the United States was reaching annual levels of a half million or more (Reimers, 1981). Hence, the impact of migration on the numbers and proportion of the elderly population is expected to play an important role in the future.

Finally, it is increasingly being realized that a major explanation for the surge in numbers of persons 85 and over in recent decades has been the remarkable improvement in mortality at older ages. Improvements in infant and childhood mortality, it has been demonstrated, increase the proportion of the population in the youthful ages; only reductions in death rates among persons in the middle or older ages bring about increases in the relative share of the population in older ages. (Mortality among the extreme aged is discussed more fully in Chapter 9.)

2 Reliability of Data

The questionable reliability of age reporting for the extreme aged population in the United States has long been considered a serious hindrance to demographic research. Observations concerning mortality among this segment of the population have traditionally included a disclaimer cautioning that reported age of the very elderly in the census is often incorrect, most frequently due to age exaggeration. Reporting of age on death certificates for extreme aged individuals is also believed to be quite inaccurate (Shryock and Siegel, 1973) and, because of this, observed death rates for this group are highly unreliable. Bayo (1972, p. 2) notes that "most textbooks in the demographic field include specific sections wherein the unreliability of the basic mortality data at the higher ages is discussed." Given this history of reliability problems, many researchers have tended to overlook the vast improvements that have been made in the accuracy of age reporting in recent years.

The deficiencies of census data for the extreme aged are well known. Common problems include: (1) overstatement of age to obtain social status and (2) rounding off of age at five-year intervals due to poor memory (Bowerman, 1939; Myers, 1966). Additional errors are introduced by under- and over-enumeration of certain population groups and through nonsampling errors that occur in the processing of census data.

Beginning with the 1960 Census, data processing errors at the Bureau of the Census have marred the published statistics for the extreme aged, most notably for centenarians. In the 1960 census, the published number of white centenarians was about two and one-half times the expected figure derived from alternative methods of estimation (Myers, 1966). Similarly, there were some unexplained excesses in the census figures among persons at certain ages in the nineties (Rosenwaike, 1979).

The census form used in the 1970 enumeration required that respondents both print their age and mark two age-identifying circles. The first circle denoted century and decade; the second circle, year of birth (see Figure 2.1). Yet, in processing these data, the Bureau of the Census ignored printed ages and instead relied solely on the encoded circles as the indicator of age. As a result close to 100,000 persons were incorrectly tabulated as centenarians because they had erred in encoding the circles. This error could have been avoided if the encodings had been cross-checked against printed ages. According to one estimate, 90 percent of these mistabulated centenarians were actually under 65 (Siegel and Passel, 1976; U.S. Bureau of the Census, 1973c).

The procedure used by the Census Bureau with those of unknown age (respondents who did not supply data for birth month or year), compounded the error in the enumeration of centenarians. That is, the Bureau failed to allocate the age of the false centenarians according to other data on the forms as it did with persons of unknown age (2.7 percent of the total population). The latter were assigned an age during computer editing that corresponded with the age stored for the last person processed with the same set of specific characteristics. The failure to replicate this procedure confounded all published 1970 census data for the population 85 and over. A pertinent illustration is that 35,774 persons were identified as the children of heads of households and also purported to be at least 85 years old (U.S. Bureau of the Census, 1973d, Table 204). False centenarians not only account for over 90 percent of all persons in the published census report identified as 100 years old and over, but comprise about 7 percent of the total population aged 85 and over.

The 1980 census questionnaire required respondents to indicate their year of birth by marking three circles: one for century, one for decade, and one for specific year of birth (see Figure 2.1). This more detailed procedure resulted in improved data. In comparison with the 1970 census results, the overstatement error in the published figures for the centenarian population was relatively minor. Nonetheless, the Census Bureau deemed the problem of sufficient significance to indicate that

FIGURE 2.1: FACSIMILE OF THE 1970 AND 1980 CENSUS QUESTIONNAIRE ITEMS ON AGE

1970 CENSUS

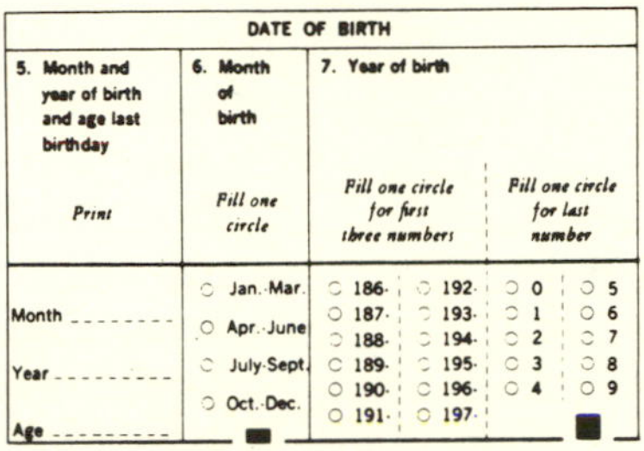

1980 CENSUS

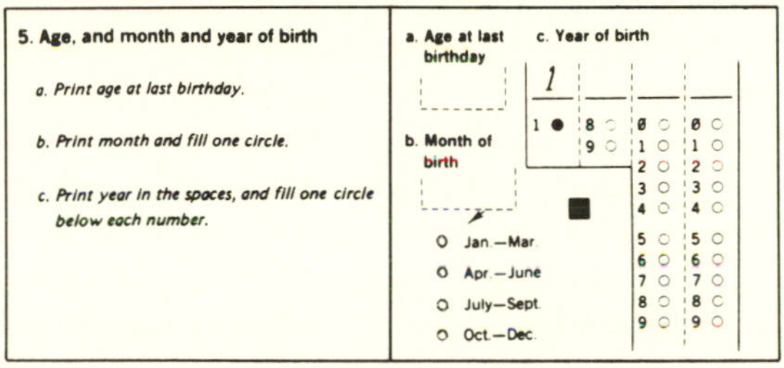

Sources: U.S. Bureau of the Census 1972a, 1983a.

a high count of centenarians resulted in large part from its allocation procedure. During computer editing, the Bureau had allocated one out of every four of the 32,000 persons reported as centenarians to this category (U.S. Bureau of the Census, 1984b). In its postcensal estimates, however, the Census Bureau decided to redistribute the allocated centenarians to ages 85 to 99 years.

The experience of the Bureau of the Census illustrates two pertinent facts: First, census data for the extreme aged are improving, and second, despite the improvement a need still exists for verification from alternative sources of data. The traditional source of age data for comparability with census statistics has been death certificates. Demographers have assumed that age exaggeration is greater in census data than on death certificates (Myers, 1966; U.S. National Center for Health Statistics, 1962). This assumption was supported by the Matched Records Study of 1960, in which death certificates for a large sample of persons who died shortly after the 1960 census were matched with census records for the same people (U.S. National Center for Health Statistics, 1968; Kitagawa and Hauser, 1973). This study showed that, among both whites and nonwhites, the overwhelming majority of decedents with age discrepancies showed an older age in the census.

The Matched Records Study found discrepancies between ages on death certificates and in census reports, but did not examine in detail the extent of age misstatement, particularly its frequency among the extreme aged population. Demographers have attempted to construct independent estimates of the number of persons 85 years and over for comparison with census figures by two specific means: (1) the method of extinct generations and (2) comparison with enrollment data from the Medicare program.

In the extinct generation method, population estimates for the aged are calculated solely from statistics of deaths cumulated until the point at which there are virtually no survivors in a cohort. Rosenwaike (1968, 1979) used this method to produce estimates of the population 85 years and over that could be compared with the 1950 and 1960 censuses. He found that estimates of the extreme aged population constructed from official mortality statistics differed by only about 2 percent from 1950 census data and by less than one percent from the 1960 figures. The high degree of agreement with the latter census largely reflects the accuracy of age reporting among white males and females aged 85–89, who constitute two-thirds of the population 85 and over. The total nonwhite population, as estimated by the extinct generation method, was 12 percent smaller than census estimates. For both races and sexes there were considerable differences in the results for persons 90 years of age and above.

Tables 2.1 and 2.2 provide slightly revised data utilizing the extinct generation method. (The previously published data compared census

TABLE 2.1:   COMPARISON OF TWO ESTIMATES OF THE POPULATION 85 YEARS OLD
AND OVER, BY RACE, AGE AND SEX: APRIL 1, 1950

| | | | Difference | |
Age group	Census	Extinct generation method	Absolute	As percent of census figure
All persons				
Total	577,450	572,014	-5,436	-0.9
85-89 years	429,605	428,949	-656	-0.2
90-94 years	118,695	117,881	-814	-0.7
95-99 years	24,675	20,570	-4,105	-16.6
100 years & over	4,475	4,614	+139	+3.1
White male				
Total	216,325	213,266	-3,059	-1.4
85-89 years	166,005	165,641	-364	-0.2
90-94 years	41,955	41,089	-866	-2.1
95-99 years	7,565	5,779	-1,786	-23.6
100 years & over	800	757	-43	-5.4
White female				
Total	315,810	318,772	+2,962	+0.9
85-89 years	235,710	238,944	+3,234	+1.4
90-94 years	66,890	67,865	+975	+1.4
95-99 years	12,005	10,693	-1,312	-10.9
100 years & over	1,205	1,270	+65	+5.4
Nonwhite male				
Total	18,105	17,059	-1,046	-5.8
85-89 years	11,755	10,921	-834	-7.1
90-94 years	3,790	3,666	-124	-3.3
95-99 years	1,735	1,586	-149	-8.9
100 years & over	825	886	+61	+7.4
Nonwhite female				
Total	27,210	22,917	-4,293	-15.8
85-89 years	16,135	13,443	-2,692	-16.7
90-94 years	6,060	5,261	-1,493	-49.6
95-99 years	3,370	2,512	-858	-25.4
100 years & over	1,645	1,701	+56	+3.4

Sources: U.S. Bureau of the Census, 1953a: Tables 38 and 94; and computations
from U.S. National Center for Health Statistics, Vital Statistics of
the United States, Annual, Vol. II - Mortality.   For method of
computation, see Rosenwaike, 1979.

populations with January 1 estimates; in the present tables, extinct
generation estimates are made for the April 1 census dates.)

The extinct generation method produced more white females 85 years
and above than were enumerated in the census. This indicates that

TABLE 2.2: COMPARISON OF TWO ESTIMATES OF THE POPULATION 85 YEARS OLD
AND OVER, BY RACE, AGE AND SEX: APRIL 1, 1960

Age group	Census-derived estimate	Extinct generation method	Difference Absolute	Difference As percent of census estimate
All persons				
Total	929,252	930,791	+1,539	+0.2
85-89 years	697,770	693,826	-3,944	-0.6
90-94 years	183,584	196,838	+13,254	+7.2
95-99 years	36,756	34,671	-2,085	-5.7
100 years & over	11,142	5,456	-5,686	-51.0
White male				
Total	330,915	324,167	-6,748	-2.0
85-89 years	255,874	249,495	-6,379	-2.5
90-94 years	61,627	64,172	+2,545	+4.1
95-99 years	10,420	9,498	-922	-8.9
100 years & over	2,994	1,002	-1,992	-66.5
White female				
Total	526,700	541,884	+15,184	+2.9
85-89 years	393,244	402,115	+8,871	+2.2
90-94 years	107,409	117,310	+9,901	+9.2
95-99 years	20,928	20,157	-771	-3.7
100 years & over	5,119	2,302	-2,817	-55.0
Nonwhite male				
Total	31,361	27,590	-3,771	-12.0
85-89 years	22,012	18,644	-3,368	-15.3
90-94 years	5,912	6,267	+355	+6.0
95-99 years	2,263	1,909	-354	-15.6
100 years & over	1,174	770	-404	-34.4
Nonwhite female				
Total	40,276	37,150	-3,126	-7.8
85-89 years	26,640	23,572	-3,068	-11.5
90-94 years	8,636	9,089	+453	+5.2
95-99 years	3,145	3,107	-38	-1.2
100 years & over	1,855	1,382	-473	-25.5

Sources: Tables 3.1, 3.2 and 3.3 and computations from U.S. National Center
for Health Statistics, Vital Statistics of the United States, Annual,
Vol. II - Mortality. For method of computation, see Rosenwaike, 1979.

very elderly white females may have been underenumerated in the census. An alternative explanation may be that the emphasis on youth in American culture is prompting older females to understate their age. This age understatement would be a reversal of the expected pattern among the elderly who tend to inflate their age for increased status.

Among nonwhites, who number less than 10 percent of the extreme aged population, Rosenwaike's application of the extinct generation method revealed much more extensive age misstatement than among whites. Although this method overstates the number of extreme aged nonwhites, there is substantially less overreporting than with census data.

An alternative source for constructing estimates of persons aged 65 and over originated with the Medicare program in 1966. Over 98 percent of the elderly population are enrolled in this program. Age reporting in the Medicare program is believed to be more accurate than in the census because, to some extent, proof of age is required to enter the program (Bayo, 1972). In a comparison of Medicare and census data, Rosenwaike, et al. (1980) found: that Medicare counts of the population 85 years and over were about 4 to 5 percent higher than census estimates for 1966–1969, that the differences dropped to no more than 1 percent for 1970–1973, and that Census Bureau estimates for 1974–1977 exceeded Medicare enrollment figures. The postcensal estimates subsequent to the 1970 census were superseded by revised estimates following the release of 1980 census baseline figures. The revised series and comparable Medicare data are shown in Figure 2.2. Tables 2.3 and 2.4 show the detailed statistics while Table 2.5 shows the percent difference between Medicare and Census Bureau figures for each year.

As with other comparisons with census data, there are distinctive patterns of variation among sex-race groups. Medicare-based estimates of white females aged 85 and over are invariably larger than those of the Census Bureau—again indicating underenumeration or understatement of age in the census. Among white males, Medicare estimates were closer to Census Bureau estimates than was true for white females at every time period. From 1966–1983 nonwhite females were generally underestimated by the Census Bureau to a greater extent than were white females. The number of nonwhite males computed from Medicare data was consistently smaller than census estimates,

FIGURE 2.2: POPULATION AGED 85 YEARS AND OVER, BY SEX,
CENSUS BUREAU ESTIMATES AND MEDICARE ENROLLMENT: 1966-1983

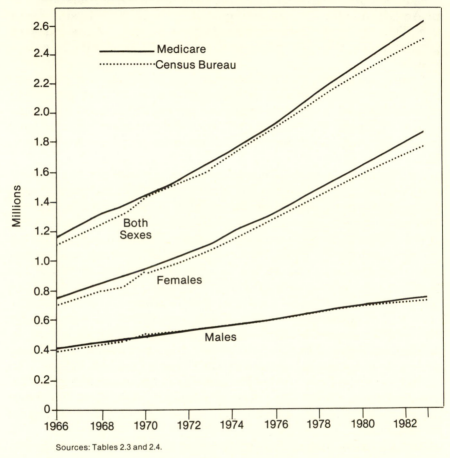

Sources: Tables 2.3 and 2.4.

with the census excess reaching as high as 9 percent in 1970. Exceptions to this pattern occurred in 1982 and 1983 when the Medicare figure exceeded the Census Bureau estimates.

In summary, whatever error exists in the estimates of the population aged 85 and over has probably been fairly small in recent years. For example, between 1970 and 1979 the difference between Census Bu-

TABLE 2.3:   POPULATION 85 YEARS OLD AND OVER ACCORDING TO CENSUS BUREAU ESTIMATES,
              BY RACE AND SEX: JULY 1, 1966 TO JULY 1, 1983

(in thousands)

Year	All persons			White			Nonwhite		
	Total	Male	Female	Total	Male	Female	Total	Male	Female
1966	1,112	409	718	1,039	373	666	89	36	53
1967	1,186	426	760	1,091	387	704	95	39	57
1968	1,241	440	800	1,139	399	739	102	41	61
1969	1,307	459	848	1,199	415	783	109	44	65
1970	1,430	496	934	1,314	450	864	117	46	70
1971	1,487	510	977	1,367	463	904	120	47	73
1972	1,542	522	1,020	1,419	475	944	123	47	76
1973	1,607	538	1,069	1,480	490	989	127	48	79
1974	1,706	565	1,141	1,571	515	1,056	135	50	85
1975	1,821	594	1,227	1,675	540	1,134	146	54	93
1976	1,896	606	1,290	1,744	551	1,192	153	55	98
1977	1,992	627	1,365	1,832	571	1,261	160	56	104
1978	2,095	652	1,443	1,927	594	1,333	168	58	109
1979	2,197	676	1,521	2,023	617	1,407	174	59	114
1980	2,271	689	1,582	2,088	627	1,461	183	62	121
1981	2,351	705	1,646	2,161	641	1,520	190	64	126
1982	2,437	723	1,714	2,240	657	1,583	198	66	131
1983	2,503	734	1,769	2,300	666	1,634	203	68	136

Sources: U.S. Bureau of the Census, 1974; 1982a: Table 2; 1984b: Table 2.

reau and Medicare aggregate population estimates was under 3 percent
in all years except one. In the last few years, estimates prepared by
the Bureau of the Census of both whites and nonwhites at the extreme
ages have been 4 or 5 percent short of the numbers compiled from
Medicare records.

Census data for the extreme aged clearly contain flaws. Age data
for the population 85 and over, however, are no longer as questionable
as they once were. Corrections can be made through the method of
extinct generations, comparisons with Medicare enrollments, and with
improved census editing. A shortcoming of the method of extinct generations is that it does not provide absolute verification of age, but
measures agreement between ages stated on death certificates and
census documents, and thus may report ages that are equally misstated
on both records. Siegel and Passel (1976) argue that age cannot be
verified through Medicare checks because the age reported by enrollees
is not commonly validated at advanced ages. This may have been more

TABLE 2.4: PERSONS 85 YEARS OLD AND OVER ENROLLED FOR HOSPITAL INSURANCE (MEDICARE PROGRAM), BY RACE AND SEX: JULY 1, 1966 TO JULY 1, 1983

Year	All persons			White[a]			Nonwhite[a]		
	Total	Male	Female	Total	Male	Female	Total	Male	Female
1966	1,168,444	414,011	754,433	1,075,177	378,343	696,834	93,267	35,668	57,599
1967	1,245,563	435,500	810,063	1,144,427	397,415	747,012	101,136	38,085	63,051
1968	1,304,091	450,946	853,145	1,198,404	411,759	786,645	105,687	39,187	66,500
1969	1,367,232	467,742	899,490	1,256,899	427,389	829,510	110,333	40,353	69,980
1970	1,441,031	488,079	952,952	1,325,276	446,269	879,007	115,755	41,810	73,945
1971	1,515,327	507,833	1,007,494	1,394,362	464,747	929,615	120,965	43,086	77,879
1972	1,580,010	521,036	1,058,974	1,455,487	477,555	977,932	124,523	43,481	81,042
1973	1,660,519	542,403	1,118,116	1,528,492	496,447	1,032,045	132,027	45,956	86,071
1974	1,745,164	559,192	1,185,972	1,606,981	511,645	1,095,336	138,183	47,547	90,636
1975	1,843,683	583,066	1,260,617	1,696,973	533,232	1,163,741	146,710	49,834	96,876
1976	1,917,676	598,412	1,319,264	1,766,434	547,600	1,218,834	151,242	50,812	100,430
1977	2,030,024	625,202	1,404,822	1,869,714	571,871	1,297,843	160,310	53,331	106,979
1978	2,134,295	649,462	1,484,833	1,965,492	594,009	1,371,483	168,803	55,453	113,350
1979	2,242,629	675,012	1,567,617	2,064,621	617,059	1,447,562	178,008	57,953	120,055
1980	2,341,978	695,602	1,646,376	2,153,417	634,849	1,518,568	188,561	60,753	127,808
1981	2,437,138	713,526	1,723,612	2,239,076	649,698	1,589,378	198,062	63,828	134,234
1982	2,540,214	735,206	1,805,008	2,331,100	668,454	1,662,646	209,114	66,752	142,362
1983	2,630,340	752,271	1,878,069	2,409,924	682,526	1,727,398	220,416	69,745	150,671

Sources: U.S. Social Security Administration, Medicare, Annual; U.S. Health Care Financing Administration, Medicare, Annual.

a. Persons of unknown color distributed each year like persons of known color.

TABLE 2.5:   PERCENT DIFFERENCE BETWEEN CENSUS BUREAU AND MEDICARE POPULATIONS
OF PERSONS 85 YEARS OLD AND OVER AS OF JULY 1, BY RACE AND SEX:
1966 TO 1983

(using census figures as base)

Year	All persons			White			Nonwhite		
	Total	Male	Female	Total	Male	Female	Total	Male	Female
1966	3.6	1.2	5.1	3.5	1.4	4.6	4.8	-0.9	8.7
1967	5.0	2.2	6.6	4.9	2.7	6.1	6.5	-2.3	10.6
1968	5.1	2.5	6.6	5.2	3.2	6.5	3.6	-4.4	9.0
1969	4.6	1.9	6.1	4.8	3.0	5.9	1.2	-8.3	7.7
1970	0.8	-1.6	2.0	0.9	-0.8	1.7	-1.1	-9.1	5.6
1971	1.9	-0.4	3.1	2.0	0.4	2.8	0.8	-8.3	6.7
1972	2.5	-0.2	3.8	2.6	0.5	3.6	1.2	-7.5	6.6
1973	3.3	0.8	4.6	3.3	1.3	4.4	4.0	-4.3	9.0
1974	2.3	-1.0	3.9	2.3	-0.7	3.7	2.4	-4.9	6.6
1975	1.2	-1.8	2.7	1.3	-1.3	2.6	0.5	-7.7	4.2
1976	1.1	-1.3	2.3	1.3	-0.6	2.3	-1.1	-7.6	2.5
1977	1.9	-0.3	2.9	2.1	0.2	2.9	0.2	-4.8	2.9
1978	1.9	-0.4	2.9	2.0	0.0	2.9	0.5	4.4	4.0
1979	2.1	-0.1	3.1	2.1	0.0	2.9	2.3	-1.8	5.3
1980	3.1	1.0	4.1	3.1	1.3	3.9	3.0	-2.0	5.6
1981	3.7	1.2	4.7	3.6	1.4	4.6	4.2	-0.3	6.5
1982	4.2	1.7	5.3	4.1	1.7	5.0	5.6	1.1	8.7
1983	5.1	2.5	6.2	4.8	2.5	5.7	8.6	2.6	10.8

Source: Derived from Tables 2.3 and 2.4.

of a problem among initial entrants in the program. Since then new
Medicare enrollees must show some identification, and it is likely that
most apply for coverage upon reaching eligibility at age 65.

Comparison of the extreme aged population calculated by the extinct
generation method with that based on Medicare enrollment is now
becoming possible. This is due to the fact that the number of years
that deaths by single years can be cumulated is now sufficient to permit
the reconstruction of the population alive in 1967—the first full calendar year for which Medicare statistics are available. An estimate of
the reconstructed population, 85 years of age and over, by sex and age,
developed to correspond with the numbers living at the beginning of
January 1967 is shown in Table 2.6. (Statistics of deaths utilized in
this reconstruction were from the years 1967 through 1981. It should
be noted that some persons aged 85 and over in 1967 were still living

TABLE 2.6: COMPARISON OF THE POPULATION 85 YEARS OLD AND OVER,BY AGE AND SEX,
AS OF JANUARY 1, 1967 - TWO METHODS

Age	Extinct generation method	Health insurance actuarial enrollment data	Difference	Percent difference
All persons				
85-89 years	868,883	882,955	14,072	1.6
85	250,445	251,988	1,543	0.6
86	209,808	218,241	8,433	4.0
87	167,922	168,792	1,870	0.5
88	132,777	136,017	3,240	2.4
89	107,931	107,917	-14	0.0
90-94 years	263,295	262,994	-301	-0.1
90	86,032	87,318	1,286	1.5
91	66,629	66,494	-135	-0.2
92	48,933	48,607	-326	-0.7
93	35,669	34,157	-1,512	-4.2
94	26,032	26,418	386	1.5
95 years & over	55,397	50,156	-5,241	-9.5
85 years & over	1,187,575	1,196,105	8,530	0.7
Male				
85-89 years	314,863	319,074	4,211	1.3
85	93,706	93,796	90	0.1
86	76,757	79,014	2,257	2.9
87	60,032	60,379	347	0.6
88	46,739	47,900	1,161	2.5
89	37,629	37,985	356	0.9
90-94 years	87,282	87,132	-150	-0.2
90	29,371	29,643	272	0.9
91	22,196	21,947	-249	-1.1
92	15,901	15,989	88	0.6
93	11,469	11,125	-344	-3.0
94	8,345	8,428	83	1.0
95 years & over	17,184	15,086	-2,098	-12.2
85 years & over	419,329	421,292	1,963	0.5
Female				
85-89 years	554,020	563,881	9,861	1.8
85	156,739	158,192	1,453	0.9
86	133,051	139,227	6,176	4.6
87	107,890	108,413	523	0.5
88	86,038	88,117	2,079	2.4
89	70,302	69,932	-370	-0.5
90-94 years	176,013	175,862	-151	0.1
90	56,661	57,675	1,014	1.8
91	44,433	44,547	114	0.3
92	33,032	32,618	-414	-1.3
93	24,200	23,032	-1,168	-4.8
94	17,687	17,990	303	1.7
95 years & over	38,213	35,070	-3,143	-8.2
85 years & over	768,246	774,813	6,567	0.9

Sources: U.S. National Center for Health Statistics, Vital Statistics
of the United States, Annual, Vol. II- Mortality; U.S. Social
Security Administration, Job 5234, Actuarial Enrollment Data,
Table 9 (unpublished). For computation of extinct generation
method, see source for Table 2.1.

at the end of 1981, the last year for which death statistics were cumulated. Estimates of this small surviving group—about 15,000 persons or 1 percent of the total—were incorporated into the reconstructed populations.)

Table 2.6 shows populations derived from the extinct generation method for January 1, 1967 with corresponding figures from unpublished statistics of persons on the Health Insurance rolls. The very close correspondence of the two independently derived series is notable: the aggregate difference is less than 1 percent. The bulk of the discrepancy of 8,530 (out of a total population of 1.2 million) between the two series occurs in the figures for age 86 where there is a difference of 8,433. A plausible explanation for this may be a tendency among the Medicare enrollees to report a round number of year of birth (1880). The fairly substantial difference in the two series at ages 95 and over (9 percent) may result from a tendency to overreport age by the next-of-kin of decedents (who are the death certificate informants) in comparison with a more accurate age recorded earlier in life by the decedent at the time of entry in the Medicare rolls.

Cross-checking census data with other records of age for the extreme aged is most beneficial when the verifying age was recorded earlier in the individual's life, when there was no motivation for age overstatement and smaller chance for faulty memory. Although Social Security or Medicare data may be contaminated by those who wish to qualify for benefits at a premature age, few are likely to attempt such fraudulent action. In addition, there is a 20–year span between the time a person enrolls in the Medicare program at age 65 and the time he enters the 85 year and older category.

One of the few studies that have attempted to match death certificate age for the extreme aged with documents completed much earlier in an individual's life found a high level of validity of age reporting, except for those age 100 and over and for nonwhites in general. Rosenwaike and Logue (1983) used a sample of 3,000 death certificates of extreme aged persons registered in Pennsylvania and New Jersey between 1968 and 1972 and linked these with records for the same individuals in the 1900 census. Despite the substantial complications involved in matching records spanning seven decades, the authors linked death certificates to census records for 53 percent of the whites and 30 percent of the nonwhites in their sample.

Almost three-fourths of the white decedents had either the identical month and year of birth on both documents or ages differing by less than one year; agreement was slightly less for white females than for white males. But only 40 percent of the black decedents showed an identical age or an age differing by less than one year, with black females having somewhat better agreement than black males. At least 85 percent of the whites with death certificate ages in the intervals 85–89, 90–94 and 95–99 had reported census ages in the same intervals. The level of agreement among blacks declined from 65 percent among those in the 85–89 interval to 56 percent for those in the 95–99 interval.

As discussed above, the extensive number of persons misclassified as centenarians in the 1970 census mar the published reports of characteristics of the extreme aged. To a large extent, through the use of age data contained on the public use sample files for the 1970 census, it has been possible to assemble statistics limited to persons 85 to 99 years old and this is so noted in the text and in the tables. The public use samples of the decennial censuses of population and housing provide social scientists with a valuable resource for examining otherwise unavailable cross-classifications of personal characteristics. At the 1970 census the Census Bureau made six files available for purchase, each containing a 1–percent national sample of persons, three "drawn from the population covered by the census 15–percent sample and three from the population in the census 5–percent sample" (U. S. Bureau of the Census 1972b). In the few instances in this volume where 1970 data for centenarians appear as published, the tables indicate that no adjustments have been made for those falsely reported. In particular, data for the institutionalized elderly generally include centenarians. It was assumed that the census forms for the institutionalized aged were prepared by facility staff rather than by the elderly themselves and, therefore, were more likely to be correct.

At the 1980 census the computerized files, now designated "public-use microdata samples," consisted of "three mutually exclusive samples: the A sample included 5 percent of all persons and housing units, and the B and C samples each included 1 percent of all persons and housing units" (U.S. Bureau of the Census 1983c). In the present work, to produce a comprehensive portrait of the extreme elderly, files containing up to 4 percent of the population from public use samples (depending on item availability) have been used for 1970 data and the combined B and C samples (except in a few instances) have been used for 1980 data. No adjustments have been made for the general problems of age misstatement for any of the census years.

Age and Sex
3   Distribution

Since 1950 the growth in the proportion of the elderly population that was 85 years and over has outpaced the proportional growth of those in the 65 to 74 and 75 to 84 categories. The "aging" of the elderly population itself is thus a fairly recent phenomenon. The population 65 and over now comprises over 11 percent of the U.S. total, and nearly 9 in every 100 persons in this group is age 85 or older. For 1900, the comparable figure was less than 4 in 100. And, as it ages, the extreme elderly population is becoming increasingly feminized. Females die at lower rates throughout life than males; hence by the oldest ages there are many more surviving women than men.

Since age misreporting at the extreme ages has characteristically been much greater for nonwhites than whites, it is difficult to discuss trends by race in the 85 and over group. The percentage of nonwhites *reported* as age 85 or above relative to those 65 and over was nearly double that for whites until 1930 (Table 3.1). But since 1970 there have been proportionally more individuals 85 and over relative to those 65 and over in the white group than the nonwhite, with both groups tending to have higher percentages at the extreme ages in more recent census years. With improvements in age reporting over time, the later figures seem to be considerably more reliable than the earlier data.

AGE DISTRIBUTION

Trends in the distribution of the extreme aged population by five-year age group must be considered in conjunction with a review of the

TABLE 3.1: POPULATION 65 YEARS OLD AND OVER AND 85 YEARS OLD AND OVER, BY RACE: 1900 TO 1980

(in thousands)

Census year	Total			White			Nonwhite		
	65 and over	85 and over Number	Percent of persons 65+	65 and over	85 and over Number	Percent of persons 65+	65 and over	85 and over Number	Percent of persons 65+
1900	3,080	122	4.0	2,807	101	3.6	274	21	7.8
1910	3,950	167	4.2	3,640	144	3.9	310	24	7.6
1920	4,933	210	4.3	4,583	185	4.0	350	25	7.2
1930	6,634	272	4.1	6,240	244	3.9	394	28	7.2
1940	9,019	365	4.0	8,379	329	3.9	640	35	5.5
1950	12,270	577	4.7	11,374	532	4.7	896	45	5.1
1960	16,560	929	5.6	15,304	858	5.6	1,256	72	5.7
1970	19,980	1,409	7.0	18,279	1,293	7.1	1,701	116	6.8
1980	25,549	2,240	8.8	22,947	2,045	8.9	2,602	195	7.5
1980[a]	25,549	2,240	8.8	23,165	2,061	8.9	2,384	179	7.5

Sources: U.S. Bureau of the Census, 1933: Volume II, Chapter 10, Table 9; 1953a: Table 38; 1982a: Table 4; 1983a: Table 45; 1984b: Table 4.

a. Consistent with 1970 census classification by race.

reliability of age reporting. While the overall reliability of age reporting among the oldest segment of the population is discussed in Chapter 2, there are several aspects of this problem peculiar to the study of five-year age groups. The rounding of age (to a multiple of five) has been a recurring problem in all but the most recent American censuses. At the older ages this problem has been compounded by another reporting error found in many populations, a tendency toward age exaggeration, in particular an upward rounding of age (Shryock and Siegel, 1973; Mathisen and Mazess, 1981).

Age exaggeration is especially pronounced among reported ages of 100 and above. The data in Table 3.2 indicate a steady decline in the proportion of centenarians from 1880 to 1940; this reflects gradual improvements in age reporting over the years. In the 1880 census the alleged centenarian population accounted for 5.4 percent of the population 85 years old and over; by 1940 the figure had fallen to only 1.0 percent. A disproportionate share of the supposed centenarians were nonwhites (see Figure 3.1); for more than half a century their representation among the 85 and over group was in excess of ten times that among whites. Although nonwhites may in fact experience preferential survivability at the older ages, it is very unlikely that it would be as exaggerated as the census data suggest. Generally poorer health and living conditions and more illiteracy among nonwhites lend additional credence to the suspicion of widespread age exaggeration among elderly nonwhites. Between 1880 and 1940 the proportion of reputed centenarians among all nonwhites reported as 85 and over fell from 20.3 percent to 6.4 percent (see Tables 3.3 and 3.4) doubtlessly reflecting improvements in age reporting.

Few demographers ever accepted census figures for persons at ages 100 years and over at their face value; Census Bureau statisticians have had few illusions about their worth. A report on the 1900 enumeration, commenting on the declining share of centenarians at each successive census, pointed out: "This regular diminution indicates, not that the longevity of the population has been decreasing, but that in this as in other particulars the accuracy of the age statistics of the census has been increasing" (U.S. Bureau of the Census, 1906, p. 143).

Careful study by census officials indicated that the steady reduction in the proportion of persons who claimed to be 100 years or more was closely correlated with the fall in illiteracy over the years (U.S. Bureau of the Census, 1913). The huge literacy gap between elderly whites

TABLE 3.2: TOTAL POPULATION 85 YEARS OLD AND OVER, BY AGE GROUP AND SEX: 1880 TO 1980

Age and sex	1880 Number	Percent	1910 Number	Percent	1940 Number	Percent	1960[a] Number	Percent	1970[b] Number	Percent	1980 Number	Percent
Both sexes												
Total	74,714	100.0	167,237	100.0	364,752	100.0	929,252	100.0	1,404,460	100.0	2,240,067	100.0
85-89 years	49,835	66.7	122,818	73.4	277,012	75.9	697,770	75.1	1,018,147	72.5	1,520,202	67.9
90-94 years	16,100	21.5	33,473	20.0	69,598	19.1	183,584	19.8	313,237	22.3	556,592	24.8
95-99 years	4,763	6.4	7,391	4.4	14,463	4.0	36,756	4.0	73,076	5.2	131,079	5.9
100+ years	4,016	5.4	3,555	2.1	3,679	1.0	11,142	1.2	--	--	32,194	1.4
Male												
Total	31,523	100.0	75,313	100.0	156,374	100.0	362,276	100.0	488,041	100.0	681,525	100.0
85-89 years	21,908	69.5	56,335	74.8	121,455	77.7	277,886	76.7	362,063	74.2	477,185	70.0
90-94 years	6,351	20.1	14,553	19.3	27,965	17.9	67,539	18.6	103,649	21.2	159,077	23.3
95-99 years	1,855	5.9	3,045	4.1	5,616	3.6	12,683	3.5	22,329	4.6	34,961	5.1
100+ years	1,409	4.5	1,380	1.8	1,338	0.9	4,168	1.2	--	--	10,302	1.5
Female												
Total	43,191	100.0	91,924	100.0	208,378	100.0	566,976	100.0	916,419	100.0	1,558,542	100.0
85-89 years	27,927	64.7	66,483	72.3	155,557	74.7	419,884	74.1	656,084	71.6	1,043,017	66.0
90-94 years	9,749	22.6	18,920	20.6	41,633	20.0	116,045	20.5	209,588	22.9	397,515	25.5
95-99 years	2,908	6.7	4,346	4.7	8,847	4.2	24,073	4.2	50,747	5.5	96,118	6.2
100+ years	2,607	6.0	2,175	2.4	2,341	1.1	6,974	1.2	--	--	21,892	1.4

Sources: U.S. Bureau of the Census, 1933: Volume II, Chapter 10, Table 7; 1943: Table 2; 1964: Table 156; 1972a: Table 50; 1983a: Table 41.

a. Figures from 25 percent sample prorated to equal population 85 and over in complete count.
b. Excludes persons reported as centenarians in the largely erroneous published figure.

26

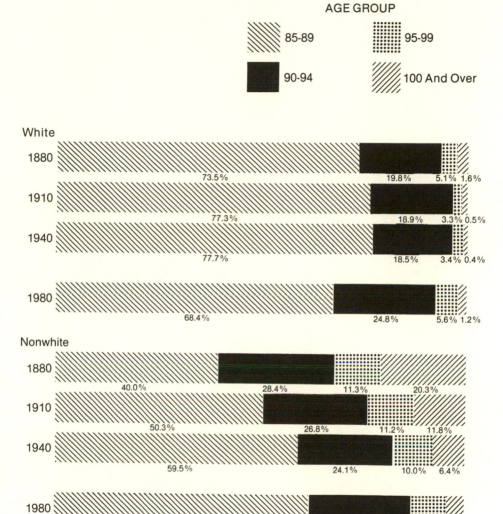

AGE GROUP

85-89   95-99

90-94   100 And Over

White

1880   73.5%   19.8%   5.1% 1.6%

1910   77.3%   18.9%   3.3% 0.5%

1940   77.7%   18.5%   3.4% 0.4%

1980   68.4%   24.8%   5.6% 1.2%

Nonwhite

1880   40.0%   28.4%   11.3%   20.3%

1910   50.3%   26.8%   11.2%   11.8%

1940   59.5%   24.1%   10.0%   6.4%

1980   61.8%   25.5%   8.6%   4.1%

Sources: Tables 3.3 and 3.4.

27

TABLE 3.3: WHITE POPULATION 85 YEARS OLD AND OVER, BY AGE GROUP AND SEX: 1880 TO 1980

Age and sex	1880 Number	Percent	1910 Number	Percent	1940 Number	Percent	1960[a] Number	Percent	1970[b] Number	Percent	1980[c] Number	Percent
Both sexes												
Total	59,607	100.0	143,618	100.0	329,339	100.0	857,615	100.0	1,287,832	100.0	2,061,424	100.0
85-89 years	43,798	73.5	110,936	77.3	255,929	77.7	649,118	75.7	939,362	72.9	1,409,810	68.4
90-94 years	11,803	19.8	27,161	18.9	61,061	18.5	169,036	19.7	285,072	22.1	511,109	24.8
95-99 years	3,051	5.1	4,757	3.3	10,938	3.4	31,348	3.7	63,398	4.9	115,689	5.6
100+ years	955	1.6	764	0.5	1,411	0.4	8,113	0.9	--	--	24,816	1.2
Male												
Total	25,642	100.0	65,074	100.0	141,348	100.0	330,915	100.0	440,942	100.0	621,051	100.0
85-89 years	19,277	75.2	50,843	78.1	112,091	79.3	255,874	77.3	330,213	74.9	439,199	70.7
90-94 years	4,756	18.6	11,970	18.4	24,498	17.3	61,627	18.6	92,024	20.9	144,172	23.2
95-99 years	1,216	4.7	1,935	3.0	4,224	3.0	10,420	3.1	18,705	4.2	30,088	4.8
100+ years	393	1.5	326	0.5	535	0.4	2,994	0.9	--	--	7,592	1.2
Female												
Total	33,965	100.0	78,544	100.0	187,991	100.0	526,700	100.0	846,890	100.0	1,440,373	100.0
85-89 years	24,521	72.2	60,093	76.5	143,838	76.5	393,244	74.7	609,149	71.9	970,611	67.4
90-94 years	7,047	20.8	15,191	19.3	36,563	19.4	107,409	20.4	193,048	22.8	366,937	25.5
95-99 years	1,835	5.4	2,822	3.6	6,714	3.6	20,928	4.0	44,693	5.3	85,601	5.9
100+ years	562	1.7	438	0.6	876	0.5	5,119	1.0	--	--	17,224	1.2

Sources: U.S. Bureau of the Census, 1933: Volume II, Chapter 10, Table 9; 1943: Table 2; 1964: Table 156; 1972a: Table 50; 1980 Census Summary Tape File 2C.

a. Figures from 25 percent sample prorated to equal population 85 and over in complete count.
b. Excludes persons reported as centenarians in the largely erroneous published figure.
c. Roughly consistent with 1970 census count by race. See "data comparability" discussion in Chapter 4.

28

TABLE 3.4: NONWHITE POPULATION 85 YEARS OLD AND OVER, BY AGE GROUP AND SEX: 1880 TO 1980

Age and sex	1880		1910		1940		1960[a]		1970[b]		1980[c]	
	Number	Percent	Number	Percent	Number	Percent	Number	Percent	Number	Percent	Number	Percent
Both sexes												
Total	15,107	100.0	23,619	100.0	35,411	100.0	71,637	100.0	116,628	100.0	178,643	100.0
85-89 years	6,037	40.0	11,882	50.3	21,083	59.5	48,652	67.9	78,785	67.6	110,392	61.8
90-94 years	4,297	28.4	6,312	26.8	8,535	24.1	14,548	20.3	28,165	24.1	45,483	25.5
95-99 years	1,712	11.3	2,634	11.2	3,525	10.0	5,408	7.5	9,678	8.3	15,390	8.6
100+ years	3,061	20.3	2,791	11.8	2,268	6.4	3,029	4.2	--	--	7,378	4.1
Male												
Total	5,881	100.0	10,239	100.0	15,026	100.0	31,361	100.0	47,099	100.0	60,474	100.0
85-89 years	2,631	44.7	5,492	53.6	9,364	62.3	22,012	70.2	31,850	67.6	37,986	62.8
90-94 years	1,595	27.1	2,583	25.3	3,467	23.1	5,912	18.9	11,625	24.7	14,905	24.6
95-99 years	639	10.9	1,110	10.8	1,392	9.3	2,263	7.2	3,624	7.7	4,873	8.1
100+ years	1,016	17.3	1,054	10.3	803	5.3	1,174	3.7	--	--	2,710	4.5
Female												
Total	9,226	100.0	13,380	100.0	20,387	100.0	40,276	100.0	69,529	100.0	118,169	100.0
85-89 years	3,406	36.9	6,390	47.8	11,719	57.5	26,640	66.1	46,935	67.5	72,406	61.3
90-94 years	2,702	29.3	3,729	27.9	5,070	24.9	8,636	21.4	16,540	23.8	30,578	25.9
95-99 years	1,073	11.6	1,524	11.3	2,133	10.5	3,145	7.8	6,054	8.7	10,517	8.9
100+ years	2,045	22.2	1,737	13.0	1,465	7.2	1,855	4.6	--	--	4,668	3.9

Sources: See sources for Table 3.3.

a. Figures from 25 percent sample prorated to equal population 85 and over in complete count.
b. Excludes persons reported as centenarians in the largely erroneous published figure.
c. Roughly consistent with 1970 census count by race. See "data comparability" discussion in Chapter 4.

and blacks, the bulk of the nonwhite category, has accounted for much of the differential in the proportion of centenarians between the two groups. The majority of the black population over 65 was illiterate as late as 1930, whereas less than one-tenth of elderly whites were so classified by 1910. Accounting for this disparity was the fact that most elderly blacks were born into a slave society where they generally were not permitted to learn to read or write. To compound the problem, reliable birth records were usually nonexistent. At the same time, some degree of status accrued to those who could claim to be long-lived; hence there was strong societal support for exaggerating one's age.

Among the white population the proportion of centenarians among the extreme aged did not decline so dramatically in the decades after 1880 (Table 3.3). Nevertheless there was a drop from 1.6 percent of those 85 and over in 1880 to 0.4 percent by 1940. Exaggeration of age was not confined to the centenarian population alone, since the proportion of extreme aged whites who were 95–99 also dropped at the same time. Between 1880 and 1940 the share of those aged 95–99 in the total group 85 and over declined from 5.1 percent to 3.4 percent. The share of the nonwhite population that was 95–99 years of age fluctuated between 10 and 12 percent of the total 85 years and over between 1880 and 1940, with little trend evident (Table 3.4). Since this was roughly three times the proportion in that category in the white population it is likely that the numbers are much inflated. Only in 1960 was there some evidence of relative decline in the numbers in this age group among nonwhites—to 7.5 percent.

The declining relative share of extreme aged in the oldest age groups—95–99 years and 100 and over—implies an increasing share for the 85–94 age group. Table 3.2 indicates that among the aggregate number of persons 85 and above the proportion reported as 85–89 years advanced from census to census between 1880 and 1940, climbing from two-thirds of the total in the former year (66.7 percent) to three-fourths (75.9 percent) in the latter. Since 1940 the representation of those in the youngest portion of the extreme aged group has slipped somewhat as the elderly population itself ages, a phenomenon now being observed for perhaps the first time in history.

Among the white population, the share of the extreme aged in the single age group 85–89 years climbed from 73.5 percent in 1880 to 77.7 percent in 1940; over the ensuing decades it has diminished to 68.4 percent (Table 3.3). Among nonwhites only 40.0 percent of the total of those 85 and above in 1880 were aged 85–89 years. The proportion advanced to an all-time peak of 67.9 percent in 1960 and has since fallen again, to 61.8 percent (Table 3.4).

Although the true number of centenarians certainly has never amounted to more than 1 percent of the total extreme aged population, interest in this oldest segment of the population has been high. It must be stressed again, however, that gross exaggeration of age has always been a conspicuous characteristic of "official" American data on this group. As enumerated by the decennial census, the centenarian population was approximately 4,000 at each count between 1880 and 1950. In reality, the true number probably was gradually increasing over the years, concomitant with general population growth and increasing life expectancy, but it undoubtedly never approached a figure of 4,000. When the number of centenarians jumped to more than 10,000 in the 1960 census, most demographers viewed the figure with disbelief, theorizing that perhaps a data processing error accounted for the sudden leap.

Robert J. Myers, former Chief Actuary of the Social Security Administration, made a careful review of the subject. He developed a method of analysis of the very aged population "by projecting, through the use of population life table survival factors, the populations reported at various advanced age groups in one census to the next census and then comparing the results with the corresponding number reported in the latter census for the same age cohort" (Myers, 1966, p. 470). For centenarians his projected populations were significantly lower than the enumerated populations. On the basis of his projections he wrote that "instead of the 10,326 centenarians reported in 1960 ... there were actually at most only about 3,700, and that, instead of, the approximately 2,800 nonwhite centenarians reported, there were only about 250" (Myers, 1966, p.474). (Myers' figures refer to the published count based on the 20 percent sample unadjusted for the discrepancy between the sample tally and the complete count. Adjusted figures are shown in Tables 3.2 to 3.4.)

Following the 1970 enumeration an obviously erroneous count of over 100,000 persons aged 100 years and over was produced by the Census Bureau. On close examination the statistical agency realized that lax editing procedures of the complex census schedule had led to a figure that was absolutely unreliable. (For discussion of the implications of this error see Chapter 2.) Two Census Bureau demographers,

TABLE 3.5:   POPULATION 100 YEARS OLD AND OVER, BY RACE AND SEX, AS PUBLISHED
AND AS ESTIMATED BY SIEGEL AND PASSEL: 1950 TO 1970

Census year	Total			White			Nonwhite		
	Both sexes	Male	Female	Both sexes	Male	Female	Both sexes	Male	Female
Published Census Figures									
1950	4,447	1,665	2,782	2,007	807	1,200	2,440	800	1,582
1960	10,369	3,800	6,539	7,538	2,755	4,783	2,831	1,075	1,756
1970	106,441	54,338	52,103	88,980	46,015	42,965	17,461	8,323	9,138
Siegel-Passel "Preferred" Estimates									
1950	2,300	800	1,500	1,350	500	850	950	300	650
1960	3,300	1,150	2,150	2,550	875	1,675	750	275	475
1970	4,800	1,550	3,250	3,900	1,250	2,650	900	300	600

Source: Siegel and Passel, 1976.

Jacob Siegel and Jeffrey Passel (1976), used several statistical methods
to estimate the true centenarian population in 1970. Their "preferred
estimate"—4,800 persons—was about one-third less than the number
of centenarians derived from Medicare enrollment records and through
population reconstruction utilizing death statistics of reputed centenarians. (For a discussion of these methods see Chapter 2.) Table 3.5
indicates very clearly the limitations of Census data for centenarians.
The top tier of the table shows the official Census figures by race and
sex for 1950, 1960 and 1970, whereas the lower tier contains Siegel
and Passel's preferred estimates. Medicare enrollment figures are believed to be more accurate than census counts since many of the beneficiaries provided proof of age at the time of entry. On the other
hand, enrollees only needed to demonstrate that they had passed the
age of 65 to qualify, not prove that they were a specific age beyond
that point, so age misstatement may be present (Myers, 1966). Despite
this flaw and obvious data processing errors for those at ages 114 and
above, the available tabulations are of particular interest to researchers. They reveal an enrollment of 6,785 persons at ages 100 through
114 on January 1, 1970, and a total of 23,033 persons in the same age

group at the beginning of 1980.The centenarian population has more than tripled in only a single decade according to these figures.

Returning to Myers' estimate, as the most reliable calculation of the white centenarian population in 1960, we find a figure of about 3,450. The maximum number of whites included in the Health Insurance centenarian population in 1970 was about 5,500. This includes all of the approximately 1,000 persons with race not reported, presumably a fraction of whom were nonwhite, so it is a maximum figure. Thus growth between 1960 and 1970 can be calculated at about 50 percent. This can be compared with the Siegel and Passel "preferred" estimate of an increase of 53 percent between the same two dates.

When death rates, using National Center for Health Statistics data by age, are calculated for persons 100 years and over according to Medicare enrollment counts the results show declines in the death rates for centenarians between 1969–71 and 1979–81 that are more than double those for nonagenarians (see Table 9.11). This is most unlikely, particularly since the resulting death rates for centenarians are as low or *lower* than those exhibited by persons 95–99 years of age. Accordingly it must be assumed that the Medicare statistics somewhat inflate the centenarian population and to a greater extent around 1980 than around 1970.

The "true" number of centenarians in 1980 therefore is considerably lower than census counts (with or without allocations) or Medicare statistics report. The total number of deaths of centenarians in the 3–year span 1969–71 was 9,017; in the 3 years, 1979–81, it was 17,911. Assuming that some decline in the centenarian death rate occurred in this time period, as it did for persons 85–99 years of age (Table 9.11), the obvious conclusion is that the "true" centenarian population more than doubled, even if improvement of age accuracy in death certificate reporting during the decade was only slight. Thus, the Siegel and Passel "preferred" 1970 estimate of 4,800 centenarians would be replaced by 1980 with a figure (perhaps well) in excess of 10,000. The files of the Social Security Administration provided a count of 15,000 centenarians for 1980, but according to Siegel and Davidson, "even this figure appears to overstate the actual figure" (U.S. Bureau of the Census, 1984d, p. 132).

Even after discounting the apparently flawed "official" statistics, the recent extraordinarily large growth in the centenarian population clearly must be viewed as an emerging trend. This trend is not confined

FIGURE 3.2: MALE AND FEMALE POPULATIONS
85 YEARS AND OVER: 1900 -1980

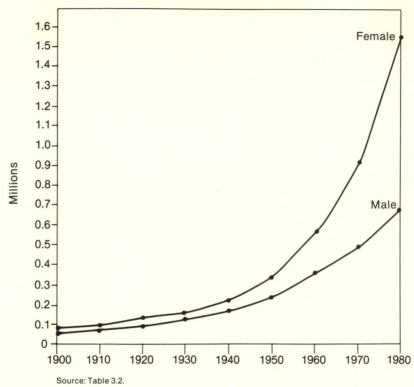

Source: Table 3.2.

to the United States. In the Netherlands, for example, a nation with particularly accurate age data, there were 165 persons aged 100 years or over in 1970 and two and one-half times that number—427—in 1982 (Tas, 1982). Similarly, in England and Wales the number of centenarians drawing pensions roughly doubled each decade between 1951 and 1981 (Thatcher, 1982).

SEX DISTRIBUTION

Because the detailed data needed to compute expected sex ratios for the extreme elderly are lacking, it is impossible to compare estimated

TABLE 3.6:   SEX RATIO (MALES PER 100 FEMALES) OF THE POPULATION 85 YEARS OLD AND
OVER, BY AGE GROUP AND RACE: 1880 TO 1980

Age and race	1880	1910	1940	1960	1970	1980
All races						
Total	73.0	81.9	75.0	63.9	53.3	43.7
85-89 years	78.4	84.7	78.1	66.2	55.2	45.8
90-94 years	65.1	76.9	67.2	58.2	49.5	40.0
95-99 years	63.8	70.1	63.5	52.7	44.0	36.4
100+ years	54.0	63.4	57.1	59.8	---	47.1
White						
Total	75.5	82.9	75.2	62.8	52.1	43.1
85-89 years	78.6	84.6	77.9	65.1	54.2	45.2
90-94 years	67.5	78.8	67.0	57.4	47.7	39.3
95-99 years	66.3	68.6	62.9	49.8	41.9	35.1
100+ years	69.9	74.4	61.1	58.5	---	44.1
Nonwhite						
Total	63.7	76.5	73.7	77.9	67.7	51.2
85-89 years	77.2	85.9	79.9	82.6	67.9	52.5
90-94 years	59.0	69.3	68.4	68.5	70.3	48.7
95-99 years	59.6	72.8	65.3	72.0	59.9	46.3
100+ years	49.7	60.7	54.8	63.3	---	58.1

Source: Calculated from Tables 3.2, 3.3 and 3.4.

ratios with the actual census figures to assess the accuracy of the latter numbers. "Because of the greater likelihood of deficiencies in the basic data and the greater dependence on the various assumptions made as one goes back in time, the estimates of expected sex ratios are subject to greater and greater error as one goes up the age scale" (Shryock and Siegel, 1973, p. 221). The accuracy of expected sex ratios depends on reliable reporting of births in each cohort and allowance for its decrements by death in the intervening years. Reliable data on migration are also required.

Since "immigration to the United States was especially male-selective during the earlier years of heavy immigration" and persons admitted between 1900 and 1910 had a sex ratio of 228 males per 100

TABLE 3.7:   SEX RATIO (MALES PER 100 FEMALES) OF THE WHITE POPULATION 85 YEARS
             OLD AND OVER, BY AGE GROUP AND NATIVITY: 1910 TO 1980

Age and nativity	1910	1940	1960	1970	1980
Native					
Total	78.7	72.8	59.3	50.3	39.3
85-89 years	80.4	75.2	61.5	51.9	41.4
90-94 years	75.1	65.1	53.5	47.3	34.7[a]
95-99 years	62.6	61.7	47.2	41.9	---
100+ years	73.8	64.4	58.2	---	---
Foreign born					
Total	91.5	82.3	73.1	68.4	59.4
85-89 years	93.4	86.5	75.4	70.8	62.3
90-94 years	86.6	72.0	69.5	61.9	53.8[a]
95-99 years	80.2	65.6	55.7	62.6	---
100+ years	75.4	56.0	54.8	---	---

Source: Calculated from Table 4.1.

a. Sex ratio for persons 90 years and over.

females (Shryock and Siegel, 1973, p. 197), this historical experience
can be expected to continue to influence sex ratios in the affected cohorts as they age. Accurate immigration statistics by age are seldom
available, and "any estimates of total births and deaths in the United
States for the years before 1930 are subject to considerable error"
(Shryock and Siegel, 1973, p. 190). Hence it is difficult to assess the
accuracy of official census data on the sex distribution of the extreme
elderly population. Errors in age reporting for this group compound
the problems of interpretation, especially for nonwhites.

Nonetheless, one inference remains incontrovertible. That is, that
males have a higher rate of mortality than females throughout the life
span. Thus, the number of males per 100 females continues to fall as
a cohort ages, resulting in the increasing feminization of the oldest
age segments (Figure 3.2). Furthermore the female advantage in sur-
vivorship has been increasing over this century, so that the gap between the sexes continues to widen. There were 73 males per 100
females age 85 and above in 1880, according to official figures (Table
3.6). Although reported ratios were somewhat higher until 1940, there

has been a steady decline since that date. In 1980 there were only about 44 males to every 100 females in this age range. Data limited to whites are the most accurate and show a decreasing sex ratio with increasing age *within* the 85-and-over group. Not surprisingly, given the poor age reporting characteristic of reputed centenarians, the sex ratio seems to change favorably for males at ages 100 and over in some census years, but these figures must be considered unreliable. Sex ratios for nonwhites are similarly unreliable at all the extreme ages. Relative to whites, sex ratios for nonwhites were generally lower until 1940, but since then a reversal seems to have occurred. In 1980 there were about eight more nonwhite males per 100 nonwhite females than was the case for whites (see Table 3.6).

Given the preponderance of males among immigrants, it is not surprising to find higher sex ratios at the oldest ages for foreign-born residents relative to natives (Table 3.7). When the survivors of the heavy immigration years before World War I have died, however, the extreme elderly population will be primarily composed of native-born individuals, and computed sex ratios for the total 85 and over group will scarcely be affected by earlier sex-specific immigration.

Race, Ethnic Group and
4   National Origin

This chapter will first present some highlights on the composition of the extreme aged population in terms of race, national origin and ethnic group. Then the state of current knowledge of the relationship between aging on the one hand and ethnic minority group membership on the other will be reviewed.

A great majority of the total population of the United States, and of those who are 85 years and over, consists of white persons, but this group includes people with diverse ethnic backgrounds. The influx of immigrants into this country during the nineteenth and early twentieth centuries included many persons of German, English, Italian, Irish and Scandinavian nativity. In recent years many have come from Latin America. Among nonwhite persons 85 years and over, almost 89 percent are black with the remainder composed of American Indians, and of Chinese, Japanese and other Asian and Pacific Island peoples, with no single group predominating.

Prior to 1950, with a single exception (in 1900), the census reports provided statistics cross-classifying age by nativity for the white population only. The percentage of the white population 85 years and over that was of foreign birth was highest in the first quarter of the twentieth century, accounting for slightly over one-third of the total at the time of the 1910 census. Since 1960 the foreign born have comprised only about one-fifth of the total extreme aged white population (Table 4.1 and Figure 4.1).

In recent censuses about 4 to 5 percent of the nonwhite population

TABLE 4.1: NATIVITY OF WHITE POPULATION 85 YEARS OLD AND OVER, BY AGE GROUP AND SEX: 1910 TO 1980

Age and sex	1910		1940		1960[a]		1970[b]		1980[c]	
	Native	Foreign born	Native	Foreign born	Native	Foreign born	Native	Foreign born	Native	Foreign born
Both sexes										
Total	95,135	48,483	242,909	86,430	636,090	160,732	1,039,975	253,550	1,599,050	384,000
85-89 years	73,503	37,433	190,588	65,341	482,342	120,762	759,600	187,525	1,112,700	256,000
90-94 years	18,127	9,034	43,946	17,115	124,923	32,131	224,750	54,400	} 486,350	} 128,000
95-99 years	3,034	1,723	7,507	3,431	22,671	6,455	55,625	11,625		
100+ years	471	293	868	543	6,154	1,384	---	---		
Male										
Total	41,907	23,167	102,326	39,022	236,724	67,879	348,075	103,000	451,050	143,100
85-89 years	32,762	18,081	81,790	30,301	183,666	51,900	259,500	77,725	325,650	98,300
90-94 years	7,777	4,193	17,331	7,167	43,524	13,180	72,150	20,800	} 125,400	} 44,800
95-99 years	1,168	767	2,865	1,359	7,269	2,309	16,425	4,475		
100+ years	200	126	340	195	2,265	490	---	---		
Female										
Total	53,228	25,316	140,583	47,408	399,366	92,853	691,900	150,550	1,148,000	240,950
85-89 years	40,741	19,352	108,798	35,040	298,676	68,862	500,100	109,800	787,050	157,750
90-94 years	10,350	4,841	26,615	9,948	81,399	18,951	152,600	33,600	} 360,950	} 83,200
95-99 years	1,866	956	4,642	2,072	15,402	4,146	39,200	7,150		
100+ years	271	167	528	348	3,889	894	---	---		

Sources: U.S. Bureau of the Census, 1933: Volume II, Chapter 10, Table 9; 1943: Table 3; 1964: Table 155; 1970 Census Public Use Sample; 1980 Census Public Use Microdata Sample.

a. Figures from 25 percent sample prorated to equal population 85 and over in complete count.
b. Excludes persons reported as centenarians in the largely erroneous published figure.
c. Consistent with 1970 census count by race.

FIGURE 4.1: PERCENT OF WHITES 85 YEARS AND OVER
OF FOREIGN BIRTH: 1900-1980

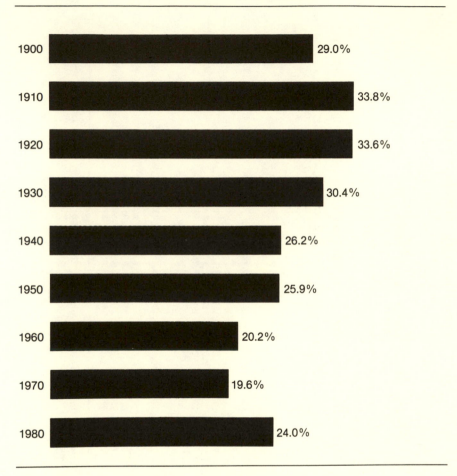

Sources: Table 4.1 and U.S. Bureau of the Census, 1953a.

85 years of age and over has been of foreign birth (Table 4.2). The 1970 census, which further distinguished the specific race of this immigrant group disclosed that most were nonblack. Like the white population of foreign birth, the nonwhite population of immigrant origin aged 85

TABLE 4.2: NATIVITY OF NONWHITE POPULATION 85 YEARS OLD AND OVER, BY AGE GROUP AND SEX: 1960 TO 1980

Age and sex	1960a Native	1960a Foreign born	1970b Native	1970b Foreign born	1980c Native	1980c Foreign born
Both sexes						
Total	64,402	2,561	126,730	6,669	159,950	17,150
85-89 years	43,549	1,928			99,750	10,900
90-94 years	13,115	484				
95-99 years	4,970	86			60,200d	6,250d
100+ years	2,768	63				
Male						
Total	27,184	1,596	49,754	3,587	52,750	6,900
85-89 years	18,995	1,215			34,050	3,900
90-94 years	5,109	309				
95-99 years	2,037	40			18,700d	3,000d
100+ years	1,043	32				
Female						
Total	37,218	965	76,976	3,082	107,200	10,250
85-89 years	24,554	713			65,700	7,000
90-94 years	8,006	175				
95-99 years	2,933	46			41,500d	3,250d
100+ years	1,725	31				

Sources: U.S. Bureau of the Census, 1964: Table 162; 1972a: Table 190; 1980 Census Public Use Microdata Sample.

a. Based on 25 percent sample.
b. Based on 15 percent sample. Includes persons erroneously reported as centenarians.
c. Consistent with 1970 census count by race.
d. Ages 90 years and over.

and above has increased in number at each successive census.

A majority of very aged Asian Americans are of foreign birth (Table 4.3). In the early part of this century males greatly outnumbered females in the immigrant streams from Asia, a fact which explains the preponderance of males among the extreme elderly of Japanese and Chinese origin as late as 1970 and those of Filipino origin as late as 1980.

Data compiled by the National Center for Health Statistics comparing the white population with Chinese Americans and Japanese Americans indicate that mortality is lower for the Asian groups at all ages (U.S. Department of Health, Education and Welfare, 1979). But these low mortality levels of the Asian groups have not yet resulted in relatively high aging of these populations because their age composition is heavily affected by the recency of their immigration. (Young persons constitute the bulk of nearly all immigrant streams.) Presumably, in future years, as the Japanese and Chinese age they will be disproportionally represented among the extreme aged population, due to their mortality advantage.

Since nearly all Americans are immigrants or the descendants of immigrants, the decennial census traditionally has subdivided the population into "generations." First-generation Americans are international migrants who remained and have been enumerated as foreign born. Their children born in the United States are second-generation Americans, classified in the census as native born of foreign or mixed parentage. Third and subsequent generation Americans (persons with both parents born in the United States) are classified as natives of native parentage.

The 1960 census was the first to show statistics of foreign-born persons 85 and above by specific country of birth. Table 4.4 indicates that between 1960 and 1980 there were significant changes in the birthplace of the foreign-born population, reflecting the major shifts in country of origin between the "old" immigrants of the nineteenth century and the "new" immigrants of the early twentieth century. Despite the sharp growth of the extreme aged population during these decades, the numbers reported as born in such countries as Germany, Ireland and Sweden showed little change; however, the number of natives of Hungary, Italy, Poland, and the U.S.S.R. quadrupled. By 1970 Italy had replaced Germany as the country from which the largest number of persons 85 and over originated.

TABLE 4.3: NONWHITE POPULATION 85 YEARS OLD AND OVER, BY RACE, SEX AND NATIVITY: 1970 AND 1980

Race	Total			Native			Foreign born		
	Total	Male	Female	Total	Male	Female	Total	Male	Female
1970a									
Total	133,399	53,341	80,058	126,730	49,754	76,976	6,669	3,587	3,082
Black	121,264	47,265	73,999	119,476	46,563	72,913	1,788	702	1,086
All other nonwhite	12,135	6,076	6,059	7,254	3,191	4,063	4,881	2,885	1,996
Japanese	4,302	2,336	1,966	1,203	508	695	3,099	1,828	1,271
American Indian	3,711	1,655	2,056	3,567	1,577	1,990	144	78	66
Chinese	1,388	787	601	616	341	275	772	446	326
Filipino	919	526	393	468	209	259	451	317	134
Other	1,815	772	1,043	1,400	556	844	415	216	199
1980b									
Total	178,643	60,474	118,169	158,700	52,000	106,700	15,500	6,000	9,500
Black	158,920	52,966	105,954	127,900	48,500	99,400	4,650	1,750	2,900
All other nonwhite	19,723	7,508	12,215	10,800	3,500	7,300	10,850	4,250	6,600
Japanese	5,759	1,859	3,900	650	300	350	5,350	1,850	3,500
American Indian	5,670	2,215	3,455	6,250	2,000	4,250	250	150	100
Chinese	3,409	1,429	1,980	650	400	250	2,500	950	1,550
Asian Indianc	1,799	376	1,423	2,700	600	2,100	850	150	700
Filipino	1,692	1,150	542	50	---	50	1,300	950	350
Other	1,394	479	915	500	200	300	600	200	400

Sources: U.S. Bureau of the Census, 1972a: Table 190; 1980 Census Summary Tape File 2C; 1980 Census Public
Use Microdata Sample.

a. Based on 15 percent sample. Includes persons erroneously reported as centenarians.
b. Consistent with 1970 census count by race (with exception noted). Data for the total nonwhite population
are from Summary Tape File 2C; data by nativity are from the Public Use Microdata Sample. Hence, figures from
the sample do not add to the totals for the full count.
c. Included with white population in 1970.

TABLE 4.4: FOREIGN-BORN POPULATION 85 YEARS OLD AND OVER, BY COUNTRY OF BIRTH AND SEX: 1960 TO 1980

Country of birth	1960[a]			1970[b]			1980		
	Total	Male	Female	Total	Male	Female	Total	Male	Female
All countries	163,293	69,475	93,818	259,701	107,605	152,096	401,200	150,000	251,200
Austria	4,954	2,399	2,555	10,449	4,343	6,106	16,300	5,400	10,900
Canada	16,716	5,885	10,831	21,078	6,507	14,571	23,650	6,400	17,250
Czechoslovakia	4,430	1,964	2,466	7,379	2,934	4,445	9,000	3,000	6,000
Germany	26,743	10,377	16,366	25,732	9,729	16,003	27,200	8,500	18,700
Hungary	2,809	1,309	1,500	7,315	2,780	4,535	11,200	3,950	7,250
Ireland	9,607	2,974	6,633	10,433	2,665	7,768	13,650	3,550	10,100
Italy	16,112	8,567	7,545	35,972	19,223	16,749	62,100	28,900	33,200
Mexico	3,617	1,502	2,115	6,751	3,123	3,628	12,700	5,300	7,400
Norway	6,254	2,811	3,443	7,998	3,286	4,712	7,550	2,600	4,950
Poland	8,051	3,643	4,408	17,202	7,696	9,506	34,850	12,350	22,500
Sweden	11,982	5,166	6,816	11,910	4,184	7,726	11,050	5,000	6,050
United Kingdom	20,396	7,718	12,678	26,773	8,997	17,776	27,350	7,550	19,800
USSR	8,905	4,380	4,525	17,472	8,253	9,219	34,250	15,450	18,800
All other[c]	22,717	10,780	11,937	53,237	23,885	29,352	110,350	42,050	68,300

Sources: U.S. Bureau of the Census, 1965: Table 9; 1973a: Table 17; 1980 Census Public Use Microdata Sample.

a. Based on 25 percent sample.
b. Based on 5 percent sample. Includes persons erroneously reported as centenarians.
c. Includes "not specified".

TABLE 4.5:   NATIVE POPULATION 85 YEARS OLD AND OVER OF FOREIGN OR MIXED PARENTAGE,
BY COUNTRY OF ORIGIN: 1960 AND 1970

Country of origin	1960[a]			1970[b]		
	Total	Male	Female	Total	Male	Female
Total	144,752	51,955	92,797	222,950	74,450	148,500
Austria	953	333	620	2,850	1,050	1,800
Canada	9,467	3,586	5,881	17,400	5,650	11,750
Czechoslovakia	1,496	506	990	3,850	1,600	2,250
Germany	57,855	20,932	36,923	78,100	27,700	50,400
Hungary	226	98	128	750	350	400
Ireland	23,907	7,476	16,431	26,650	7,150	19,500
Italy	994	354	640	3,650	1,300	2,350
Mexico	616	318	298	1,800	650	1,150
Norway	4,430	1,675	2,755	9,450	3,550	5,900
Poland	1,284	488	796	4,300	1,350	2,950
Sweden	3,443	1,274	2,169	9,350	3,200	6,150
United Kingdom	26,797	9,695	17,102	32,650	9,950	22,700
USSR	550	242	308	3,550	1,400	2,150
All other[c]	12,734	4,978	7,756	21,700	7,300	14,400
Not specified	-	-	-	6,900	2,250	4,650

Sources: U.S. Bureau of the Census, 1965: Table 9; 1970 Census Public Use Sample.

a. Based on 25 percent sample.
b. Ages 85 to 99 years only.
c. Includes "not specified" in 1970.

The 1960 census was also the first (and thus far the only) census for which statistics were published for the population 85 years of age and over that subdivided the native population into two major classes: native of foreign or mixed parentage and native of native parentage. Earlier censuses, and that of 1970, used 75 years of age and over as the oldest age category. Data for persons 85 years and over, however, are available from the 1970 Census Public Use sample. The 1970 statistics of the second-generation American population included among the extreme aged indicated three-fifths of this group consisted of individuals with parents originating in Germany, Ireland or the United Kingdom (Table 4.5). This clearly reflects the predominance of natives of these countries in the migrant stream to the United States in the late nineteenth century.

Among the extreme aged whites in 1970 the population categorized as native of foreign or mixed parentage was slightly smaller in number

TABLE 4.6:   POPULATION 85 YEARS OLD AND OVER, BY NATIVITY AND PARENTAGE:
1960 AND 1970

Race	Total	Foreign born	Native	
			Foreign or mixed parentage	Native parentage
1960[a]				
All races	863,785	163,293	144,752	555,740
White	796,822	160,732	144,196	491,894
Nonwhite	66,963	2,561	556	63,846
1970[b]				
All races	1,418,500	263,700	222,950	931,850
White	1,299,200	257,400	221,100	820,700
Nonwhite	119,300	6,300	1,850	111,150
Black	107,800	1,750	950	105,100
All other	11,500	4,550	900	6,050

Sources: U.S. Bureau of the Census, 1965; Table 3; 1970 Census Public Use
Sample.

a.   Based on 25 percent sample.
b.   Ages 85 to 99 years only.

than that of foreign birth. Those natives of native parentage were substantially more numerous than the two foreign stock groups combined. In fact about two-thirds of white persons and nine-tenths of nonwhite persons were natives of native parentage (Table 4.6).

Decennial census data that would provide information on the national origin of all persons, not only the first and second generation in the United States, but also subsequent generations, has long been advocated by interested observers. The first step in this direction was the inclusion in the 1970 census of a question designed to identify those of Mexican, Puerto Rican, Cuban or other Spanish origin (or ancestry); the question was directed only at a 5 percent sample of the population. At the 1980 census, in contrast, 100 percent of the population were queried as to Spanish origin, while a sample was asked a general question on ancestry.

TABLE 4.7: POPULATION IN SELECTED ANCESTRY GROUPS, 65 YEARS AND OVER AND 85 YEARS
AND OVER: 1980

(population in thousands)

Ancestry groups[a]	Population			Percent of population		Percent of 65+ who are 85+
	All ages	65 years and over	85 years and over	65+	85+	
English	23,749	3,629	348	15.3	1.5	9.6
French	3,069	429	38	14.0	1.2	8.8
German	17,943	2,802	283	15.6	1.6	10.1
Irish	10,337	1,617	134	15.6	1.3	8.3
Italian	6,883	1,073	77	15.6	1.1	7.2
Polish	3,806	685	50	18.0	1.3	7.3

Source: U.S. Bureau of the Census, 1983b: Table 172.

a. Includes only respondents who reported a single ancestry. Data based on
approximately 19 percent sample.

Data on age by ancestry in 1980 have been published for six non-Spanish European groups (Table 4.7). The data refer only to respondents who reported a single specific ancestry; persons who reported more than one ancestry group are considered as of multiple ancestry. Persons classified among the single ancestry groups tend to be older than those of multiple ancestry since they include relatively more first and second-generation Americans. Table 4.7 shows substantially greater than average proportions in both the 65 and over and 85 and over categories for the selected ancestry groups than for the total U.S. white population.

For persons of Spanish origin, information on the extreme aged is available for 1970 as well for 1980. Table 4.8 provides data from both censuses. The three major Spanish categories—Mexicans, Puerto Ricans, and Cubans—are all groups which have had large-scale migration to the United States in the recent past and which have a history of high fertility. Accordingly, the percent of the population which is elderly is extremely low. About half of the Mexican-American population enumerated as 85 and over in 1970 was born in Mexico; most of the extreme aged Puerto Ricans and Cuban-Americans were born in the Caribbean.

In general, although minority groups have grown much more rapidly

TABLE 4.8:   POPULATION IN SPECIFIC SPANISH ORIGIN GROUPS, 65 YEARS OLD AND OVER
AND 85 YEARS AND OVER: 1970 AND 1980

Age group	Mexican		Puerto Rican		Cuban	
	1970[a]	1980	1970[a]	1980	1970[a]	1980
All ages	4,532,435	8,740,439	1,429,396	2,013,945	544,600	803,226
65 years and over	188,563	367,476	34,180	69,425	35,066	97,067
85 years and over	13,240	25,385	2,700	4,267	2,120	6,552
Percent of Population:						
65 years and over	4.2	4.2	2.4	3.4	6.4	12.1
85 years and over	0.3	0.3	0.2	0.2	0.4	0.8
Percent of 65 and over						
who are 85 and over	7.0	6.9	7.9	6.1	6.0	6.7

Sources: U.S. Bureau of the Census, 1973b: Table 1; 1980 Census Summary Tape File 2C.

a. Data based on 5 percent sample. Includes persons erroneously reported as
centenarians.

in recent decades than has the white population in the United States,
they are underrepresented among the aged. At the most recent census,
12 percent of all whites were aged 65 and over, whereas only 8 percent
of blacks were in this category. Among Asians, many of whom were
recent immigrants, only 6 percent were 65 or over, whereas the proportion among American Indians, who historically have had high fertility and relatively high mortality, was only 5 percent (Table 4.9). As
might be expected, the proportion in the extreme old ages (85 and over)
among each nonwhite group was sharply lower than among the white
population. On the other hand, the share of all elderly blacks and
Indians represented by those 85 and over was only slightly lower than
the corresponding percentage among whites. Of the total population
85 years and over in 1980, some 92 percent were white, 7 percent were
black and 1 percent Asian and American Indian combined.

ROLE OF AGE MISSTATEMENT

As seen in Chapters 2 and 3, age misstatement is often a significant
problem in studies of the extreme elderly, and this is most frequently

TABLE 4.9:   POPULATIONS BY RACE, 1980 CENSUS, AT SELECTED AGES, COMPARABLE
WITH EARLIER CENSUSES[a]

Age group	White	Black	Asian	American Indian[b]
All ages	195,129,941	26,495,025	3,500,439	1,420,400
65 years and over	23,175,914	2,086,858	211,736	74,919
85 years and over	2,061,424	158,920	13,852	5,871
Percent of population:				
65 years and over	11.9	7.9	6.0	5.3
85 years and over	1.1	0.6	0.4	0.4
Percent of 65 and over who are 85 and over	8.9	7.6	6.5	7.8

Source: 1980 Census Summary Tape File 2C.

a.   See "data comparability" discussion.
b.   American Indian includes Eskimo and Aleut.

seen in individuals incorrectly identifying themselves as centenarians.
It is probable, considering their lower literacy rates, that foreign-born
whites in the past were more likely to exaggerate their age than native-
born whites. At the 1900 census, almost half of the white centenarian
population were of foreign birth; probably overstatement of age played
some role in accounting for this high proportion. The percentage diminished in later censuses; however, as late as 1950 it was still more
than 35 percent.

But age exaggeration has declined markedly during the twentieth
century. This is exemplified by the sharp reduction in the proportion
that centenarians represent among blacks and other nonwhites in the
aggregate population reported as 85 years and over at decennial enu-
merations. According to Table 4.10 the percentage alleged to be centenarians slipped from about 12 percent in 1900 to a more modest and
realistic 4 percent by 1960.

It seems hardly coincidental that as the percentage of illiterates in
the population dwindled the proportion of centenarians also declined.
In fact it is very likely that much of the problem of age misreporting
stems from the fact that elderly blacks—until quite recently—were

TABLE 4.10:   PERCENT OF SELECTED POPULATIONS 85 YEARS OLD AND OVER REPORTED
AS 100 YEARS AND OVER: 1900 TO 1960

Year	Population 85 years and over	Population 100 years and over	Percent
Black			
1900	20,363	2,553	12.5
1910	22,138	2,675	12.1
1920	23,625	2,935	12.4
1930	26,358	2,467	9.4
Other Nonwhite			
1900	1,109	114	10.3
1910	1,481	116	7.8
1920	1,492	164	11.0
1930	1,812	151	8.3
All Nonwhite			
1940	35,411	2,268	6.4
1950[a]	45,315	2,470	5.5
1960[b]	71,637	3,029	4.2

Sources: U.S. Bureau of the Census, 1933: Volume II, Chapter 10, Table 9;
1943: Table 2; 1953a: Table 94; 1964: Table 156.

a. Based on 20 percent sample.
b. Based on 25 percent sample.

largely products of a slave society. Slaves, with only a few exceptions, were illiterate. A number of studies (e.g., U.S. Bureau of the Census, 1906) have demonstrated that the proportion of centenarians in the population—highly symptomatic of misreporting—is directly corre-lated with illiteracy. In many societies where illiteracy is common-place, age is not an important phenomenon and hence tends to be poorly reported.

The bulk of all individuals in every cohort of American blacks 85 years and over prior to that enumerated in 1950 spent their years of school age under the slavery system and failed to learn to read and write. U.S. census data indicate how widespread illiteracy was and how dramatically it has plummeted. Almost four-fifths of all blacks 55 to 64 years of age enumerated at the 1900 census were reported as illiterate (Table 4.11). These blacks were the generation aged 85 and

TABLE 4.11:   PERCENT ILLITERATE AMONG BLACK POPULATION AT SELECTED AGES:
1890 TO 1930

Census year	Percent illiterate by age		
	35-44 years	45-54 years	55-64 years
1890	70.5	80.8	86.3
1900	52.0	68.1	78.4
1910	32.3	47.0	63.0
1920	23.3	34.1	49.4
1930	16.8	24.2	34.4

Sources: U.S. Bureau of the Census, 1897:   p. 312; 1933: p. 1226.

over in 1930. If the figures for blacks 55 to 64 years of age in 1920 are
used as a guide, it was not until 1950 that perhaps half of the extreme
aged black population was able to read and write. Literacy has not
been queried in U.S. censuses since 1930, but based on data for individual age cohorts at that date, even in 1970 one-fourth of the very
elderly blacks were illiterate. As in the case of the black population,
American Indians have a historic background in which illiteracy was
commonplace and age overstatement a prominent feature of the decennial census statistics.

Other factors also may contribute to misreporting of age in some
nonwhite elderly populations. Hendricks and Hendricks (1977) point
out that one of the differential features of older blacks compared with
older whites is the "seemingly greater prestige accorded black elderly
within the family context" (p. 356). Older people are "granted a measure of respect not reaped by most whites." This high status commanded
by the elderly in the black subculture could be a motivating factor in
inducing blacks to wish to be considered among the very elderly.

DATA COMPARABILITY OVER TIME

Although race has been a traditional item in the decennial census,
an innovation in the 1980 census led to the publication of statistics
that produced a serious break in comparability. Although the effects
on the published counts of the population 85 years of age and older are
relatively minor compared with those for some other age groups, aware-

FIGURE 4.2: FACSIMILE OF THE 1970 AND 1980 CENSUS QUESTIONNAIRE
ITEMS ON RACE

1970 CENSUS

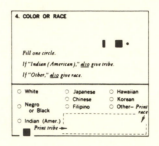

1980 CENSUS

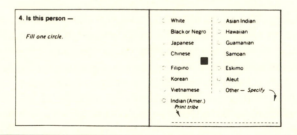

Sources: U.S. Bureau of the Census, 1972a, 1983a.

ness of the problem will aid in understanding some discrepancies in
the statistics.

The 1970 census was the first to obtain information on race principally through self-enumeration. (A facsimile of the questionnaire item
is shown in Figure 4.2.) Persons who did not classify themselves in one
of the eight specific categories on the questionnaire but entered such
responses as Mexican, Puerto Rican or a European origin were categorized as white by the Census Bureau before data processing. At the

1980 census several modifications were made in the race item. (A facsimile of this questionnaire also is shown in Figure 4.2.) These included the deletion of the word "race" from the query and the expansion of the number of specific categories from eight to fourteen. Apparently millions of persons, observing check boxes for such entries as Samoan and Guamanian, mistook the query for one of ethnic origin, and wrote such an entry after checking the "other" category. Unlike the procedure in 1970, the Census Bureau did not reclassify such persons prior to data processing.

As a result, the published counts of the 1980 census include some 6.7 million people in the "other races" category. The bulk of these persons were of Hispanic origin (5.8 million have classified themselves as Mexican, Puerto Rican or another specific Spanish group on the Spanish origin question.) For comparability with earlier censuses and for use in computing vital statistics, modified census counts were estimated by the Census Bureau. The modification procedures resulted in the addition of 6.4 million persons to the published "white" category, 135,000 persons to the black population and 183,000 persons to the category "Asian and Pacific Islander"; the count of American Indians was not altered (U.S. National Center for Health Statistics, 1983a; U.S. Bureau of the Census, 1982a). These modified counts have been used in Chapters 1 and 2 whenever appropriate since they have appeared in Census Bureau publications. In Chapter 3 and in subsequent chapters another means is used to prepare race data that corresponds to historical definitions from previous censuses and to vital statistics data. This method uses the 1980 census Summary Tape Files (computer counts containing detailed summaries) in place of published statistics. Combining the file data for "whites" with those for "other" persons (i.e., the population not classified as black, American Indian, Eskimo, Aleut, or Asian and Pacific Islander) yields a figure roughly comparable to the "white" category of prior censuses. For data tabulated on a 100 percent basis, a small number of individuals (e.g., several thousand Cambodians, Thais, etc.) who gave a write-in entry of an Asian and Pacific Islander group not specified in the census schedule (see Figure 4.2) are included among the "corrected" white population. In the census sample tabulations, and in the public use microdata tapes such write-in entries have been assigned to Asian and Pacific Islander categories and excluded from the "other" race category (U.S. Bureau of the Census, 1982c).

STATE OF CURRENT KNOWLEDGE

As a nation of immigrants, the population of the United States includes persons from a wide range of ethnic, cultural and racial groups. It is an established premise in gerontology that different groups have variant patterns of aging and health decrements, but the area of ethnic minority aging in social gerontology—that is, whether and how ethnicity and minority status affects aging—is only beginning to be explored. Little is known about the relationship between aging and ethnicity among whites, and less is available on blacks and Hispanics (Markides, 1983). Where racial and ethnic data are available and pertinent, they are included in this study. (See, for example, various tables in Chapters 5, 6, 7, 9 and 11.)

In a 1977 work Hendricks and Hendricks remarked on the neglect of the study of aged blacks by the professional gerontological community: "For a group whose size would place it among the two dozen or so largest independent nations of the world, there is remarkable lack of knowledge about the processes of aging among blacks" (p. 352). In the years since 1977, fortunately, such writers as Jackson (1980), Place (1981) and Manuel (1982) have focused on minority groups, especially blacks, thus helping to fill the gap in research. Although the volume of research has been increasing in recent years, Markides (1983, p. 115) has noted its shortcomings: "Careful examination of the literature discloses that many conclusions regarding the existence of ethnic or cultural differences are not based on scientific evidence because many studies either lack appropriate data or perform inappropriate data analyses for establishing the existence of ethnic differences."

The central interest of many studies to date is how membership in a particular ethnic minority group makes aging different from majority experience (Markides, 1983). With respect to old age, the main concern has been to document and remedy the disadvantages of ethnic membership, with little attention given to the possible advantages of belonging to an ethnic group (Meyers, 1980; Shryock and Siegel, 1973, p. 252).

Two major hypotheses have emerged in the literature: (1) the "age as leveller" concept, which "predicts a decline with age in the relative disadvantage of minority persons since all older people experience similar deprivations regardless of ethnicity" (Markides, 1983, p. 116); and (2) the "double jeopardy" hypothesis, the dominant model in current research, which maintains that the disadvantages experienced by minorities in youth and middle age are exacerbated in old age. Dowd and Bengtson (1981), who conducted the most frequently cited study to date, confirmed the double jeopardy hypothesis in respect to income and health, but other evidence is contradictory (Markides, 1983). The fact that Dowd and Bengston's analysis was confined to only one city (Los Angeles) and excluded those over age 75 should also be noted.

There is little doubt that race and ethnicity exert a considerable influence on the old-age experience of individuals. Meyers (1980, p. 66) notes that "there is evidence of profound and consistent difference, in terms of a number of social and epidemiological indicators, among different ethnic groups." Such differences do not wait to emerge only in old age however, but reflect cumulative lifetime experience. According to Place (1981, p. 196), "our cultural heritage shapes our expectations about life, about relationships with our family and friends. It guides our responses to pain and death; it provides content and purpose to our days." In addition, social values affect attitudes held by and about the elderly and thus can either ease the inevitable negative experiences of old age or make them more stressful. Thus, although the elderly regardless of background may face similar problems in old age, their responses to those problems are often conditioned by their cultural heritage.

Whether the negative aspects of old age are exacerbated by ethnic minority status, as concepts of double or multiple jeopardy suggest, is still an open question. Meyers (1980, pp. 69–70) has cautioned that:

Studies of multiple jeopardy must be interpreted with great caution to avoid confounding the effects of ethnicity with those of social class. Indeed ethnicity in the United States, as in most settings, is closely related to class.... These data reflect lifelong social and economic differences that have affected old age and the aging process in their own rights, independent of the effects of language, national origin, or race. Nevertheless their caveat notwithstanding, there appear to be more than chance associations between ethnicity and the health and social status of older adults.

With this criticism in mind and the additional cautionary note that wide variations exist *within* ethnic categories as well as between them (Place, 1981) a summary of existing knowledge on how ethnic membership may affect the elderly is presented here. White Americans are an extremely diverse group, and too little information is available to permit generalizations about the relationship between aging and ethnicity. However, it is commonly believed that non-Hispanic whites have lower levels of mutual assistance between elderly parents and children than do either blacks or Spanish-Americans; "the family remains the primary source of support and assistance for many ethnic elderly," and "the extended family has been especially important to the black elderly " (Place, 1981, pp. 209, 220). For American Indians "kinship obligations and respect for elders as embodiments of wisdom and special knowledge... continue to be significant values" (Place, 1981, p. 207). The situation is similar for Asian groups:

Respect for elders was central to the ancient value system of Oriental society and was institutionalized in elaborate rules of conduct governing virtually every aspect of life. Orientals have traditionally placed great emphasis on an authoritative family structure and obligations of young to old, child to parent. ... Adult children for the most part still feel an enormous sense of responsibility—sometimes reinforced by guilt and group pressures—toward the elderly. Few are institutionalized (Place, 1981, p. 215).

But, according to Markides (1983, p. 124), "there is considerable disagreement and controversy over how supportive the family is of the individual, particularly the older person, among minority groups." He suggests that supportive roles by minorities may have been overemphasized or romanticized in the literature. Even if one assumes that ethnic families are more supportive of their elderly, "the literature has not clarified the extent to which greater involvement with kin on the part of minority aged constitutes an advantage in family relations." If ties are mainly economic and not affectionate, life satisfaction may not be enhanced (Markides, 1983, p. 129). Meyers (1980) also notes that, whereas ethnic background may have a significant impact on family relationships, the qualitative aspects of such intergroup differences remain unknown:

There is ample evidence that there are differences in the structure and function of ethnic families and that they have a significant impact on many aspects of domestic life. However, there is no evidence that these differences are related to either the length or the quality of older peoples' lives (p. 69).

Ethnic background can influence an individual's responses to significant life events, such as reactions to illness and death. Following widowhood, for example, the elderly in some ethnic groups are more likely to live with adult children than their non-ethnic group counterparts. Such differences "stem from culturally influenced family organization and attitudes toward friendship and neighboring, as well as residence, economic status, and level of education" (Place, 1981, p. 203).

Cultural attitudes toward work and leisure can affect occupation and lifetime earnings and hence income levels in old age. Among Spanish-Americans, for example:

The tendency toward early retirement has been accounted for in both cultural and socioeconomic terms, revealing once again the often compounding effect of ethnicity and other factors in the life of an old person. Many Spanish-American men are engaged in lower-class manual labor, and physical decline means the end of employment. At the same time, work has not traditionally had the same value in Spanish cultures that it has in those influenced by the Protestant ethic, and, at least in the more rural areas, one's worth as a person is not necessarily linked to productivity (Place, 1981, pp. 213–214).

The interactions between ethnicity and social class have yet to be clarified. Place (1981, p. 208) has noted that "there is often greater similarity between blacks and whites of the same socioeconomic status than between people of the same race who differ widely in socioeconomic background." Such phenomena as the relatively low death rates observed among Asian groups may also reflect differences in socioeconomic status, since these groups have the highest levels of income and education of any population subgroup in the United States (U.S. Department of Health, Education and Welfare, 1979). Meyers (1980, p. 68) notes that although "ethnicity is clearly associated with relatively high rates of late-life morbidity, mortality, and social stress" ethnicity does not necessarily *cause* these problems; but "the treatment that an ethnic group may receive from the majority society compounds the risk."

In summary, despite general agreement among social scientists that ethnic minority group membership is a significant factor in old age and aging, the precise dimensions of the relationship have not yet been established. Likewise, the effects of race and ethnicity on the specific characteristics, needs, and expectations of the extreme elderly, as distinct from the young-old or the middle-aged, await the efforts of researchers.

5 *Geographic Distribution*

The extreme elderly, like the rest of the population, are unevenly distributed throughout the country. Moreover, the spatial distribution of this group as well as their motivations for moving (or aging in place) differ in some ways from those of the younger old and the general population. Migration rates of the elderly, while much lower than those of younger adults, are becoming increasingly important as the size of the aged population increases and their demographic and socioeconomic characteristics change over time. This chapter will present available data on the geographic distribution and mobility of persons 85 and over.

After 1970, the United States experienced a shift in population to small towns, nonmetropolitan areas, and to two major regions: the South and West. The shift to nonmetropolitan areas was greater than to either small towns or other regions. These trends in the geographic distribution of all age groups have sparked interest in the distribution of the elderly (Heaton, 1983, p. 95). The number of studies on aged migration is increasing, and there is growing recognition of the implications of the spatial distribution of elderly "consumers" versus working-age "producers." It is apparent that this topic will be a focus of scholarly interest for the coming years.

The trend away from metropolitan areas began among the elderly in the 1950s, two decades before the general population began leaving large urbanized areas (Heaton, 1983, p. 95). The population composition of a given locale is a product of both natural increase and in- and out-migration. Thus, the ages at which migration occurs have a significant impact on the composition of both sending and receiving areas. Current evidence indicates that migration of both old and young may be more important than fertility and mortality as a determinant of the geographical distribution of the aged. For example, the movement of young families to the suburbs has been largely responsible for the aging of central cities (Heaton, 1983).

Whether the oldest old are more concentrated geographically—in central cities or rural areas, for example—than other age categories is important in order to determine their needs and to allocate resources. It is equally important to ascertain the *characteristics* of the extreme elderly residing in a given locality. State-level data are inadequate for such assessments, since within a state wide variations may exist between central cities and the urban fringe, metropolitan and nonmetropolitan counties, and urban and rural areas. The particular mix of elderly in the area resulting from aging in place, as well as the migration patterns of both young and old, must be known in considerable detail for effective service planning and delivery. Davis, for instance, noted that "despite the national uniformity of the Medicare program, substantial variations in benefits occur according to geographical location. Elderly persons residing in the South and the North Central regions receive far fewer benefits than elderly persons in the Northeast and the West" (Davis, 1975, pp. 449–450). These discrepancies in benefits may be due in part to indirect factors such as regional disparities in levels of income and education, and in part to direct factors such as the geographic availability of medical resources.

GEOGRAPHIC DISTRIBUTION: STATES

In 1980 almost 49 percent of those aged 85 and over lived in eight states: California, New York, Pennsylvania, Florida, Illinois, Texas, Ohio, and Michigan. These same states contained nearly the same proportion (48 percent) of the general population (Table 5.1). In contrast slightly over 1.5 percent of the extreme elderly lived in seven of the least populated states—Alaska, Nevada, Wyoming, Delaware, Hawaii, North Dakota, Vermont—and the District of Columbia, which accounted for 2.2 percent of the population of all ages. The ranking of states according to their proportion of the extreme elderly population differs somewhat from their rank in terms of total population (Table

TABLE 5.1:   STATES WITH THE LARGEST NUMBERS OF EXTREME ELDERLY: 1980

State	Percent of U.S. population aged 85+	U.S. population of all ages Percent	Rank
California	9.7	10.4	1
New York	8.6	7.8	2
Pennsylvania	5.8	5.2	4
Florida	5.2	4.3	7
Illinois	5.1	5.0	5
Texas	5.0	6.3	3
Ohio	4.8	4.8	6
Michigan	3.6	4.1	8
Massachusetts	3.3	2.5	11
New Jersey	3.2	3.3	9

Source: U.S. Bureau of the Census, 1983a: Table 67.

5.1). For example, Florida ranks fourth in the nation in the proportion of extreme elderly but falls to seventh place in terms of total population. Texas, on the other hand, ranks sixth in its proportion of the very old but is the third most populous state in the nation.

From about 1.4 million in 1970, the population 85 and over increased to over 2.2 million by 1980. There was much state-to-state variation in this growth. Table 5.2 presents the numbers of extreme elderly in each state in 1970 and 1980 and the percentage change over the decade. Due to the substantial increase in the number of extreme elderly in the United States, no state has had a decline in the *number* of extreme elderly. What has occurred is a considerable change in the *proportionate* distribution of the population 85 and over due to old and young migration over time. From 1970 to 1980, 22 states gained in their proportionate share of this population, 1 state (Colorado) remained the same, and 28 states and the District of Columbia declined. Intercensal growth varied from a low of 5.4 percent in Alaska to a high of 129.4 percent in Arizona. California gained close to 86,000 extreme elderly,

TABLE 5.2: POPULATION AGED 85 AND OVER AND INTERCENSAL CHANGE, BY STATE: 1970 AND 1980

State	1970a	1980	Increase	Percent increase
United States	1,404,460	2,240,067	835,607	59.5
Alabama	22,550	34,019	11,469	50.9
Alaska	587	619	32	5.4
Arizona	8,667	19,878	11,211	129.4
Arkansas	17,626	26,354	8,728	49.5
California	132,084	218,017	85,933	65.1
Colorado	15,270	24,363	9,093	59.5
Connecticut	20,796	35,729	14,933	71.5
Delaware	3,152	5,269	2,117	67.2
Dist. of Columbia	5,002	6,385	1,383	27.6
Florida	52,569	117,342	64,773	123.2
Georgia	24,830	39,434	14,604	58.8
Hawaii	2,800	5,561	2,761	98.6
Idaho	5,312	8,476	3,164	59.6
Illinois	75,643	114,682	39,039	51.6
Indiana	37,540	54,410	16,870	44.9
Iowa	30,312	44,940	14,628	48.3
Kansas	22,758	33,455	10,697	47.0
Kentucky	24,855	35,036	10,181	41.0
Louisiana	20,379	30,535	10,156	49.8
Maine	9,311	14,099	4,788	51.4
Maryland	19,503	32,665	13,162	67.5
Massachusetts	48,208	73,908	25,700	53.3
Michigan	50,164	81,653	31,489	62.8
Minnesota	32,078	52,789	20,711	64.6
Mississippi	16,016	23,509	7,493	46.8
Missouri	43,207	61,072	17,865	41.3
Montana	5,934	8,837	2,903	48.9
Nebraska	15,540	23,744	8,204	52.8
Nevada	1,685	3,640	1,955	116.0
New Hampshire	6,071	9,650	3,579	59.0
New Jersey	43,935	72,231	28,296	64.4
New Mexico	4,583	8,783	4,200	91.6
New York	122,740	192,983	70,243	57.2
North Carolina	26,240	45,203	18,963	72.3
North Dakota	5,439	8,140	2,701	49.7
Ohio	73,011	108,426	35,415	48.5
Oklahoma	23,321	33,981	10,660	45.7
Oregon	17,532	28,431	10,899	62.2
Pennsylvania	85,155	129,960	44,805	52.6
Rhode Island	7,246	11,978	4,732	65.3
South Carolina	11,749	20,004	8,255	70.3
South Dakota	6,410	10,427	4,017	62.7
Tennessee	26,719	41,443	14,724	55.1
Texas	68,632	112,022	43,390	63.2
Utah	5,436	8,852	3,416	62.8
Vermont	3,981	6,007	2,026	50.9
Virginia	24,742	41,131	16,389	66.2
Washington	25,858	41,476	15,618	60.4
West Virginia	14,172	19,409	5,237	37.0
Wisconsin	35,025	55,637	20,612	58.8
Wyoming	2,067	3,473	1,406	68.0

Sources: U.S. Bureau of the Census, 1972a: Table 19; 1983a: Table 67.
a. Excludes persons reported as centenarians in the largely erroneous published figure.

while Florida gained nearly 65,000—percentage gains of 65.1 and 123.2 respectively. Some states, like Nevada and New Mexico, experienced very small numerical gains but large changes in percentage terms. Table 5.2 provides a very good indication of the uneven growth of the 85 and over group within the United States. Doubtlessly, figures calculated on a county or other substate basis would exhibit equal or even greater variability within many states.

Deimling has noted that "the age distribution after age 65 years varies considerably by race, sex, and geographical location" (1982, p. 151). The aging of the elderly population and the uneven distribution of the young old relative to the old old are both reflected in Table 5.3. The proportion aged 65 and over in 1980 varied from a low 2.9 percent in Alaska to a high of 17.3 percent in Florida. The range is considerably narrower, however, from 7.5 to 13.7 percent, when these two states are excluded. Arkansas, Iowa, Missouri, Nebraska, Rhode Island, and South Dakota all had proportions 65 and over in excess of 13 percent. States with elderly proportions in excess of the national average of 11.3 percent tended to be in the New England, Middle Atlantic, and West North Central sections of the country. States with the lowest proportions of elderly residents, on the other hand, tended to be in the South Atlantic (with the important exception of Florida) and Mountain states. There was considerable variation from state to state in the proportions 85 and over and in the ratio of persons 85 and above to those 65 and above. States with high proportions 65 and over generally tended to have high proportions of old old residents also. Yet Florida, which has the highest proportion of the total elderly in the nation, was not among the ten states with the highest proportion of extreme aged and had the fourth *lowest* ratio of 85 + /65 + of the fifty states. Arizona, another popular retirement state, also had a comparatively low proportion of its population aged 85 and over and similarly, a very low ratio of 85 + /65 + . For California, figures in both categories were close to the national average.

Between 1970 and 1980, the proportion 85 and over increased in every state except Alaska, which experienced a heavy in-migration of younger age groups. The proportion 65 and above also increased in every state although the amount of change varied widely. Percentage changes from 1970 to 1980 in the ratio of those 85 + to the group 65 and over are also shown in Table 5.3. Percentage increases of one-third or more occurred in twelve states, states as diverse as New York and

TABLE 5.3: PERCENT OF THE TOTAL POPULATION AGED 65 AND OVER, AGED 85 AND OVER,
AND RATIO OF 85+/65+, BY STATE: 1970 AND 1980

State	1970			1980			Percent change in ratio of 85+/65+
	65+	85+	85+/65+	65+	85+	85+/65+	
U.S.	9.87	0.69	7.00	11.28	0.99	8.77	25.3
Alabama	9.46	0.65	6.92	11.30	0.87	7.73	11.7
Alaska	2.29	0.20	8.52	2.87	0.15	5.36	-37.1
Arizona	9.12	0.49	5.37	11.31	0.73	6.47	20.5
Arkansas	12.36	0.92	7.41	13.67	1.15	8.43	13.8
California	9.03	0.66	7.33	10.20	0.92	9.03	23.2
Colorado	8.51	0.69	8.13	8.56	0.84	9.85	21.2
Connecticut	9.53	0.69	7.20	11.74	1.15	9.79	36.0
Delaware	8.00	0.58	7.19	9.96	0.89	8.90	23.8
Dist. of Col.	9.36	0.66	7.06	11.64	1.00	8.60	21.8
Florida	14.56	0.77	5.31	17.31	1.20	6.95	30.9
Georgia	8.01	0.54	6.76	9.46	0.72	7.63	12.9
Hawaii	5.74	0.36	6.35	7.89	0.58	7.30	15.0
Idaho	9.51	0.75	7.84	9.92	0.90	9.05	15.4
Illinois	9.84	0.68	6.92	11.04	1.00	9.09	31.4
Indiana	9.51	0.72	7.60	10.66	0.99	9.29	22.2
Iowa	12.40	1.07	8.65	13.30	1.54	11.59	34.0
Kansas	11.85	1.01	8.55	12.96	1.42	10.92	27.7
Kentucky	10.48	0.77	7.37	11.19	0.96	8.55	16.0
Louisiana	8.42	0.56	6.64	9.61	0.73	7.55	13.7
Maine	11.55	0.94	8.13	12.53	1.25	10.01	23.1
Maryland	7.64	0.50	6.51	9.38	0.77	8.26	26.9
Mass.	11.18	0.85	7.58	12.66	1.29	10.17	34.2
Michigan	8.48	0.57	6.66	9.85	0.88	11.24	68.8
Minnesota	10.75	0.84	7.84	11.77	1.30	11.01	40.4
Mississippi	10.03	0.72	7.20	11.48	0.93	8.12	12.8
Missouri	11.99	0.92	7.71	13.18	1.24	9.42	22.2
Montana	9.90	0.85	8.63	10.75	1.12	10.45	21.1
Nebraska	12.37	1.05	8.47	13.10	1.51	11.54	36.2
Nevada	6.34	0.34	5.44	8.21	0.45	5.53	1.7
New Hamp.	10.63	0.82	7.74	11.18	1.05	9.37	21.1
New Jersey	9.72	0.61	6.30	11.67	0.98	8.40	33.3
New Mexico	6.95	0.45	6.49	8.90	0.67	7.58	16.8
New York	10.75	0.67	6.26	12.31	1.10	8.93	42.7
N. Carolina	8.15	0.52	6.34	10.26	0.77	7.49	18.1
N. Dakota	10.74	0.88	8.20	12.32	1.25	10.12	23.4
Ohio	9.37	0.69	7.32	10.83	1.00	9.27	26.6
Oklahoma	11.71	0.91	7.78	12.43	1.12	9.03	16.1
Oregon	10.84	0.84	7.73	11.52	1.08	9.37	21.2
Pennsylvania	10.79	0.72	6.69	12.90	1.09	8.49	26.9
Rhode Island	10.98	0.77	6.97	13.40	1.26	9.44	35.4
S. Carolina	7.37	0.45	6.15	9.20	0.64	6.96	13.2
S. Dakota	12.09	0.96	7.96	13.18	1.51	11.46	44.0
Tennessee	9.78	0.68	6.96	11.27	0.90	8.01	15.1
Texas	8.86	0.61	6.92	9.64	0.79	8.17	18.1
Utah	7.32	0.51	7.01	7.48	0.61	8.10	15.5
Vermont	10.69	0.90	8.38	11.37	1.17	10.33	23.3
Virginia	7.87	0.53	6.76	9.45	0.77	8.14	20.4
Washington	9.45	0.76	8.03	10.44	1.00	9.61	19.7
W. Virginia	11.15	0.81	7.29	12.20	1.00	8.16	11.9
Wisconsin	10.70	0.79	7.41	11.99	1.18	9.86	33.1
Wyoming	9.09	0.62	6.84	7.92	0.74	9.34	36.5

Sources: U.S. Bureau of the Census, 1972a: Table 19; 1983a: Table 67.

Nebraska, Massachusetts and Iowa. Significantly, percentage changes in states like California, Arizona and Texas were below the national average of 25 percent. Hence the phenomenon of the aging of the elderly population is not affecting every state equally. The largest change in the ratio of extreme elderly to total elderly occurred in Michigan (69 percent), followed by South Dakota, New York, and Minnesota, all in excess of 40 percent.

GEOGRAPHIC DISTRIBUTION: REGIONS

Percentages of extreme elderly living in the various regions of the United States have also changed over time. (The areas included in each region are shown in Figure 5.1). Generally, the proportions have decreased steadily in the Northeast and North Central regions and increased in the South and West. These changes parallel recent overall population shifts in the United States. Between 1950 and 1980 the proportion of the extreme elderly living in the North Central region declined from 34.6 to 29.0 percent of the total in the U.S. During the same period, the proportion living in the Northeast decreased from 27.8 to 24.4 percent. The proportion resident in the South increased from 24.4 percent in 1950 to 29.6 percent in 1980 and that in the West from 13.2 to 17.0 percent over the same period (U.S. Bureau of the Census, 1953a, Table 62, 1983a, Table 54).

A closer look at the period 1970 to 1980 indicates that gains and losses in percentages varied in the divisions *within* the four major regions (Table 5.4). In the Northeastern region the share of the extreme aged living in the New England division declined by less than 1 percent, whereas that in the Middle Atlantic division decreased by 1.6 percent. In the Southern region only the South Atlantic division increased its proportion of extreme elderly, by 12.6 percent. Both the East South Central and the West South Central divisions declined. In the West both the Mountain and Pacific divisions increased their proportions during the 1970s.

The general population was distributed somewhat differently than the old old in both 1970 and 1980, with lower proportions of the population of all ages in the Northeast and North Central regions and higher proportions in the South and West. By 1980, the discrepancies between the distribution of total population and the extreme elderly group were even greater. The South and West regions gained more

FIGURE 5.1: CENSUS REGIONS AND GEOGRAPHIC DIVISIONS
OF THE UNITED STATES

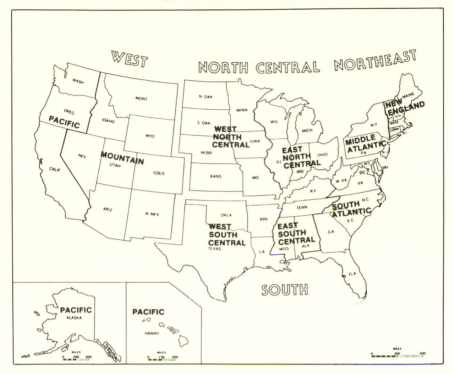

Source: U.S. Bureau of the Census, 1983a.

total population than extreme elderly during the intercensal period, and the Northeast and North Central regions lost more total population than those 85 and over. Only the South Atlantic division (and within it the single state of Florida) gained significantly more old old than total population. The East South Central and West South Central divisions both lost extreme elderly and gained total population. The gain of 11.3 percent in total population in the West far surpassed the gain of 4.7 percent in the proportion 85 and over.

The regional distribution of the 65–84 age group with that of the extreme elderly is contrasted in Table 5.5. Relative to persons 65–84 years, greater proportions of the oldest old live in the Northeast (es-

TABLE 5.4:   PERCENT DISTRIBUTION OF TOTAL POPULATION AND OF PERSONS 85 YEARS OLD
AND OVER, BY U.S. REGION AND DIVISION: 1970 AND 1980

Region and division	Percent of U.S. total: 1970[a]		Percent of U.S. total: 1980		Percent change in proportion 1970-1980	
	All ages	85+	All ages	85+	All ages	85+
Total	100.00	100.00	100.00	100.00	--	--
Northeast	24.13	24.74	21.69	24.40	-10.1	-1.4
New England	5.83	6.81	5.45	6.76	- 6.5	-0.7
Middle Atlantic	18.13	17.93	16.24	17.64	-10.4	-1.6
North Central	27.84	30.41	25.98	28.99	- 6.7	-4.7
East N. Central	19.81	19.32	18.48	18.52	- 6.7	-4.1
West N. Central	8.03	11.09	7.58	10.47	- 5.6	-5.6
South	30.90	28.63	33.27	29.63	7.7	3.5
South Atlantic	15.09	12.96	16.31	14.59	8.1	12.6
East S. Central	6.30	6.42	6.47	5.98	2.7	-6.9
West S. Central	9.50	9.25	10.48	9.06	10.3	-2.1
West	17.13	16.22	19.06	16.98	11.3	4.7
Mountain	4.08	3.49	5.02	3.85	23.0	10.3
Pacific	13.05	12.74	14.04	13.13	7.6	3.1

Source: See Table 5.2.

a.   Excludes persons reported as centenarians in the largely erroneous published figure.

pecially New England) and North Central regions. The younger old
are more concentrated in the South, especially the South Atlantic division (and in particular the state of Florida). The proportions of 65–
84 year-olds and those 85 and above who live in the West are almost
identical. These distribution patterns conform with recent theories on
the migration of the elderly: namely, that it is primarily the healthier,
higher socioeconomic status, *younger* old who move to the Sunbelt
states soon after retirement; whereas the "frail elderly" tend to age in
place, to make only local moves or, if they did migrate to Sunbelt states
when young old, return to their state of origin when they can no longer
maintain their independence (Biggar, 1980; Longino and Biggar, 1982;
Wiseman and Roseman, 1979; Collins, 1984).

GEOGRAPHIC DISTRIBUTION: URBAN/RURAL

The distribution by race and urban-rural residence of persons 85 and
over is shown in Table 5.6.These data indicate that during the 1970s

TABLE 5.5: DISTRIBUTION OF PERSONS AGED 65-84 YEARS AND 85 YEARS OLD AND OVER, BY
U.S. REGION AND DIVISION: 1980

Region and division	65-84 years		85 years and over	
	Number	Percent of U.S. population	Number	Percent of U.S. population
Total	23,304,066	100.00	2,240,067	100.00
Northeast	5,525,170	23.70	546,545	24.40
New England	1,368,997	5.87	151,371	6.76
Mid Atlantic	4,156,173	17.83	395,174	17.64
North Central	6,041,945	25.93	649,375	28.99
East N. Central	4,077,763	17.50	414,808	18.52
West N. Central	1,964,182	8.43	234,567	10.47
South	7,819,775	33.55	663,741	29.63
South Atlantic	4,036,650	17.32	326,842	14.59
East S. Central	1,522,665	6.53	134,007	5.98
West S. Central	2,260,460	9.70	202,892	9.06
West	3,917,176	16.81	380,406	16.98
Mountain	974,064	4.18	86,302	3.85
Pacific	2,943,112	12.63	294,104	13.13

Source: U.S. Bureau of the Census, 1983a: Table 67.

the number and the proportion of extreme elderly rose in urban areas but the proportion declined in rural areas. The proportion of extreme aged blacks in urban areas increased from 74.4 percent in 1970 to 78.6 percent in 1980, a gain of 4.2 percentage points, whereas the percentage for whites increased by only 3.8 points from 73.1 percent to 76.9 percent. Greater proportions of blacks than whites were classified as urban in both 1970 and 1980. This finding is of interest since blacks historically were concentrated in the rural South. It was only after 1910 that large numbers migrated to metropolitan areas outside the South.

A further refinement of the urban-rural data for 1980 shows the distribution of the total, elderly, and extreme elderly populations within urban areas by race (Table 5.7). For whites, the proportion urban increases steadily with age, as the proportion rural simultaneously falls. Within the urban sector, extreme elderly whites are more concentrated in central cities than either the population 65 and over as a whole or the general population. The proportion of extreme elderly who live outside urbanized areas is greater for whites than for blacks.

The proportions urban for blacks show an opposite pattern from that

TABLE 5.6:   RESIDENCE OF POPULATION BY SELECTED AGE GROUP AND RACE, URBAN AND
              RURAL: 1970 AND 1980

Race and age	Number (in thousands)				Percent distribution			
	1970[a]		1980		1970[a]		1980	
	Urban	Rural	Urban	Rural	Urban	Rural	Urban	Rural
Total								
All ages	149,325	53,887	167,051	59,495	73.5	26.5	73.7	26.3
65 years and over	14,631	5,434	19,046	6,503	72.9	27.1	74.5	25.5
85 years and over	1,106	405	1,727	513	73.2	26.8	77.1	22.9
White								
All ages	128,773	48,976	134,322	54,050	72.4	27.6	71.3	28.7
65 years and over	13,309	5,021	16,932	6,015	72.6	27.4	73.8	26.2
85 years and over	1,007	370	1,572	473	73.1	26.9	76.9	23.1
Black								
All ages	18,367	4,213	22,594	3,901	81.3	18.7	85.3	14.7
65 years and over	1,192	367	1,682	405	76.5	23.5	80.6	19.4
85 years and over	87	30	125	34	74.4	25.6	78.6	21.4

Sources: U.S. Bureau of the Census, 1972a: Table 50; 1983a: Table 43.

a.   Includes persons erroneously reported as centenarians.

of whites—the urban share of the total falls with increasing age. With advancing age, more blacks are concentrated in rural areas and the black urban proportion decreases. This reflects both youthful out-migration from rural areas and the aging-in-place of older blacks. Inside urban areas, oldest old blacks are somewhat less concentrated in central cities than blacks in the general population or the total elderly population. Nevertheless, in 1980 over half of all blacks aged 85 and above were living in the central cities of urbanized areas compared to less than one-third of whites in that age category. A slightly greater proportion of whites than blacks among the oldest old were classified as rural in 1980.

The urban/rural distribution of extreme elderly is significant from the point of view of poverty levels and consequent needs for special services. According to the Bureau of the Census (1980 Census Public Use Microdata Sample), about one in three (13.2 percent) urban blacks

TABLE 5.7:   PERCENT DISTRIBUTION OF POPULATION BY SELECTED AGE GROUP AND RACE, BY
             TYPE OF RESIDENCE: 1980

Urban-rural residence and race	All ages	65 and over	85 and over
White			
Urban	71.3	73.8	76.9
Inside urbanized areas	58.5	58.4	58.8
Central cities	24.6	28.7	30.7
Urban fringe	33.8	29.7	28.1
Outside urbanized areas	12.8	15.4	18.1
Rural	28.7	26.2	23.1
Black			
Urban	85.3	80.6	78.5
Inside urbanized areas	75.9	68.1	63.6
Central cities	57.2	55.6	51.5
Urban fringe	18.7	12.5	12.1
Outside urbanized areas	9.4	12.5	14.8
Rural	14.7	19.4	21.5

Source: U.S. Bureau of the Census, 1983a: Table 43.

aged 85 and above (exclusive of the institutionalized) were below the poverty level in 1980, compared to fewer than one in five whites (17.2 percent). In rural areas, half (49.0 percent) of all extreme aged blacks were below the poverty level, compared to about one in four whites (26.7 percent).

GEOGRAPHIC MOBILITY

Population redistribution through internal migration is not a random process in any age group. Traditionally, given the domination of economic factors in the push-pull of population redistribution, geographic mobility has been related to labor markets and upward social mobility (Heaton, Clifford, and Fuguitt, 1980). Lee has noted that migration after age 60 differs from moves that take place earlier in a person's life. "It smacks more of an end than a beginning; the sloughing off rather than the taking on of responsibilities; retrenchment rather than expansion" (Lee, 1980, p. 132). The movement of the elderly population is clearly not related to employment prospects. For the young old, retirement is an important determinant. As greater numbers of the elderly receive retirement benefits, plan for their retirement, and place increasing emphasis on the quality of retired life, migration of the elderly will "increase with time, and the migrating streams of the elderly will continue to be diffuse in origin and highly specific in destination. What we have so far witnessed is only the beginning of a movement" (Lee, 1980, p. 135).

Whereas elderly *inter*community moves are often voluntary responses to better climate and amenities at the destination, local or *intra*community moves often involve involuntary factors, such as loss of income, widowhood, and illness. Such involuntary factors are closely related to increasing age and hence affect the old old much more frequently than the young old. According to Biggar (1980, p. 89), "local mobility selects the more dependent elderly." Wiseman (1980) cites failing health and the need for assistance as major reasons for local moves among the aged. The propensity to move increases during the final stage of old age, but this is the result of "biological decline and loss of independent residential status, e.g., institutionalization, 'moving in' with relatives, or relocation to a limited care facility" (Wiseman and Roseman, 1979, p. 327). Longino and Biggar (1981) also note that increases in mobility at the oldest ages are related to increasing dependence, rather than positive, voluntary choices. Persons such as relatives, social workers, and physicians may make or strongly influence the decision to move under these circumstances (Wiseman and Roseman, 1979). The same authors further note that women have higher mobility rates than men at the oldest ages. This mobility doubtless reflects the lack of a spouse. Many extreme elderly males are currently married, but the great majority of women are widowed. If these elderly widows require assistance, they are more often compelled to move in order to obtain it. On the other hand, elderly males in need of assistance often have spouses to turn to and do not need to change residence.

Dependency-related moves are mainly local in nature. As with the decision to move, the decision of where to go may also be constrained:

That group of older persons who have little control over the decision to move have little control in the decision of where to move. Many of these people are being institutionalized. Their locational choices, if not dictated by others, are limited to the few facilities available to them.... Someone who has just lost a spouse or recently suffered significant health decline is likely to rely on kinship or familial ties not only for emotional support but also as a potential or actual source of many other kinds of assistance. Such migrants would have very limited search spaces—limited to the residential communities of their immediate kin who have migrated from the home community earlier (Wiseman and Roseman, 1979, pp. 329–330).

Both the numbers of movers and their characteristics must be considered in gauging the impact of migration on sending and receiving areas. The assumption that all the elderly need special services of the same type or degree is unwarranted. Service demand does not necessarily increase or decrease in proportion to the influx or outflow (or aging-in-place) of elderly residents. The out-migration of younger old may, in fact, concentrate the demand for services among the older, less healthy, poorer and less educated components of the elderly population left behind (Biggar, 1980, p. 89).

Longino and Biggar note that variations in the characteristics of migrants and nonmigrants may be even greater at the local level than at the state level (1982, p. 156). Furthermore, "the changing characteristics of older people in a metropolitan county or in a cluster of rural counties that result from population redistribution have been invisible in census data. It is only at this scale that one can talk meaningfully and usefully about migration impacts" (Longino and Biggar, 1982, p. 158). Thus, planners need to know the age distribution *within* the 65 and over population, and their sociodemographic characteristics to plan intelligently on a *local* level. Aggregate state-level data are inadequate for such purposes due to the tremendous local variations within each state.

In order to determine the residential mobility of the population, decennial censuses from 1960 on have included a question on the usual place of residence five years before the census. If residence was not in "this house" at the earlier date, the location was coded in terms of state, county or foreign country. At each census the proportion of those recorded as having moved was higher for the extreme elderly than for those who were between the ages of 65–69 years (Table 5.8). In 1955–60, 30.0 percent of those age 65–69 years old moved compared to 34.6 percent of persons 85 years and over. The figures for 1975–80 were 22.9 percent (65–69 years) and 29.3 percent (85 and over).

TABLE 5.8: MOBILITY OF THE POPULATION 65 TO 69 YEARS AND 85 YEARS AND OVER:
1955-60, 1965-70, AND 1975-80

Mobility status	1955-1960[a]		1965-1970		1975-1980	
	65 to 69 years	85 years and over	65 to 69 years[b]	85 years and over[c]	65 to 69 years[d]	85 years and over
	Number (in thousands)					
Total	6,186	864	6,983	1,419	8,876	2,183
Non-movers	4,330	565	5,041	913	6,841	1,543
Movers	1,856	299	1,942	506	2,035	640
	Percent distribution					
Total	100.0	100.0	100.0	100.0	100.0	100.0
Non-movers	70.0	65.4	72.2	64.3	77.1	70.7
Movers	30.0	34.6	27.8	35.7	22.9	29.3

Sources: U.S. Bureau of the Census, 1964: Table 164; 1973d: Table 196; 1984a:
Table 259; 1970 Census Public Use Sample; 1980 Census Public Use
Microdata Sample.

a. Based on 25 percent sample.
b. Based on 15 percent sample.
c. Ages 85 to 99 only.
d. Based on approximately 19 percent sample.

The types of moves made by the two age groups were somewhat different. In 1975–80, 22.8 percent of all migrants aged 65–69 moved to another state, whereas only 13.7 percent of the extreme elderly movers were interstate migrants. It should be noted that by age 85 most voluntary migration is probably ended. After 85 a change of residence results from the need for nursing care and other forms of assistance. Indeed it is the high proportion of the very elderly population located in institutions that accounts for the fact that the extreme elderly appear to be more "mobile" than the young-old. Table 5.9 indicates that only 20 percent of all persons 85 years and over residing in households in 1980 had moved to their current residence during the previous five years. However, almost 60 percent of that large share of the extreme elderly residing in group quarters had moved from another residence during the prior half decade. Such moves tend to be local moves, the large majority occurring within the same county.

Those 85 and over, usually retired for many years, have long since adjusted to changes in employment status. Thus geographic mobility

TABLE 5.9:   MOBILITY OF PERSONS 85 YEARS OLD AND OVER, BY RESIDENCE IN GROUP
             QUARTERS AND HOUSEHOLDS: 1965-70 AND 1975-80

(percent distribution)

Mobility status	In group quarters		In households	
	1965-70[a]	1975-80	1965-70[a]	1975-80
Total	100.0	100.0	100.0	100.0
Non-movers	24.1	40.3	73.8	79.9
Movers	75.9	59.7	26.1	20.1

Sources: U.S. Bureau of the Census, 1970 Census Public Use Sample; 1980 Census
           Public Use Microdata Sample.

[a]   Ages 85 to 99 years only.

of the old old, when it does occur, must be attributable to different factors. In fact, migration at the extreme old ages is in sharp contrast to that occurring earlier in life. There may seldom be any real choice at all for the individuals involved. Rather, inability to function independently because of disability from chronic illness, perhaps combined with the loss of a spouse and other kin able and willing to assist them, seems to be the critical determinant of movement in the final stage of life.

Countermigration, defined as return to the state of origin by persons who had previously moved elsewhere, especially to the Sunbelt states, is also a highly selective phenomenon. An analysis of 1980 census data shows that elderly people returning to New York from Florida, for example, were older, poorer, and more likely to be widowed than those moving to Florida from New York (Collins, 1984). The return migrants were more often female, less likely to live independently, and more likely to be disabled or institutionalized. Countermigration trends are likely to mitigate somewhat the concern of officials in states like Florida, some of whom have expressed doubts about "whether the state's long romance with retirees may be reaching a point of diminishing returns" as once healthy and self-reliant younger inmigrants become increasingly ill and in need of expensive services with advancing age (Stuart, 1983). At the same time, countermigration may affect the original sending states, such as New York, Pennsylvania, and New Jersey, in a negative manner. Unlike countermigrants, migrants to

Florida tend to be younger, more independent, and better off financially, whereas countermigrants are often the opposite. Thus states like Florida may benefit from the migration streams in *both* directions, whereas other states, like Ohio and New York, stand to lose out on both counts. The latter lose the economic benefits of younger old, healthy and well-off consumers of housing, recreation, and other amenities, only to gain back the same people when they are old old consumers of expensive health and welfare services. Thus whether or not elderly migration is good for a particular area depends heavily on the characteristics of the movers.

CONCLUSION

The numbers, proportions, and characteristics of extreme elderly residents affect aspects of life within a state or local area. Hence the uneven distribution of the extreme aged throughout the nation has an important bearing on policymaking and the establishment and financing of health and other facilities serving the aged. State-level dependency burdens are affected by the distribution of extreme aged between states. If delivery of services is to be equitable and effective, federal, state and local service agencies must take account of the within-state population distribution of the old old, as well as their sociodemographic characteristics. Conditions that affect the ability of individual states to provide services to needy elderly include the size of the working-age population relative to the state's burden of child and old-age dependency, its unemployment rate, wage and price structure, and its quality and quantity of housing. The demand for services by the extreme aged is affected by such variables as income, education, health status, and the proportion living alone.

The geographic distribution of population and the migration processes underlying that distribution affect the extreme elderly on three levels: individual, familial and societal. Where the individual is geographically situated affects his conditions of life in every respect. When independence is no longer feasible and assistance is required in extreme old age, the geographic proximity of surviving kin is a factor in avoiding or delaying institutionalization or reliance on outside agencies. Lastly, on an aggregate level, the availability of health and welfare services is not uniform over the nation. Where people live will continue to influence the kinds, extent, and quality of services available to them.

6 Social and Economic Characteristics

No single set of statistics so well reflects the earlier life of the extreme aged, and predict the quality of life during their remaining years, as do social and economic characteristics. This chapter will consider such factors as marital status, income and educational attainment, as well as their interrelations and trends. Projected changes in these factors over time will also be considered since the "carry-over" effect of the advantages or deprivations of youth and middle age into old age is an important component. For example, those with low socioeconomic status jobs during their middle years generally have neither savings for retirement nor private pensions to supplement retirement income from government programs. Those with little formal education may also be handicapped in learning about benefits available in social welfare programs for the elderly. When these economic and educational factors are combined with the poorer health that usually accompanies advancing age, the result is that many who were at the lower end of the socioeconomic scale during their earlier years see their status fall even further behind at ages 85 and above.

The elderly are not a homogeneous group. A comparison of the "young old" (aged 65–74) to the "old old" (85 and over), reveals "many sharp differences with respect to such characteristics as living arrangements, marital status, work status, income, education, health, kinship support, and use of leisure time" (Siegel, 1979). More of the "young old" are married since mortality is lower among this group, and their better health enables them to supplement their retirement income with part-time employment if they choose—or perhaps even postpone retirement for a few years beyond age 65. Better health also means that more persons age 65–74 years are able to live independently. In addition, census statistics indicate that the rapidly expanding 85 years and over population, as well as the 75 to 84–year-olds who will soon enter the extreme aged category, are better educated and have higher income levels than these groups had in the past. Rising levels of income and education among the elderly imply a demand for more and better health care and other governmental programs tailored to their needs, as well as a greater ability to seek out such services.

MARITAL STATUS

Table 6.1 shows the marital status distribution of the population 65 and over by age and sex from 1940 to 1980. For both sexes, percentages currently married increased substantially over time in nearly every age group. Nonetheless, there are sizable differences by sex within each age category. At ages 85 and over, almost 1 out of 2 males were married compared to only about 1 in 12 women in 1980 (Figure 6.1). The differential by sex for the currently married has widened over time. In 1940 the gap was about 26 percentage points, by 1970 it was close to 33 points and by 1980, 40 points. Much higher percentages of women are widowed relative to men at every date. These statistics and the trends over time reflect the greater survival potential for females, their tendency to marry men older than themselves, and the decreased likelihood of remarriage following widowhood or divorce (Glick, 1979).

Even if women over 85 wished to remarry, a decreasing sex ratio over time will limit their options. (From 68 males per 100 females over 85 in 1950, the ratio fell to 44 per 100 by 1980, and is projected to decline even more by 2000.) Since widowhood and divorce have considerable negative impact on women's income, such trends imply an increasing need for social services for elderly females. The important role of marital status in affecting the likelihood of an individual's entry into a nursing home and the probable outcome of that event are discussed further in Chapter 7.

The rates of widowhood reflect a sex differential similar to that found for marriage (Table 6.1). In 1980 7.3 percent of all males age 65 to 69 were widowed, whereas 33.8 percent of all women were widows. For the 85 and over population the figures are 44 percent for males and

TABLE 6.1: PERCENT DISTRIBUTION OF THE POPULATION 65 YEARS OLD AND OVER BY
MARITAL STATUS, BY AGE GROUP AND SEX: 1940 TO 1980

Age and marital status	Male					Female				
	1940	1950[a]	1960[b]	1970[c]	1980[d]	1940	1950[a]	1960[b]	1970[c]	1980[d]
Married										
65-69 years	71.9	74.0	79.4	80.6	83.0	46.5	48.9	51.6	52.0	54.8
70-74 years	64.9	67.5	73.1	75.8	79.6	34.3	36.6	39.1	40.0	42.7
75-79 years	56.1	59.0	64.7	68.8	73.6	23.0	24.7	27.4	27.9	29.5
80-84 years	45.8	48.2	53.7	58.0	64.4	13.5	14.2	16.2	17.2	17.7
85 and over	33.0	33.6	38.7	42.4	48.4	6.7	7.0	8.2	9.9	8.4
Widowed										
65-69 years	16.2	15.0	10.2	8.8	7.3	43.1	41.1	37.9	36.5	33.8
70-74 years	23.8	22.2	16.8	13.8	11.2	55.5	53.3	50.4	49.0	46.2
75-79 years	33.3	31.4	25.3	21.2	17.6	67.3	65.1	62.2	61.1	60.0
80-84 years	44.7	43.3	37.2	32.0	27.3	77.1	75.9	73.1	71.9	72.3
85 and over	58.5	57.9	52.8	47.0	43.8	85.1	82.9	81.4	79.0	81.8
Divorced										
65-69 years	1.6	2.3	2.7	3.5	4.4	1.0	1.5	2.7	4.1	5.5
70-74 years	1.3	1.9	2.4	3.1	3.7	0.7	1.1	2.1	3.3	4.5
75-79 years	1.1	1.5	2.1	2.7	3.2	0.4	0.7	1.5	2.7	3.6
80-84 years	0.8	1.1	1.7	2.4	2.6	0.3	0.5	1.1	2.1	2.7
85 and over	0.6	0.8	1.4	2.3	2.1	0.2	0.4	0.8	1.6	2.0
Never married										
65-69 years	10.3	8.7	7.7	7.1	5.4	9.4	8.4	7.9	7.4	5.9
70-74 years	9.9	8.3	7.8	7.3	5.5	9.5	9.0	8.4	7.8	6.6
75-79 years	9.5	8.1	7.9	7.3	5.6	9.2	9.4	8.8	8.4	7.0
80-84 years	8.7	7.4	7.4	7.6	5.7	9.2	9.4	9.5	8.8	7.3
85 and over	7.9	7.7	7.1	8.3	5.6	8.0	9.7	9.6	9.5	7.9

Sources: U.S. Bureau of the Census, 1943: Volume II, Table 6; 1953a: Table 4;
1964: Table 176; 1973d: Table 203; 1984a: Table 264; 1970 Census
Public Use Sample

a. Based on 20 percent sample.
b. Based on 25 percent sample.
c. Based on 5 percent sample for ages 65 to 84 years and on Public Use Sample
for ages 85 to 99 years only.
d. Based on approximately 19 percent sample.

FIGURE 6.1: MARITAL STATUS OF MALE AND FEMALE POPULATIONS 85 YEARS AND OVER: 1980

(in thousands)

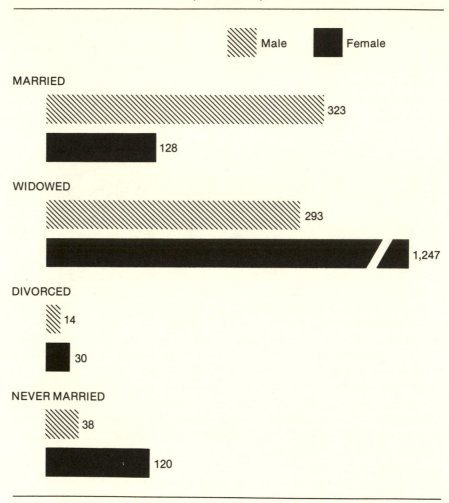

Source: U.S. Bureau of the Census 1984a, Table 264.

82 percent for females. During the decades since 1940 the rate of widowhood has decreased somewhat for all age levels, more so for males than for females reflecting the sex-specific increases in length of life. Among the extreme elderly the proportions who were divorced has, as would be expected, increased since 1940, but the figures are still very low.

Although divorce is now uncommon among the elderly, Uhlenberg and Meyers (1981) have predicted that "the number of older persons with an earlier divorce, the number whose marital status is 'divorced,' and the number who experience a divorce in old age can all be expected to increase rapidly in coming years." Cherlin (1983, p. 14) asserts that "it is reasonable to expect that by the turn of the century, one-fourth of all persons reaching old age will have experienced divorce" and believes that even this figure may be too low. The percentage of the population 85 and over who have never married has tended to fluctuate moderately, with relatively low levels for males and females observed in 1980.

According to Table 6.2, at each census date extreme aged nonwhites of both sexes were more likely to be married than were whites. The only exceptions occurred in 1950 when nonwhite women were slightly less likely to be currently married than their white counterparts and in 1980 when nonwhite men were less likely. Nonwhite males were less likely to be widowed than white males, (except in 1980) whereas the reverse was true for the two female groups. In every group, the percentage classified as divorced was very small but shows some tendency to increase over time. White women were more likely to be single than white males. For nonwhites the difference by sex was just the opposite, with males more likely to have never married. For both sexes in each racial category, greater percentages generally were currently married and fewer widowed at each successive census date, but there were several exceptions to this pattern (some of which may have been due to sampling variation).

A cautionary note about the data in Table 6.2 is necessary. Age misreporting, particularly for nonwhite males, may affect the statistics on marital status. Age exaggeration among extreme elderly nonwhites (Rosenwaike, 1979) may help to explain the larger percentages at censuses prior to 1980 currently married and lower percentages who were divorced relative to white males. For example, some nonwhite males classified as age 85 and over may actually have been under 85. Non-

TABLE 6.2:   MARITAL STATUS OF THE POPULATION 85 YEARS OLD AND OVER, BY RACE
AND SEX: 1940 TO 1980

(percent distribution)

Race and marital status	Male					Female				
	1940	1950[a]	1960[b]	1970[c]	1980[d]	1940	1950[a]	1960[b]	1970[c]	1980[d]
White										
Total	100.0	100.0	100.0	100.0	100.0	100.0	100.0	100.0	100.0	100.0
Married	32.4	33.4	38.3	42.3	48.8	6.6	7.0	8.1	9.8	8.3
Widowed	58.9	58.3	53.0	47.4	43.7	84.7	82.9	81.0	78.9	81.6
Divorced	0.6	0.8	1.4	2.2	2.0	0.2	0.4	0.8	1.5	1.9
Never Married	8.1	7.5	7.2	8.1	5.6	8.5	9.7	10.0	9.8	8.1
Black[e]										
Total	100.0	100.0	100.0	100.0	100.0	100.0	100.0	100.0	100.0	100.0
Married	38.7	35.7	42.9	43.8	44.8	7.2	6.6	9.3	11.9	8.6
Widowed	54.4	53.3	49.7	42.3	46.0	89.0	83.4	85.4	80.3	83.2
Divorced	0.5	0.9	1.3	3.4	3.3	0.2	0.4	1.0	2.2	2.7
Never Married	6.4	10.1	6.1	10.5	5.9	3.5	9.7	4.3	5.6	5.5

Sources: U.S. Bureau of the Census, 1943: Volume II, Table 6; 1953a: Table 4;
1964: Table 176; 1984a: Table 264; 1970 Census Public Use Sample.

a.   Based on 20 percent sample.
b.   Based on 25 percent sample.
c.   Ages 85 to 99 years only.
d.   Based on approximately 19 percent sample.
e.   Figures for years prior to 1970 for all nonwhites.

white females, however, are characterized by slightly less age misreporting at the extreme ages than males.

Data concerning the presence or absence of a spouse among currently married couples reveal the tenuous nature of life for the extreme elderly (Table 6.3). Somewhat less than half of men 85 years and over are married. Of that number, however, approximately 13 percent are not living with their wives for reasons other than separation such as hospitalization or institutionalization of the spouse. Slightly over 8

TABLE 6.3:   PRESENCE OF SPOUSE AMONG CURRENTLY MARRIED PERSONS 85 YEARS OLD AND OVER,
              BY RACE AND SEX: 1970 AND 1980

Census year and presence of spouse	Number				Percent distribution			
	White		Black		White		Black	
	Male	Female	Male	Female	Male	Female	Male	Female
1970[a]								
Currently married	190,925	82,500	17,375	7,900	100.0	100.0	100.0	100.0
Spouse present	163,725	64,450	14,200	5,750	85.8	78.1	81.7	72.8
Spouse absent-separated	4,825	3,375	1,775	1,250	2.5	4.1	10.2	15.8
Spouse absent-other	22,375	14,700	1,400	900	11.7	17.8	8.1	11.4
1980[b]								
Currently married	294,486	116,769	22,916	8,982	100.0	100.0	100.0	100.0
Spouse present	251,091	86,858	18,552	5,470	85.3	74.4	81.0	60.9
Spouse absent-separated	3,850	3,680	1,714	1,803	1.3	3.2	7.5	20.1
Spouse absent-other	39,545	26,231	2,650	1,709	13.4	22.5	11.6	19.0

Sources: U.S. Bureau of the Census, 1970 Census Public Use Sample; 1984a: Table 264.

a.   Ages 85 to 99 years only.
b.   Based on approximately 19 percent sample.

percent of very elderly women are married but approximately one fifth of these married women have spouses absent for reasons other than separation. (Persons reported as separated are those living apart because of marital discord, with or without a legal separation.) In short, about 40 percent of very old men and 6 percent of very old women are married *and* living with their spouses.

EDUCATIONAL ATTAINMENT

Table 6.4 shows years of school completed by sex for those age 85 and above in 1980; statistics for those 65–74 and 75–84 are also shown. Approximately 1 in 18 males 85 and over have had no formal education compared to close to 1 in 23 females. Two-fifths of the males and about three-tenths of the females had less than an eighth-grade education. Higher percentages of females than males had completed high school

TABLE 6.4:   YEARS OF SCHOOL COMPLETED BY PERSONS 65 YEARS OLD AND OVER, BY
AGE GROUP AND SEX: 1980

(percent distribution)

Years of school completed	Male			Female		
	65-74 years[a]	75-84 years[a]	85 years and over	65-74 years[a]	75-84 years[a]	85 years and over
Total	100.0	100.0	100.0	100.0	100.0	100.0
Elementary						
None	1.6	3.1	5.7	1.4	2.8	4.4
1 to 4 years	6.4	9.5	13.7	4.4	6.8	8.6
5 to 7 years	14.6	19.2	20.5	12.9	16.7	17.5
8 years	17.7	23.0	23.0	17.1	22.3	24.4
High School						
1 to 3 years	18.5	14.7	11.1	20.2	16.3	13.3
4 years	21.7	14.5	12.7	26.0	19.2	17.8
College						
1 to 3 years	8.9	7.2	5.9	10.1	9.3	8.0
4 years or more	10.5	8.8	7.4	7.8	6.6	5.8

Sources: U.S. Bureau of the Census, 1984a: Table 262; 1980 Census Public
Use Microdata Sample.

a.   Data for ages 65 to 84 years based on approximately 19 percent sample.

and attended college. However, a higher percentage of males had completed college.

A trend toward increasing levels of formal education can be clearly seen in the cohorts approaching extreme old age. Persons 75–84 years old have more education than those 85 and over, and those 65–74 are still better educated. Ten percent of the 65–74-year-old males had finished college compared to less than 8 percent of those 85 and over.

Minorities are disproportionately affected by lack of schooling. Of those 85 years and over in 1980, the percentages of those who had no schooling or less than eight years were much higher for blacks than for whites (Table 6.5). Whereas almost one-third of whites had finished high school, only 12 percent of black males and 15 percent of black females had done so. Thus, although the older population as a whole has experienced substantial gains in educational status, significant differences exist among racial, ethnic, and age groupings (White House Conference on Aging, 1981).

TABLE 6.5:   YEARS OF SCHOOL COMPLETED BY PERSONS 85 YEARS OLD AND OVER, BY
             RACE AND SEX: 1970 AND 1980

(percent distribution)

Years of school completed and race	1970[a]		1980	
	Male	Female	Male	Female
White				
Total	100.0	100.0	100.0	100.0
Elementary				
None	7.0	4.9	4.8	3.9
1 to 4 years	8.2	4.9	11.9	7.5
5 to 7 years	28.5	23.5	20.3	16.7
8 years	26.0	26.9	24.2	25.4
High School				
1 to 3 years	10.0	13.5	11.5	13.6
4 years	10.1	16.1	13.3	19.6
College				
1 to 3 years	4.9	6.4	6.1	8.4
4 years or more	5.2	3.8	7.8	6.0
Black				
Total	100.0	100.0	100.0	100.0
Elementary				
None	17.0	14.0	12.1	9.2
1 to 4 years	26.5	21.5	35.4	23.9
5 to 7 years	33.3	34.8	23.9	28.9
8 years	9.0	11.3	9.6	13.6
High School				
1 to 3 years	6.0	8.6	7.4	9.7
4 years	4.2	5.5	5.2	8.2
College				
1 to 3 years	2.4	2.2	3.1	3.6
4 years or more	1.5	2.2	3.3	2.9

Sources: U.S. Bureau of the Census, 1970 Census Public Use Sample; 1980 Census
           Public Use Microdata Sample.

a.   Ages 85 to 99 years only.

INCOME

The living standard and overall economic status of the elderly have
improved in the last 20 years. Major contributing factors have been

increased Social Security coverage and benefits for the retired population and expanded private pension payments and annuities (White House Conference on Aging, 1981; Cherlin, 1983). While noncash benefits such as Medicare, Medicaid, food stamps and housing programs are important to the elderly, their exact monetary impact "is extremely difficult to determine since there is no universal agreement as to their monetary valuation, or to the true extent of multiple benefits to the same household" (White House Conference on Aging, 1981, p. 58). The economic well-being of the elderly is, in fact, very difficult to measure. Espenshade and Braun (1983, pp. 40–41) have noted the complex problems involved in constructing such a measure and have called attention to the fact that "previous research on the economic well-being of older persons has been handicapped by equating it with money income, ignoring such considerations as net worth, home equity, leisure, and possession of durable goods."

Although personal income declines with increasing age for all elderly, the decrease is much greater for men (Table 6.6). For males in 1979, less than 40 percent of those aged 65 to 74, over half of those 75 to 84 years, and almost two-thirds of those 85 years and over had personal income of less than $6,000. The proportions of males with personal income of $10,000 or more decreased with advancing age from 37 percent of men 65–74 years to less than 16 percent of those 85 and over.

At all ages, the personal income of men is greater than that of women. However, because most women enter old age with a very low amount of personal income, the decline with age is not so dramatic. Almost three-fourths of the women aged 65 to 74 had personal income of less than $6,000. Among women 85 and over, the proportion was slightly over 83 percent. Relatively few elderly women had personal income of $10,000 or more (12.5 percent for women aged 65 to 74 and 7.5 percent for those 85 and over). These personal income changes primarily reflect the fact that it is the "young" elderly who remain in the labor force past age 65 and that after age 70 participation declines rapidly (Hendricks and Hendricks, 1977). Labor force participation rates are negligible at the oldest ages (Table 6.7); most who do work do so only on a part-time basis. Given prevailing social norms about suitable ages for retirement and the likelihood of disabling health problems with increasing age, this situation is unlikely to change significantly in years to come.

TABLE 6.6:   PERSONAL INCOME IN PREVIOUS YEAR OF THE POPULATION 65 YEARS OLD AND
              OVER, BY AGE GROUP AND SEX: 1980

Personal income	65-74 years[a]		75-84 years[a]		85+ years	
	Male	Female	Male[b]	Female[b]	Male	Female
Number (in thousands):						
Total	6,740	8,850	2,869	4,879	654	1,506
No income	140	703	108	458	45	194
Under $2,000	242	1,464	155	615	60	272
$ 2,000-$ 3,999	1,010	2,814	635	1,757	177	563
$ 4,000-$ 5,999	1,159	1,431	627	928	142	226
$ 6,000-$ 9,999	1,722	1,334	670	641	126	140
$10,000-$14,999	1,114	626	324	266	51	62
$15,000-$24,999	813	344	209	146	32	33
$25,000 and over	540	134	141	70	21	18
Percent distribution:						
Total	100.0	100.0	100.0	100.0	100.0	100.0
No income	2.1	7.9	3.8	9.4	6.9	12.9
Under $2,000	3.6	16.5	5.4	12.6	9.2	18.0
$ 2,000-$ 3,999	15.0	31.8	22.2	36.0	27.0	37.3
$ 4,000-$ 5,999	17.2	16.2	21.9	19.0	21.8	15.0
$ 6,000-$ 9,999	25.5	15.1	23.3	13.1	19.2	9.3
$10,000-$14,999	16.5	7.1	11.3	5.4	7.8	4.1
$15,000-$24,999	12.1	3.9	7.3	3.0	4.9	2.2
$25,000 and over	8.0	1.5	4.9	1.4	3.2	1.2

Sources: U.S. Bureau of the Census, 1984a: Table 293; 1980 Census Public Use
           Microdata Sample.

a. Ages 65 to 84 years based on approximately 19 percent sample.
b. Estimated by subtracting from published data for persons 75 years and over the
    numbers for persons 85 years and over in public use sample.

Table 6.8 indicates the extent of multiple sources of income among
the extreme elderly. Three-quarters of persons 85 years and over receive Social Security benefits. In the decade of the 1970s, the proportion
of extreme elderly who received public assistance (including Supplementary Security Income, a program instituted in 1974 to provide a
minimum income to the elderly) decreased from 18.2 percent in 1970
to 12.6 percent in 1980. Throughout this period, women were more
likely than men to receive these payments. Over one-third of the oldest
old received income from interest, dividends and rentals. Men were
much more likely than women to receive income from pensions. Ac-

TABLE 6.7: LABOR FORCE PARTICIPATION RATES OF PERSONS 85 YEARS AND OVER,
            BY RACE AND SEX: 1950 TO 1980

(percent of extreme aged in labor force)

Race and sex	1950	1960	1970[a]	1980
White				
Male	6.6	6.9	6.6	4.2
Female	1.2	1.9	3.2	1.5
Nonwhite				
Male	9.8	8.0	8.8	4.3
Female	2.1	3.1	5.7	3.0

Sources: U.S. Bureau of the Census, 1953a: Table 118; 1964: Table 194;
          1970 Census Public Use Sample; 1980 Census Public Use Microdata
          Sample.

a.   Ages 85 to 99 years only.

cording to a recent survey commissioned by the National Council on
Aging (1981) that specified some sources of income in addition to those
delineated separately in the U.S. Census, very few of the elderly receive
money from relatives, but the proportion increases with age. Among
those households containing persons 80 years of age and older, in 7
percent some money was received from relatives.

In the National Council on the Aging study 93 percent of all households with persons 80 years and over reported receiving income from
Social Security. (This contrasts with the 1980 Census figure indicated
above of only 75 percent of persons 85 and over with income from this
source. It is unlikely that conceptual differences alone account for this
sizable discrepancy. Conceivably, in the Census, income from Social
Security may have been underreported or misreported in another category.) Although the oldest age category reported was 80 and above,
rather than 85 and over, there seems little reason to suspect large
changes in income sources between ages 80 to 85. Social Security benefits are the major source of income for the majority of all elderly,
particularly with increasing age (National Council on the Aging, 1981).
The second most frequent source of income of surveyed households
containing those in the 80 and over category was personal savings,

TABLE 6.8:   SOURCES OF INCOME IN PREVIOUS YEAR OF PERSONS 85 YEARS OLD AND
OVER, BY SEX: 1970 AND 1980

(percent with any income from each source)

Source	1970[a]			1980		
	Total	Male	Female	Total	Male	Female
Social Security	73.3	80.9	69.2	75.0	79.2	73.2
Public assistance[b]	18.2	15.1	19.8	12.6	9.5	14.0
Earnings						
Wages	5.1	7.3	3.9	3.6	5.6	2.6
Non-farm income	1.1	2.1	0.5	0.7	1.8	0.3
Farm income	0.7	1.7	0.2	1.3	2.1	1.0
Interest, dividends,						
rental incomes[c]	-	-	-	34.5	40.1	32.0
All other income[d]	36.3	40.8	33.8	20.3	31.3	15.6

Sources: U.S. Bureau of the Census, 1970 Census Public Use Sample; 1980 Census
Public Use Microdata Sample.

a.   Ages 85 to 99 years only.
b.   For 1980 data, these payments are generally labeled "Supplementary Security
Income."
c.   For 1970, interest, dividend and rental income included with "all other income."
d.   Includes income from pensions.

with 34 percent utilizing some money from this source. This percentage
was identical to that reported for households with persons 70–79 years
of age. About one-fifth of those surveyed in the two elderly age groups
reported that investments were a source of their household income.

The limited statistics available on income levels and sources mask
sizable differences by race and sex. Women, the majority of the extreme
aged population, have been less likely than men to hold long-term or
well-paid jobs. This employment factor has had an adverse effect on
their Social Security and pension benefits in old age. Moreover, private
pension coverage of women continues to lag far behind that of men,
despite the recent large-scale increase in the number of women in the
work force. "Part of the difference in coverage between men and women
results from the fact that a higher proportion of women work part-time
and are employed in small establishments and low coverage industries"
(White House Conference on Aging, 1981, p. 64).

TABLE 6.9:   FAMILY INCOME IN PREVIOUS YEAR OF PERSONS 85 YEARS OLD AND OVER
RESIDING IN FAMILY HOUSEHOLDS, BY SEX: 1980

| Family | Number | | Percent distribution | |
income	Male	Female	Male	Female
Total in families	395,750	562,000	100.0	100.0
No income	2,750	2,850	0.7	0.5
Under $2,000	4,200	3,700	1.1	0.7
$ 2,000-$ 3,999	23,000	22,400	5.8	4.0
$ 4,000-$ 5,999	49,400	46,750	12.5	8.3
$ 6,000-$ 9,999	102,750	106,550	26.0	19.0
$10,000-$14,999	66,650	98,000	16.8	17.4
$15,000-$24,999	70,100	128,850	17.7	22.9
$25,000 and over	76,900	152,900	19.4	27.2

Source: U.S. Bureau of the Census, 1980 Census Public Use Microdata Sample.

The vast majority of older women who live with their children are widows. The presence of these women in their children's homes may result in part from economic pressures of widowhood, since for elderly women in particular, marital status is closely related to income. According to Hendricks and Hendricks (1977), over 80 percent of private pension plans do not award benefits to the surviving spouse of the pensioner. Since the surviving spouse is most often the wife, and the pensioner is most often the husband, the fact that widowed women are the subgroup of the aged most likely to be in poverty (Jackson, 1980) is not surprising. Among those currently age 85 and over, divorced or single women may be somewhat better off than widows. This is due to the effect of greater lifetime labor force participation on post-retirement income.

For males 85 and over, pension coverage and amounts received doubtless reflect their lower earnings prior to retirement relative to more recent retirees under 85. Elderly blacks tend to be poorer than whites. They are also less likely to have paid-off mortgages and more likely to rent than to own their homes. Whereas only 5 percent of elderly whites receive Supplemental Security Income (SSI), 22 percent of blacks do so (National Council on the Aging, 1981).

Family income levels—the total income of all related persons living in a household—are shown in Table 6.9. Although extremely old men had higher personal incomes than did women, among those living in family households, over two-thirds of the women but only slightly over one-half of the men were in households with family income of $10,000 or more in 1979. Among the extreme elderly approximately 59 percent of men and 37 percent of women lived in family households. The men were much more likely to be married and living with a spouse than with other relatives. Only a small percentage of women in such households, however, were married and living with spouses. The vast majority of women living in family settings were widows and lived with other relatives. Elderly women were twice as likely as were men to be living with their children (Tables 7.3 and 7.4). For elderly men in family households, family income was more likely to include their own personal income and the relatively low personal income of their spouses. Although the personal income for elderly women in family households was low, their larger family income probably reflected the relatively higher earnings of the relatives with whom they lived.

Table 6.10 shows personal income of noninstitutionalized persons 85 years and over by their relationship to the household head (householder). The data indicate that approximately 30 percent of heads of households and of those who live in group quarters (but not in institutions) had personal income of at least $6,000. Approximately 21 percent of those who live in households with nonrelatives and only 15 percent of those who live with spouses or other relatives had personal income of $6,000 or more. Median income in 1979 was highest for householders ($4,360), followed by those in group quarters ($4,040) and those in nonfamily households ($3,590). It was lowest for persons not household heads living with spouses or other relatives ($2,220 and $3,200 respectively). It appears that those with very low personal income were more likely to live in the households of others.

Most elderly Americans seem to prefer to live independently, but their ability to do so depends heavily on their income and state of health (Glick, 1979). Many elderly must confront the problem of reduced income and health care costs that are likely to increase dramatically, due to chronic illnesses (Susser, 1969). An increase in the average life span beyond retirement means that any assets the elderly bring with them to retirement must be spread over a longer period. If the additional years are characterized by chronic health problems and limited mobility, income needs will be compounded.

TABLE 6.10:   PERSONAL INCOME IN PREVIOUS YEAR OF NONINSTITUTIONALIZED PERSONS 85 YEARS
OLD AND OVER, BY RELATIONSHIP TO HOUSEHOLDER: 1980

Personal income	House- holder	Spouse of house- holder	Other relative of householder	Non- relative of householder	Noninmate of group quarters
Number					
Total	1,070,200	104,650	431,100	27,250	26,400
No income	22,900	23,750	20,450	1,900	2,100
< $2,000	71,250	24,500	67,700	2,800	3,450
$ 2,000-$ 3,999	385,500	30,300	203,300	11,150	7,500
$ 4,000-$ 5,999	246,400	10,350	75,800	5,550	5,600
$ 6,000-$ 9,999	186,750	8,250	41,350	3,550	4,200
$10,000-$14,999	77,650	3,450	13,100	1,450	2,250
$15,000-$24,999	48,550	2,500	6,350	650	1,050
$25,000 and over	31,200	1,550	3,050	200	250
Percent distribution					
Total	100.0	100.0	100.0	100.0	100.0
No income	2.1	22.7	4.7	7.0	8.0
< $2,000	6.7	23.4	15.7	10.3	13.1
$ 2,000-$ 3,999	36.0	29.0	47.2	40.9	28.4
$ 4,000-$ 5,999	23.0	10.0	17.6	20.4	21.2
$ 6,000-$ 9,999	17.5	7.9	9.6	13.0	15.9
$10,000-$14,999	7.3	3.3	3.0	5.3	8.5
$15,000-$24,999	4.5	2.4	1.5	2.4	4.0
$25,000 and over	2.9	1.5	0.7	0.7	0.9
Median income	$ 4,360	$2,220	$3,200	$3,590	$4,040

Source: U.S. Bureau of the Census, 1980 Census Public Use Microdata Sample.

SUMMARY AND CONCLUSION

Aging is not an event but a lifelong process. Therefore the individual brings to old age the cumulative experiences of a lifetime. Race, sex, early training and education, occupation and earnings, and health status over the years have a strong influence on this cumulative experience. These factors affect not only the probability of reaching extreme old age, but also the quantity and quality of the remaining years of life. Differences within the extreme elderly population largely reflect earlier differences in the life course. In fact, it has been said that "the study of the middle-aged group [those 45–64] is of both theoretical and practical interest, particularly for gerontologists, because experiences during these years lay the economic, social, and psychological foundations for later years " (U.S. Bureau of the Census, 1981b).

For women, educational attainment influenced whether and at what age they married, the social and economic characteristics of their spouse, their labor force experience or lack of it, and the number of children they bore. These early choices had a large impact on their income prospects and marital status in old age, as well as the likelihood of having kin, especially daughters, available to provide physical and psychological services in their advanced years. Whereas those women now at extreme old age had relatively large numbers of offspring, the percentage of elderly women with small families will increase sharply as women whose childbearing period coincided with the Depression (those born 1906–15) reach age 85. The family's capacity to provide support for the aged is thus expected to decline, a trend which will be reversed only temporarily with the aging of mothers of the baby-boom years (White House Conference on Aging, 1981; Cherlin, 1983).

Elderly men, who are much more likely to be currently married and to have higher incomes, face somewhat fewer constraints in old age. Again, as for women, it is their opportunities and choices in early life that continue to influence their prospects at the end. Income prospects for the elderly are expected to improve as more are covered by retirement and health care plans. Nevertheless, as late as 1979 sizable disparities by race and sex were observed in pension plan and group health insurance coverage for younger persons. Such disparities in youth and middle age will not disappear as the individual advances to retirement and extreme old age unless significant societal changes take place. From the point of view of future income prospects, it is important to note that between one-third and one-half of the work force in 1979 were covered by *neither* a pension plan *nor* employer-subsidized group health insurance. Again, women and blacks were worse off than white males (U.S. Bureau of the Census, 1981b).

The data indicate that income is rising for the extreme aged but that it remains very unequally distributed. The fact that proportionally more younger females than males are currently working at jobs that do not provide a pension plan indicates that this imbalance in income between males and females will not change radically in the near future. Since most extreme aged persons are female, the implications are that a majority of the 85 and over population will be required to live on income that is derived from the Social Security program, supplemented by whatever savings are available and any assistance that can be provided by other family members. For the major expenses incurred for health care, it is expected that the population 85 years and over will continue to be heavily dependent on government sponsored programs.

7   *Living Arrangements*

Although the "old" are customarily considered as a single homogeneous age category, evidence points to substantial differences in the life styles of those who live beyond 60 or 65—a period that can span 25 to 30 years or more. In this chapter, the living arrangements of the extreme elderly, defined as those who are 85 years and over, are described. The following topics will be discussed: family status, living alone or with nonrelatives in households, and institutional living. Some data will also be analyzed in terms of sex and race.

Popular opinion long held that old age was a period of peace and serenity. The idea of old age serenity is now seen as a myth by social gerontologists and others who are aware of the social, economic and physical changes that have seriously affected the life style and living arrangements of the elderly.

Conventional opinions are that elderly life styles are quite different from those of younger age groups. Many elderly people, however, have life styles that correspond closely to those of *nonworking* people in other age groups. Specifically, a major distinguishing feature of both non-elderly and elderly life styles (until the later periods of old age) is whether or not the person works. These life styles, whether of the nonworking young, middle aged or old, are largely determined by income and health.

The extreme elderly seldom work, and most have chronic disabilities that limit their life style to some degree and may affect their living arrangements. Partial losses of health, mobility, hearing, and sight, plus the death of spouse, friends and neighbors have a powerful impact on living arrangements and life style.

For those 85 and over, simply taking care of the personal tasks of daily living consumes a large part of their day. Activities such as getting up and going to bed and associated grooming needs can take a substantial part of each day. Add to this the time required for meal preparation, eating, and household cleaning, in addition to doing errands, resting or taking a nap, and the bulk of a day is gone. These necessary everyday activities may take the extreme elderly about six and one half to eight hours, approximately the same amount of time that the non-elderly working population spends at work.

For the extreme elderly, living arrangements reflect the realities associated with loss of energy, decreased mobility and various chronic disabilities. A large minority also face poverty, and many must cope with the effects of price increases on a declining or more slowly rising income. These contingencies give the living arrangements of the extreme elderly a turbulent quality comparable to those of non-elderly adults who also must live with physical disabilities, chronic debilitating diseases, poverty and widowhood. The extreme elderly are thus faced with the challenge of finding living arrangements that are appropriate, comfortable, affordable and located in satisfactory neighborhoods or institutions. But, like their younger counterparts, they are often forced to accommodate themselves to circumstances that are only minimally satisfactory.

HOUSEHOLDS AND FAMILIES

For census purposes, all persons are classified as living in either households or group quarters. All individuals occupying a single housing unit constitute a household. Two or more persons living in the same household who are related by blood, marriage or adoption are considered a family. Unrelated individuals and individuals who live alone may constitute households but are not considered as families. All persons who are not members of households are considered to be living in group quarters, which include institutions such as homes for the aged, mental hospitals, general hospitals, as well as other types of group living arrangements.

The vast majority of all elderly people live in households of one kind or another, as distinct from group quarters. The extreme elderly, however, are less likely to live in households than are the young old. In 1980, 98 percent of all persons age 65 to 69 resided in households, whereas for the population 85 years and over the percentages were 83.0 for males and 72.3 for females (Table 7.1). The figures for the censuses from 1950 to 1980 show relatively little change for the young-old (65–69) in this aspect of living arrangements. The major differences during the period occurred for women over 85, who experienced a decline in household living—from 87.3 percent in 1950 to 72.3 percent in 1980. For men the change over the same period was less than 6 percentage points.

The proportion resident in group quarters declined for the young old (65–69 years) from 5.4 percent for males in 1950 to 1.7 percent in 1980, and from 3.5 percent for females in 1950 to 1.7 percent in 1980. However, for the extreme aged the figures for women in group quarters showed a sizable increase over the same period: from 12.7 percent in 1950 to 27.7 percent in 1980. The figures for extreme aged males showed a sizable but smaller increase—from 11.3 to 17.0 percent.

Although residence in a household and living as a member of a married couple are statistically related, there are notable differences between the sexes. For instance, the proportions of young old men and women living in households have been similar in recent censuses, but a much higher proportion of men than of women live as part of a married couple. The share of males, age 65 to 69, who lived in a married couple family increased from 70.3 percent in 1950 to 79.9 percent in 1980 while the proportion of females living with their husbands showed a smaller increase: from 46.0 percent in 1950 to 52.2 percent in 1980 (Table 7.2).

For the extreme elderly married life is relatively rare. Only about 2 of every 5 men and 1 of every 16 women lived in a married couple family. Census figures reveal that the proportion of extremely old men living in married couple families increased from 30.4 percent in 1950 to 41.1 percent in 1980. For extremely old women, the proportion who lived with their husbands showed only a small increase from 5.3 percent in 1950 to 6.1 percent in 1980 (Table 7.2).

The wide disparities in marital status between elderly men and women are reflected in their respective likelihoods of living in family housholds (as shown in Table 7.3). Family life is the norm for the majority of men aged 85 years and over in the United States, but not for the women. Among the extreme elderly males, 59 percent live in family households,

TABLE 7.1: PERSONS RESIDING IN HOUSEHOLDS AND IN GROUP QUARTERS FOR THE POPULATION 65 TO 69 YEARS AND 85 YEARS AND OVER, BY SEX: 1950 TO 1980

Census year, sex, and age group	Total	Living in households Number	Living in households Percent	Living in group quarters Number	Living in group quarters Percent
1950[a]					
Male					
65 to 69 years	2,399,645	2,269,830	94.6	129,815	5.4
85 years and over	234,430	207,925	88.7	26,505	11.3
Female					
65 to 69 years	2,598,145	2,505,300	96.4	92,845	3.5
85 years and over	343,020	299,360	87.3	43,660	12.7
1960[b]					
Male					
65 to 69 years	2,883,433	2,796,540	97.0	86,893	3.0
85 years and over	333,383	290,378	87.1	43,005	12.9
Female					
65 to 69 years	3,303,330	3,222,213	97.5	81,117	2.5
85 years and over	530,402	437,895	82.6	92,507	17.4
1970					
Male					
65 to 69 years[a]	3,113,144	3,042,347	97.7	70,797	2.3
85 years and over[c]	496,300	412,650	83.1	83,650	16.9
Female					
65 to 69 years[a]	3,878,119	3,795,823	97.9	82,296	2.1
85 years and over[c]	914,425	698,750	76.4	215,675	23.6
1980[d]					
Male					
65 to 69 years	3,880,624	3,813,514	98.3	67,110	1.7
85 years and over	667,978	554,356	83.0	113,622	17.0
Female					
65 to 69 years	4,887,335	4,805,679	98.3	81,656	1.7
85 years and over	1,524,701	1,102,647	72.3	422,054	27.7

Sources: U.S. Bureau of the Census, 1953a: Table 108; 1964: Table 181; 1973d: Table 204; 1984a: Table 265; 1970 Census Public Use Sample.

a. Based on 20 percent sample.
b. Based on 25 percent sample.
c. Ages 85 to 99 years only.
d. Based on approximately 19 percent sample.

TABLE 7.2:   PERSONS RESIDING AS HUSBAND-WIFE FAMILIES FOR THE POPULATION
              65 TO 69 YEARS AND 85 YEARS AND OVER, BY SEX: 1950 TO 1980

Census year, sex, and age group	Husband-wife families	
	Number	Percent of persons in age group
1950[a]		
Male		
65 to 69 years	1,686,200	70.3
85 years and over	71,210	30.4
Female		
65 to 69 years	1,196,350	46.0
85 years and over	18,060	5.3
1960[b]		
Male		
65 to 69 years	2,181,016	75.6
85 years and over	113,864	34.1
Female		
65 to 69 years	1,602,440	48.5
85 years and over	33,597	6.3
1970		
Male		
65 to 69 years[c]	2,397,729	77.0
85 years and over[d]	179,875	36.2
Female		
65 to 69 years[c]	1,912,992	49.3
85 years and over[d]	70,600	7.7
1980[e]		
Male		
65 to 69 years	3,102,364	79.9
85 years and over	274,363	41.1
Female		
65 to 69 years	2,553,350	52.2
85 years and over	93,570	6.1

Sources: U.S. Bureau of the Census, 1953a: Table 104; 1964: Table
            176; 1973d: Table 203; 1984a: Table 264; 1970 Census Public
            Use Sample.

a. Based on 20 percent sample.
b. Based on 25 percent sample.
c. Based on 5 percent sample.
d. Ages 85 to 99 years only.
e. Based on approximately 19 percent sample.

either with their wives (40 percent) or with other relatives (19 percent).
However, only 37 percent of all women 85 years and over live in family
settings (6 percent with spouses and 31 percent with other relatives).
Among very old persons who live in households (i.e., excluding those

TABLE 7.3: LIVING ARRANGEMENTS FOR THE POPULATION 85 YEARS OLD AND OVER, BY TYPE OF HOUSEHOLD, RACE AND SEX: 1980[a]

Race and sex	Total persons	Total in households	In family households		In non-family households		In group quarters
			With spouse	With other relatives	Alone	With non-relatives	
All persons							
Total	2,192,679	1,657,003	356,989	596,144	652,698	51,172	535,676
Male	667,978	554,356	266,863	126,525	144,689	16,279	113,622
Female	1,524,701	1,102,647	90,126	469,619	508,009	34,893	422,054
White							
Total	2,003,716	1,493,366	324,180	523,206	602,441	43,539	510,350
Male	603,663	496,811	244,473	108,354	130,837	13,147	106,852
Female	1,400,053	996,555	79,707	414,852	471,604	30,392	403,498
Nonwhite							
Total	188,963	163,637	32,809	72,938	50,257	7,633	25,326
Male	64,315	57,545	22,390	18,171	13,852	3,132	6,770
Female	124,648	106,092	10,419	54,767	36,405	4,501	18,556
Percent distribution of total population:							
All persons							
Total	100.0	---	16.3	27.2	29.8	2.3	24.4
Male	100.0	---	40.0	18.9	21.7	2.4	17.0
Female	100.0	---	5.9	30.8	33.3	2.3	27.7

White						
Total	100.0	16.2	26.1	30.1	2.2	25.5
Male	100.0	40.5	17.9	21.7	2.2	17.7
Female	100.0	5.7	29.6	33.7	2.2	28.8
Nonwhite						
Total	100.0	17.4	38.6	26.6	4.0	13.4
Male	100.0	34.8	28.3	21.5	4.9	10.5
Female	100.0	8.4	43.9	29.2	3.6	14.9

Percent distribution of population living in households:

All persons						
Total	--	21.5	36.0	39.4	3.1	--
Male	--	48.1	22.8	26.1	2.9	--
Female	--	8.2	42.6	46.1	3.2	--
White						
Total	--	21.7	35.0	40.3	2.9	--
Male	--	49.2	21.8	26.3	2.6	--
Female	--	8.0	41.6	47.3	3.0	--
Nonwhite						
Total	--	20.0	44.6	30.7	4.7	--
Male	--	38.9	31.6	24.1	5.4	--
Female	--	9.8	51.6	34.3	4.2	--

Source: U.S. Bureau of the Census, 1984a: Tables 265 and 266.

a. Based on approximately 19 percent sample.

99

who live in group quarters), 71 percent of males and 51 percent of females live in family settings. Whereas 48 percent of very old men in households live with their wives, only 8 percent of very old women in households live with a spouse.

Excluding persons who live in group quarters, the proportion of extreme aged white and nonwhite males living in family households is similar. Nonwhite males, however, are less likely than white males to live with spouses and are more likely to live with other relatives. Among extreme aged females in households, nonwhites are much more likely to live in family settings than are whites. As with males, a higher proportion of nonwhite females live with other relatives than do white women.

Census data indicate that the likelihood of living alone for persons of both sexes, whether widowed, divorced or single, increases steadily with the onset of middle age. The vast majority of persons 85 years and over residing in nonfamily households live alone (Table 7.3). Among those extreme aged who live in the community, almost 40 percent live alone. While the probability of living alone increases with age the likelihood that a woman, not in group quarters, will live alone is roughly twice that for men. The proportion of very aged males in households who live alone is approximately 26 percent; for females the corresponding proportion living alone is 46 percent.

As noted in Chapter 6, most females outlive their spouses and become widows late in life, and this has a serious effect on the living arrangements among the extreme aged (Table 6.1). Most married men remain married to the end of their lives and the vast majority of them live with their wives. Conversely, most elderly women are widows and a substantial proportion of them live alone. Higher mortality rates for males, and the pronounced tendency in our society for women to marry men several years older than themselves simultaneously increase for women the probability of widowhood and prolong the period of living alone or with someone other than a spouse.

Data on the marital status of those extreme elderly who lived in nonfamily households in 1980 reveal some interesting similarities. The figures show that 39.1 percent of widowed persons, 41.8 percent of divorced persons and 39.6 percent of separated persons lived in nonfamily households. A slightly smaller proportion of never married persons (33.7 percent) lived in nonfamily settings. Only 2.3 percent of married persons lived in nonfamily households. The data for males and females, and for whites and nonwhites, are quite similar.

Although most extremely aged females without spouses, who are not in group quarters, live alone, it does not necessarily follow that they are living in isolation. A number of changes have occurred in housing for the elderly in recent years. There has been a sizable increase in the number of housing complexes for the elderly constructed both by government and private industry. These housing clusters often take the form of an apartment complex, where each elderly person has a private apartment or townhouse, but shares community areas where residents of the complex may socialize. Also, an unknown number of widows move to apartments which are in close proximity to the homes of their children so they can have more frequent contact with them. In both of these examples although the elderly persons would be categorized as living alone, or as not living with their families, the amount of contact they have with others may far exceed the amount implied by the term "living alone."

Census data on heads of households reveal further changes that have occurred in the living arrangements of the extreme elderly. Table 7.4 provides data on heads of households for 1950 through 1980. The most obvious changes during this period are in the proportions of extreme elderly who are heads of households and those who are a parent of the head of the household. In 1950, 31.2 percent of the women (85 and over) living in households were also the *head* of the household. In 1960 the percentage increased to 37.5 percent and by 1980 it had increased to 59.2 percent. The proportion of extremely old males who were heads of households showed an even greater increase, from 54.6 percent in 1950 to 81.9 percent in 1980. The proportion of males and females in each age group who are parents of the head of the household (or parents of the wife of the household head) has decreased steadily since 1950. For all elderly age groups, women are much more likely to live with their children than are men, a reflection of the higher proportions of men that live with their spouses during old age.

An examination of the differences in the living arrangements of urban and rural residents reveals that the extreme aged in rural areas, regardless of race or sex, are more likely than their urban counterparts to be living in households than in group quarters (Table 7.5). Of all rural persons 85 years and over, 81.8 percent live in households and

TABLE 7.4: PERSONS 65 TO 69 YEARS AND 85 YEARS AND OVER IN HOUSEHOLDS, BY RELATIONSHIP TO HEAD OF HOUSEHOLD AND SEX: 1950 TO 1980

Census year and age	Male				Female				
	Total	Head of household	Parent of head or wife	Other	Total	Head of household	Parent of head or wife	Wife of Head	Other
1950a									
65 to 69 years	2,269,830	1,961,610	115,275	192,945	2,505,300	754,420	353,390	1,133,425	264,065
85 years and over	207,925	113,445	67,160	27,320	299,360	93,440	140,060	14,480	51,380
1960b									
65 to 69 years	2,796,540	2,553,505	84,623	158,412	3,222,213	1,084,976	317,393	1,569,507	250,337
85 years and over	290,378	186,180	73,025	31,173	437,895	164,054	175,677	30,442	67,722
1970									
65 to 69 years[a]	3,042,347	2,859,531	51,697	131,119	3,795,823	1,451,931	244,906	1,873,858	225,128
85 years and over[c]	412,650	310,900	77,300	24,450	698,750	322,525	237,700	67,250	71,275
1980d									
65 to 69 years	3,813,514	3,632,206	38,966	142,342	4,805,679	1,990,300	138,968	2,418,405	258,006
85 years and over	554,356	453,783	51,118	49,455	1,102,647	652,647	199,258	84,931	165,631
Percent distribution:									
1950a									
65 to 69 years	100.0	86.4	5.1	8.5	100.0	30.1	14.1	45.2	10.5
85 years and over	100.0	54.6	32.3	13.1	100.0	31.2	46.8	4.8	17.2
1960b									
65 to 69 years	100.0	91.3	3.1	5.6	100.0	33.7	9.8	48.7	7.8
85 years and over	100.0	64.1	25.0	10.7	100.0	37.5	40.1	6.9	15.5
1970									
65 to 69 years[a]	100.0	94.0	1.7	4.3	100.0	38.3	6.5	49.4	5.9
85 years and over[c]	100.0	75.3	18.7	5.9	100.0	46.2	34.0	9.4	10.2
1980d									
65 to 69 years	100.0	95.2	1.0	3.7	100.0	41.4	2.9	50.3	5.4
85 years and over	100.0	81.9	9.2	8.9	100.0	59.2	18.1	7.7	15.0

Sources: U.S. Bureau of the Census, 1953a: Table 107; 1964: Table 181; 1973d: Table 204; 1984a: Table 265; 1970 Census Public Use Sample.

a. Based on 20 percent sample.
b. Based on 25 percent sample.
c. Ages 85 to 99 years only.
d. Based on approximately 19 percent sample.

102

TABLE 7.5: PERSONS RESIDING IN HOUSEHOLDS AND IN GROUP QUARTERS FOR THE POPULATION 85 YEARS AND OVER, BY URBAN/RURAL STATUS, RACE AND SEX: 1980

Urban/rural and living arrangement	All persons			White			Nonwhite		
	Total	Male	Female	Total	Male	Female	Total	Male	Female
All persons									
Total	2,173,500	659,700	1,513,800	1,999,900	600,400	1,399,500	173,600	59,300	114,300
In households	1,640,300	550,000	1,090,300	1,488,300	496,200	992,100	152,000	53,800	98,200
In group quarters	533,200	109,700	423,500	511,600	104,200	407,400	21,600	5,500	16,100
Urban									
Total	1,666,700	482,000	1,184,700	1,534,800	439,800	1,095,000	131,900	42,200	89,700
In households	1,225,500	394,700	830,800	1,112,300	357,500	754,800	113,200	37,200	76,000
In group quarters	441,200	87,300	353,900	422,500	82,300	340,200	18,700	5,000	13,700
Rural									
Total	506,800	177,700	329,100	465,100	160,600	304,500	41,700	17,100	24,600
In households	414,800	155,300	259,500	376,000	138,700	237,300	38,800	16,600	22,200
In group quarters	92,000	22,400	69,600	89,100	21,900	67,200	2,900	500	2,400
Percent distribution:									
All persons									
Total	100.0	100.0	100.0	100.0	100.0	100.0	100.0	100.0	100.0
In households	75.5	83.4	72.0	74.4	82.6	70.9	87.6	90.7	85.9
In group quarters	24.5	16.6	28.0	25.6	17.4	29.1	12.4	9.3	14.1
Urban									
Total	100.0	100.0	100.0	100.0	100.0	100.0	100.0	100.0	100.0
In households	73.5	81.9	70.1	72.5	81.3	68.9	85.8	88.2	84.7
In group quarters	26.5	18.1	29.9	27.5	18.7	31.1	14.2	11.8	15.3
Rural									
Total	100.0	100.0	100.0	100.0	100.0	100.0	100.0	100.0	100.0
In households	81.8	87.4	78.9	80.8	86.4	77.9	93.0	97.1	90.2
In group quarters	18.2	12.6	21.1	19.2	13.6	22.1	7.0	2.9	9.8

Source: U.S. Bureau of the Census, 1980 Census Public Use Microdata Sample.

103

18.2 percent live in group quarters. For urban extreme elderly, the comparable proportions are 73.5 and 26.5 percent respectively. In both rural and urban areas, nonwhites are much less likely than whites to live in group quarters. Among very old whites, 19.2 percent of those in rural areas and 27.5 percent of those in urban areas live in group quarters. Among extreme aged nonwhites, the comparable percentages are 7.0 and 14.2.

INSTITUTIONAL LIVING

Census data on living arrangements, as noted, distinguish between living in various types of households on the one hand, and group quarters, including institutions, on the other. This discussion is generally limited to data on the elderly institutionalized population. Data on inmates of long-term care institutions (nursing homes, homes for the physically or mentally handicapped, psychiatric cases and others) indicate that the overwhelming number of the extremely old in this population reside in nursing homes; in 1980 the proportion was 95.8 percent of those 85 and over (Table 7.6).

Although less than 5 percent of the elderly (65 and over) live in institutions at any one time, the proportion increases with advancing age, most rapidly after age 75. In the last 30 years the proportion of the elderly in institutions has risen as the numbers of old and extremely old have increased.

From 1950 to 1980 the proportion of persons 65 to 74 years old who were institutionalized remained constant at approximately 2 percent. Furthermore, the differences by race and sex in that age group are very small (Table 7.7). The proportion of institutionalized 75 to 84 year olds rose between 1950 and 1970 (from 4.7 percent to 7.1 percent), but decreased slightly to 6.9 percent in 1980. Approximately 5 percent of all men and 8 percent of all women in this age group were living in institutions in 1980.

The greatest increase was in the share of very elderly (85 and over) who were institutionalized. The proportion of extreme elderly living in institutions rose dramatically between 1950 and 1980, especially in the decade of the 1960s. Although the total population 85 and over was 3.5 times larger in 1980 than in 1950, the institutionalized population was 9.5 times larger at the end of the period. In 1950, 9.4 percent of persons 85 years and over were living in institutions; by 1980, the percentage had risen to 23.2 percent. For whites the increase was from 9.9 percent to 24.2 percent, for nonwhites, from 3.2 percent to 13.2 percent. Despite the greater increase in the absolute numbers of institutionalized elderly nonwhites, their percentages in all age groups remained much lower than those for whites (Figure 7.1).

For 1950 through 1980, among whites 85 and over a much larger percentage of women were institutionalized as compared with men and the gap has widened. In 1950, 10.8 percent of white women 85 and over were institutionalized. The percentage rose to 16.2 percent in 1960 and to 27.4 percent by 1980. For white men, the percentages institutionalized were 8.7, 11.8 and 16.7 percent, respectively. Among nonwhites, however, the percentages of institutionalized males and females have remained somewhat similar. For 1950, 1960 and 1980, the percentages of institutionalized females 85 and over were 3.1, 5.2, and 14.4 percent. For nonwhite males the percentages were 3.4, 5.1 and 10.9 percent.

The sex distribution of extremely old inmates of institutions has also changed markedly since 1950. In 1950 there were approximately 56 males 85 years and over in institutions for every 100 females; in 1980 the sex ratio had fallen to about 27 males for 100 females. These data may reflect the increasing survival potential of elderly women relative to elderly men.

The proportion of all institutionalized persons 85 and over residing in homes for the aged has increased steadily during the past four decades (Table 7.6). This is true for both extreme elderly whites and nonwhites. In 1950, 78.5 percent of institutionalized whites and 54.0 percent of institutionalized nonwhites lived in homes for the aged. By 1980 the proportions had risen to 96.1 percent and 91.3 percent respectively. Conversely, the share of the institutionalized 85 and over population living in mental hospitals has declined from 17.8 percent of whites in 1950 to 1.3 percent in 1980, and from 38.3 percent of nonwhites in 1950 to 3.5 percent in 1980. The major decline in importance of the mental hospital as an institution for the chronically ill reflects the deliberate policy, beginning in the 1960s, of returning mental hospital patients to the community. Some of the deinstitutionalized individuals were placed in nursing homes (Kane and Kane, 1980).

Comparisons between residence in homes for the aged and mental hospitals reveal striking differences between whites and nonwhites between 1950 and 1980 (Table 7.6). The extreme elderly nonwhite population has been twice as likely as the white population to live in mental hospitals. The long-term lack of adequate old age homes for

TABLE 7.6: PERSONS 85 YEARS OLD AND OVER IN INSTITUTIONS BY SEX, RACE AND TYPE OF INSTITUTION: 1950 TO 1980

Census year, sex and race	Number				Percent distribution			
	Total	Homes for the aged	Mental hospitals	Other	Total	Homes for the aged	Mental hospitals	Other
1950								
All Races								
Total	54,314	42,307	9,955	2,052	100.0	77.9	18.3	3.8
Male	19,578	14,916	3,830	832	100.0	76.2	19.6	4.2
Female	34,736	27,391	6,125	1,220	100.0	78.9	17.6	3.5
White								
Total	52,878	41,532	9,405	1,941	100.0	78.5	17.8	3.7
Male	18,942	14,565	3,604	773	100.0	76.9	19.0	4.1
Female	33,936	26,967	5,801	1,168	100.0	79.5	17.1	3.4
Nonwhite								
Total	1,436	775	550	111	100.0	54.0	38.3	7.7
Male	636	351	226	59	100.0	55.2	35.5	9.3
Female	800	424	324	52	100.0	53.0	40.5	6.5
1960[a]								
All Races								
Total	118,937	98,299	15,026	5,612	100.0	82.6	12.6	4.7
Male	37,258	29,902	5,034	2,322	100.0	80.3	13.5	6.2
Female	81,679	68,397	9,992	3,290	100.0	83.7	12.2	4.0
White								
Total	115,476	96,369	13,919	5,188	100.0	83.5	12.1	4.5
Male	35,797	29,108	4,563	2,126	100.0	81.3	12.7	5.9
Female	79,679	67,261	9,356	3,062	100.0	84.4	11.7	3.8
Nonwhite								
Total	3,461	1,930	1,107	424	100.0	55.8	32.0	12.3
Male	1,461	794	471	196	100.0	54.3	32.2	13.4
Female	2,000	1,136	636	228	100.0	56.8	31.8	11.4

1970b								
All Races								
Total	271,725	248,938	11,613	11,174	100.0	91.6	4.3	4.1
Male	70,304	62,761	3,992	3,551	100.0	89.3	5.6	5.2
Female	201,421	186,177	7,651	7,593	100.0	92.4	3.8	3.8
White								
Total	261,881	241,174	10,466	10,241	100.0	92.1	4.0	3.9
Male	66,700	60,117	3,384	3,199	100.0	90.1	5.1	4.8
Female	195,181	181,057	7,082	7,042	100.0	92.8	3.6	3.6
Nonwhite								
Total	9,844	7,764	1,147	933	100.0	78.9	11.7	9.5
Male	3,604	2,644	608	352	100.0	73.4	16.9	9.8
Female	6,240	5,120	569	551	100.0	82.1	9.1	8.8
1980c								
All Races								
Total	508,918	487,746	7,022	14,150	100.0	95.8	1.4	2.9
Male	107,638	100,958	2,582	4,098	100.0	93.8	2.4	3.8
Female	401,280	386,788	4,440	10,052	100.0	96.4	1.1	2.5
White								
Total	484,356	465,312	6,174	12,870	100.0	96.1	1.3	2.7
Male	101,153	95,265	2,229	3,659	100.0	94.2	2.2	3.6
Female	383,203	370,047	3,945	9,211	100.0	96.6	1.0	2.4
Nonwhite								
Total	24,562	22,434	848	1,280	100.0	91.3	3.5	5.2
Male	6,485	5,693	353	439	100.0	87.8	5.4	6.8
Female	18,077	16,741	495	841	100.0	92.6	2.7	4.7

Sources: U.S. Bureau of the Census, 1953b: Tables 5, 7; 1963: Tables 3, 5, 7; 1973e: Tables 2, 4, 6; 1984a: Table 266.

a. Based on 25 percent sample.
b. Based on 20 percent sample. May include minimal number of persons incorrectly reported as centenarians.
c. Based on approximately 19 percent sample.

107

TABLE 7.7: POPULATION 65 YEARS OLD AND OVER IN INSTITUTIONS BY AGE GROUP, SEX AND RACE: 1950 TO 1980

(Numbers in thousands)

Census year, race and age group	Both Sexes			Male			Female		
	Total population	Inmates of institutions	Percent in institutions	Total population	Inmates of institutions	Percent in institutions	Total population	Inmates of institutions	Percent in institutions
1950									
Total									
65-74 years	8,414	176	2.1	4,053	91	2.2	4,361	85	1.9
75-84 years	3,277	155	4.7	1,507	65	4.3	1,771	91	5.1
85 and over	577	54	9.4	237	20	8.3	340	35	10.2
White									
65-74 years	7,767	165	2.1	3,736	85	2.3	4,031	80	2.0
75-84 years	3,074	150	4.9	1,406	62	4.4	1,669	88	5.3
85 and over	532	53	9.9	218	19	8.7	314	34	10.8
Nonwhite									
65-74 years	648	10	1.6	317	6	1.9	331	4	1.4
75-84 years	203	5	2.4	101	3	2.5	102	2	2.3
85 and over	45	1	3.2	19	1	3.4	26	1	3.1
1960a									
Total									
65-74 years	10,848	238	2.2	5,022	117	2.3	5,825	122	2.1
75-84 years	4,496	258	5.7	1,953	94	4.8	2,542	163	6.4
85 and over	864	119	13.8	333	37	11.2	530	82	15.4
White									
65-74 years	9,981	221	2.2	4,610	106	2.3	5,371	114	2.1
75-84 years	4,181	248	5.9	1,806	90	5.0	2,375	158	6.7
85 and over	797	115	14.5	305	36	11.8	492	80	16.2
Nonwhite									
65-74 years	867	18	2.0	412	10	2.5	454	8	1.7
75-84 years	315	10	3.2	147	5	3.2	167	5	3.2
85 and over	67	3	5.2	29	1	5.1	38	2	5.2

1970[b]									
Total									
65-74 years	12,447	264	2.1	5,442	113	2.1	7,005	151	2.2
75-84 years	6,124	432	7.1	2,438	131	5.4	3,686	302	8.2
85 and over	1,409	272	19.3	489	70	14.3	919	201	21.9
White									
65-74 years	11,304	240	2.1	4,927	100	2.0	6,377	139	2.2
75-84 years	5,682	413	7.3	2,248	123	5.5	3,435	290	8.4
85 and over	1,293	262	20.3	443	67	15.1	850	195	22.9
Nonwhite									
65-74 years	1,143	24	2.1	515	12	2.3	628	12	1.9
75-84 years	442	19	4.3	190	8	4.2	251	12	4.8
85 and over	116	10	8.6	46	4	8.7	69	6	8.7
1980[c]									
Total									
65-74 years	15,590	288	1.8	6,740	119	1.8	8,850	169	1.9
75-84 years	7,715	543	6.9	2,854	146	5.1	4,861	397	8.2
85 and over	2,193	509	23.2	668	108	16.2	1,525	401	26.3
White									
65-74 years	13,943	256	1.8	6,036	104	1.7	7,907	152	1.9
75-84 years	6,995	506	7.2	2,571	132	5.1	4,424	374	8.5
85 and over	2,004	484	24.2	604	101	16.7	1,400	383	27.4
Nonwhite									
65-74 years	1,647	32	1.9	704	15	2.1	943	17	1.8
75-84 years	720	37	5.1	283	14	4.9	437	23	5.3
85 and over	189	25	13.2	64	7	10.9	125	18	14.4

Sources: U.S. Bureau of the Census, 1953b: Table 3; 1963: Table 3; 1973e: Table 2; 1982a: Table 4; 1984a: Table 266.

a. Based on 25 percent sample.
b. Inmates based on 20 percent sample; may include minimal number incorrectly reported as centenarians.
c. Based on approximately 19 percent sample.

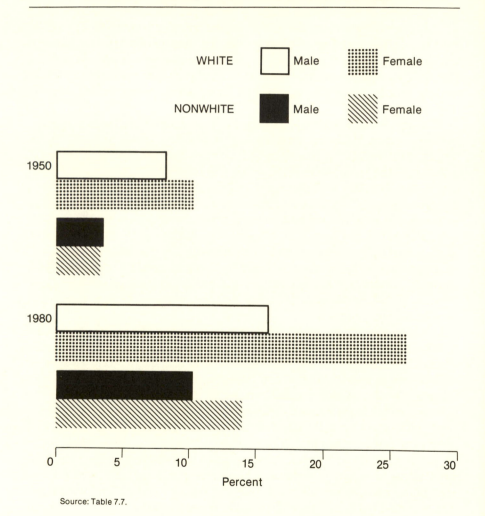

FIGURE 7.1: PERCENT OF PERSONS 85 YEARS AND OVER
IN INSTITUTIONS, BY SEX AND RACE: 1950 AND 1980

Source: Table 7.7.

nonwhites, especially in the South, is supported by these data. The paucity of homes that would admit elderly blacks was such that many chronically ill elderly blacks were condemned to live their last years in custodial type mental hospitals (Watson, 1982).

In 1980, extremely elderly males comprised 23.9 percent and females 38.5 percent of the overall nursing home population in the U.S. Part of this sex difference is the result of the greater longevity of women and the larger number of elderly widows compared with the number of widowers. This situation means that considerably more old women move into institutions for reasons ranging from various disabilities, lack of family or spouse, and fear of living alone or the inability to do so.

The presence of a spouse is directly related to the likelihood of an elderly person entering, and leaving, a nursing home or other institution. Hickey (1980) has reported that marital status figures significantly in the institutionalization of the elderly. Married persons, he found, consistently represented a smaller percentage of the total nursing home population than the unmarried. These married persons, usually private patients with their own physicians to care for them, had a higher mortality rate soon after entry (perhaps indicating a reluctance to institutionalize a spouse until absolutely necessary). However, married survivors were more likely to be discharged (20 percent of the married residents were eventually discharged compared with only 13 percent of all residents). Married persons were also more active in rehabilitation programs.

In 1980 among the institutionalized extreme elderly the great majority—78 percent—were widowed and only 8 percent were married (Table 7.8). The figures are similar for whites and nonwhites. The major differences in marital status are between males and females. Whereas 22 percent of institutionalized males 85 and over were married, the proportion for females was just 4 percent. The very low percentage of married women undoubtedly reflects the fact that among those 85 and over very few are married.

For those without a spouse, the presence of children can help prevent premature or lengthy institutionalization. Barberis (1981) has noted that many persons are placed in nursing homes to receive nontechnical and nonmedical assistance that could be delivered at home. Without families to provide these services, such individuals enter nursing homes where these tasks are performed and insurance programs provide financial assistance. Estimates of the number of inappropriately institutionalized elderly range from 16 to 35 percent.

TABLE 7.8: MARITAL STATUS OF INSTITUTIONALIZED PERSONS 85 YEARS OLD AND OVER, BY AGE GROUP, RACE AND SEX: 1980

Age group and marital status	All persons			White			Nonwhite		
	Total	Male	Female	Total	Male	Female	Total	Male	Female
All persons 85 and over									
Total	500,600	102,200	398,400	478,250	97,200	381,050	22,350	5,000	17,350
Married	40,500	23,200	17,300	38,500	22,150	16,350	2,000	1,050	950
Widowed	391,650	63,500	328,150	374,600	60,650	313,950	17,050	2,850	14,200
Divorced	9,800	3,250	6,550	9,050	2,950	6,100	750	300	450
Separated	2,300	750	1,550	1,950	700	1,250	350	50	300
Never married	56,350	11,500	44,850	54,150	10,750	43,400	2,200	750	1,450
85 to 89 years									
Total	283,300	59,100	224,200	271,150	56,300	214,850	12,150	2,800	9,350
Married	26,650	14,750	11,900	25,700	14,350	11,350	950	400	550
Widowed	216,300	34,350	181,950	207,250	32,750	174,500	9,050	1,600	7,450
Divorced	6,550	2,450	4,100	6,100	2,200	3,900	450	250	200
Separated	1,250	450	800	1,000	400	600	250	50	200
Never married	32,550	7,100	25,450	31,100	6,600	24,500	1,450	500	950
90 years and over									
Total	217,300	43,100	174,200	207,100	40,900	166,200	10,200	2,200	8,000
Married	13,850	8,450	5,400	12,800	7,800	5,000	1,050	650	400
Widowed	175,350	29,150	146,200	167,350	27,900	139,450	8,000	1,250	6,750
Divorced	3,250	800	2,450	2,950	750	2,200	300	50	250
Separated	1,050	300	750	950	300	650	100	0	100
Never married	23,800	4,400	19,400	23,050	4,150	18,900	750	250	500

Percent distribution:

All persons 85 and over

Total	100.0	100.0	100.0	100.0	100.0	100.0	100.0	100.0	100.0
Married	8.1	22.7	4.3	8.1	22.8	4.3	8.9	21.0	5.5
Widowed	78.2	62.1	82.4	78.3	62.4	82.4	76.3	57.0	81.8
Divorced	2.0	3.2	1.6	1.9	3.0	1.6	3.3	6.0	2.6
Separated	0.5	0.7	0.4	0.4	0.7	0.3	1.6	1.0	1.7
Never married	11.3	11.3	11.3	11.3	11.1	11.4	9.8	15.0	8.4

85 to 89 years

Total	100.0	100.0	100.0	100.0	100.0	100.0	100.0	100.0	100.0
Married	9.4	25.0	5.3	9.5	25.5	5.3	7.8	14.3	5.9
Widowed	76.4	58.1	81.2	76.4	58.2	81.2	74.5	57.0	79.7
Divorced	2.3	4.1	1.8	2.2	3.9	1.8	3.7	8.9	2.1
Separated	0.4	0.8	0.4	0.4	0.7	0.3	2.1	1.8	2.1
Never married	11.5	12.0	11.4	11.5	11.7	11.4	11.9	17.9	10.2

90 years and over

Total	100.0	100.0	100.0	100.0	100.0	100.0	100.0	100.0	100.0
Married	6.4	19.6	3.1	6.2	19.1	3.0	10.3	29.5	5.0
Widowed	80.7	67.6	83.9	80.8	68.2	83.9	78.4	56.8	84.4
Divorced	1.5	1.9	1.4	1.4	1.8	1.3	2.9	2.3	3.1
Separated	0.5	0.7	0.4	0.5	0.7	0.4	1.0	0.0	1.3
Never married	11.0	10.2	11.1	11.1	10.1	11.4	7.4	11.4	6.3

Source: U.S. Bureau of the Census, 1980 Census Public Use Microdata Sample.

TABLE 7.9: PERSONAL INCOME IN PREVIOUS YEAR OF NONINSTITUTIONALIZED AND INSTITUTIONALIZED PERSONS 85 YEARS OLD AND OVER, BY RACE AND SEX: 1980

Living arrangement and income	All persons			White			Nonwhite		
	Total	Male	Female	Total	Male	Female	Total	Male	Female
Noninstitutionalized									
Total	1,659,600	551,600	1,108,000	1,504,850	496,950	1,007,900	154,750	54,650	100,100
No income	71,100	12,800	58,300	61,600	11,050	50,550	9,500	1,750	7,750
< $2,000	169,700	31,400	138,300	142,300	24,000	118,300	24,400	7,400	20,000
$ 2,000-$ 2,999	311,100	67,650	243,450	259,150	53,700	205,450	51,950	13,950	38,000
$ 3,000-$ 4,999	545,000	168,500	376,500	501,100	149,650	351,450	43,900	18,850	25,050
$ 5,000-$ 9,999	369,450	172,550	196,900	352,800	162,900	189,900	16,650	9,650	7,000
$10,000-$14,999	97,900	47,850	50,050	94,550	45,850	48,700	3,350	2,000	1,350
$15,000-$24,999	59,100	30,800	28,300	57,750	30,000	27,750	1,350	800	550
$25,000 and over	36,250	20,050	16,200	35,600	19,800	15,800	650	250	400
Institutionalized									
Total	500,600	102,200	398,400	478,250	97,200	381,050	22,350	5,000	17,350
No income	168,050	32,350	135,700	161,200	30,800	130,400	6,850	1,550	5,300
< $2,000	161,800	28,550	133,250	152,200	26,900	125,300	9,600	1,650	7,950
$ 2,000-$ 2,999	78,000	14,900	63,100	74,600	14,000	60,600	3,400	900	2,500
$ 3,000-$ 4,999	39,100	10,350	28,750	37,750	10,000	27,750	1,350	350	1,000
$ 5,000-$ 9,999	30,850	10,650	20,200	30,000	10,200	19,800	850	450	400
$10,000-$14,999	15,050	3,450	11,650	14,800	3,400	11,400	250	50	200
$15,000-$24,999	5,550	1,100	4,450	5,500	1,050	4,450	50	50	0
$25,000 and over	2,200	850	1,350	2,200	850	1,350	0	0	0

Percent distribution:

Noninstitutionalized

	Total								
Total	100.0	100.0	100.0	100.0	100.0	100.0	100.0	100.0	100.0
No income	4.3	2.3	5.3	4.1	2.2	5.0	6.1	3.2	7.7
< $2,000	10.2	5.7	12.5	9.5	4.8	11.7	17.7	13.5	20.0
$ 2,000-$ 2,999	18.7	12.3	22.0	17.2	10.8	20.4	33.6	25.5	38.0
$ 3,000-$ 4,999	32.8	30.5	34.0	33.3	30.1	34.9	28.4	34.5	25.0
$ 5,000-$ 9,999	22.3	31.3	17.8	23.4	32.8	18.8	10.8	17.6	7.0
$10,000-$14,999	5.9	8.7	4.5	6.3	9.2	4.8	2.2	3.6	1.3
$15,000-$24,999	3.6	5.6	2.6	3.8	6.0	2.8	0.9	1.5	0.5
$25,000 and over	2.2	3.6	1.5	2.4	4.0	1.6	0.4	0.5	0.4

Institutionalized

	Total								
Total	100.0	100.0	100.0	100.0	100.0	100.0	100.0	100.0	100.0
No income	33.6	31.7	34.1	33.7	31.7	34.2	30.6	31.0	30.5
< $2,000	32.3	27.9	33.4	31.8	27.7	32.9	43.0	33.0	45.8
$ 2,000-$ 2,999	15.6	14.6	15.8	15.6	14.4	15.9	15.2	18.0	14.4
$ 3,000-$ 4,999	7.8	10.1	7.2	7.9	10.3	7.3	6.0	7.0	5.8
$ 5,000-$ 9,999	6.2	10.4	5.1	6.3	10.5	5.2	3.8	9.0	2.3
$10,000-$14,999	3.0	3.4	2.9	3.1	3.5	3.0	1.1	1.0	1.1
$15,000-$24,999	1.1	1.1	1.1	1.2	1.1	1.2	0.2	1.0	1.1
$25,000 and over	0.4	0.8	0.3	0.5	0.9	0.3	0	0	0

Source: U.S. Bureau of the Census, 1980 Census Public Use Microdata Sample.

The personal income of the extreme elderly has significant implications for institutionalization. In 1980 persons 85 and over who resided in institutions had extremely low incomes when compared to the noninstitutionalized. Of those in institutions 65.9 percent had either no income or incomes of less than $2,000 per year; whereas only 14.5 percent of the noninstitutionalized were in these income categories (see Table 7.9). The data do not indicate, however, that the noninstitutionalized elderly are affluent. Only 11.7 percent had incomes of $10,000 or more (4.5 percent of the institutionalized were in these categories). The modal income category for the noninstitutionalized was $3,000 to $4,999 (32.8 percent), and that for the institutionalized was "no income" (33.6 percent). Noninstitutionalized females were generally poorer than males, with the greatest discrepancies in the lowest and highest income brackets (8.0 percent of the males and 17.8 percent of the females had incomes under $2,000 and 17.9 percent of the males had incomes of $10,000 and over, whereas only 8.6 percent of the females were in this bracket). Although institutionalized males had higher incomes than females, the differences were relatively small.

Income differences of the noninstitutionalized and institutionalized by race showed similar variations. Among all noninstitutionalized extreme aged nonwhites, 23.8 percent had incomes under $2,000, whereas the percentage for whites was 13.6. Comparable percentages for the extreme aged institutionalized were 73.6 percent for nonwhites and 65.5 percent for whites (Table 7.9).

Although a significant portion of the extreme aged population is institutionalized, the majority of those 85 years and over reside in the community, either living alone or with their children. With the increased percentage of the population that is surviving to age 85 and beyond, the numbers of extreme aged persons living in noninstitutional settings will be much larger in the future. Currently, most of the extreme aged living in the community receive whatever help they require with the tasks of everyday living from relatives and friends. When this assistance is not available, the elderly frequently turn to nursing homes as an alternative. With rising costs making institutionalization an unaffordable alternative at the very time that the elderly population is expanding, there is likely to be increased demand for assistance to the extreme aged that is delivered in community settings.

8 Health

Health status, both of individuals and societies, is a measure of *quality* of life, as distinct from such measures as increases in survival rates or average years of remaining life, which refer to progress on a purely quantitative dimension. Examples of improvements in the quality of life include reductions "in the incidence and prevalence of morbidity, mental illness, and physical disability, in the incidence of hospitalization and institutionalization, or having functional limitations, and in the proportions widowed or living alone" (U.S. Bureau of the Census, 1984d, p. 43). The World Health Organization also defines health broadly, as "a state of complete physical, mental and social well-being" (United Nations, 1973, p. 107). It is not simply being alive which is important, but the individual's capacity for functioning fully as a human being. Given these definitions, it is possible that increases in the quantity of life (attributable to advances in medical technology) may coincide with decreases in its *quality*. This potentially negative aspect of continuing medical progress is only beginning to be recognized by researchers, but will inevitably receive more attention as populations in the more developed nations continue to age.

Despite society's considerable progress in controlling the aging process and improving health care, there will usually be a period of dependency and a need for specialized care at the very end of life. Furthermore, there is little basis for predicting that the period of disability characterizing the last part of life will become shorter in the future (Neugarten, 1978). The tendency, in fact, is for this period to become longer.

The United Nations noted the need for an adequate measure of the health status of a population, but also recognized the difficulties of constructing such an index:

Analyses of the health status of the population have generally been neglected in demographic research, . . . largely because of the poor development of the data and techniques used in measuring health. . . . In the first place, the concept of health as a measurable variable is rather vague. Because of the difficulties involved in measuring the positive characteristics of health, the opposite concept of ill-health or morbidity is usually adopted . . . [but] even this concept, however, does not lend itself to precise definition and measurement, since the delimitation between health and illness in a particular individual is frequently uncertain (1973, p. 107).

Although it is recognized that aging is accompanied by a progressive yet variable deterioration of health (Markides, 1983), measuring health status is a complex task. According to Hickey (1980), an index of health status for the elderly must simultaneously account for the person's actual physical condition, his functional level on various dimensions, and the factors needed to predict his future status. Despite the obvious need for a meaningful index, "the theory and practice of health-status measurement with regard to older people are still at an elementary level" (Hickey, 1980, p. 75). This chapter draws from a number of sources and a variety of measures in the assessment of the health of the extreme aged.

Data that follow are taken from Medicare statistics, the National Nursing Home Survey, the National Health Interview Survey and the one-time National Long-Term Care Survey. The Medicare data, prepared by the Health Care Financing Administration, refer to both the institutionalized and noninstitutionalized elderly. Data from the 1977 Nursing Home Survey conducted by the National Center for Health Statistics refer only to residents of nursing homes, the type of institution most utilized by the elderly. The continuing National Health Interview Survey (NHIS) conducted by the U.S. Bureau of the Census for the National Center for Health Statistics has data only for the civilian, noninstitutionalized population, collected through household interviews. The sample of households interviewed each week is representative of the target population, and weekly samples are added over time. About 42,000 households are interviewed each year, but, because the number of persons 85 years and older is small, in some tables data for two years have been combined, producing a sample of about 1,200 individuals for 1970–71 and 1,600 individuals for 1979–80.

The NHIS data base for persons 85 and over is too small to permit discussion of health status by race. It should be noted, however, that "older blacks report considerably poorer health than whites as measured by percent with limitation of activity, days of restricted activity, and bed disability days." On the other hand the disadvantage for blacks is greater in middle age than in old age, suggesting a leveling of differences with increasing age (Markides, 1983, pp. 122–123).

For the elderly population as a whole, NHIS statistics are available on five general topics: (1) self-assessed health status, (2) acute and chronic conditions, (3) physician visits, (4) limitation of activity, and (5) the ability of those with chronic health problems to function at home. These are obviously all interrelated. Limitation of activity may or may not involve bed disability days or hospitalization, and may be temporary or permanent. Permanent limitation may necessitate institutionalization or other long-term specialized care. Each of these five topics is discussed in turn below. The institutionalized elderly are considered in a separate section.

Caution must be exercised in comparing health status data over extended periods of time. Comparability may be affected by such factors as modifications in data collection procedures, changes in health care delivery, changes in the way various health measures are defined and valued, and sociodemographic changes in the population. In the National Health Interview Surveys, differences in the wording of the questionnaire or differences in the recall period used may affect data comparability. Increased reports of some chronic conditions, for instance, may be partially attributed to more specific diagnostic categories, to periodic revisions in the International Classification of Diseases, and to more accurate diagnosis resulting from increased access to care (Wilson and Drury, 1984).

SELF-ASSESSED HEALTH STATUS

Increasing use has been made of data from individuals' self-assessment of their health status. This variable is highly associated with actual health status, utilization of health care services, and longevity (U.S. National Center for Health Statistics, 1983d; Mossey and Shapiro, 1982; Palmore, 1982). Mossey and Shapiro, in examining an elderly population in Canada, found that the number of reported health problems was the best predictor of self-rated health. Life satisfaction was the next strongest predictor. They also found that only age had a stronger correlation with mortality than self-assessed health. In a 25–year follow-up study, using multivariate analyses which included psychosocial and functional health measures, Palmore found that the strongest predictor of longevity for men was self-rated health; the strongest predictor for women, health satisfaction. Self-rated health was a better predictor of longevity than functional health. For Palmore, this finding suggested that how people react to their health was more important than objective health and that those who learn to compensate and minimize health impairments may live longer (Palmore, 1982).

Since 1972, the NHIS has asked respondents to rate their health in comparison with others of the same age. The survey results indicate that generally the proportion of persons assessing their health as excellent or good decreases as age increases. In the 1978 survey (Table 8.1), over 91 percent of respondents age 20 to 44 years rated their health as excellent or good, with the proportion decreasing for each five-year age group. For those age 45 to 64 years, 78 percent rated their health as excellent or good. By age 65, the proportion with a favorable self-rating dropped to approximately 70 percent. From age 65 on, however, there was little change in the ratings. Among those 85 years and over there was a slight increase in those rating their health favorably. As pointed out by Ries (U.S. National Center for Health Statistics 1983d), this increase may reflect a number of factors. A relatively large percentage of the very ill among the 85 years and over population are institutionalized and, therefore, are not included in the NHIS survey. The survey question, however, asks respondents to assess their health in relation to *all* persons of the same age, and this would include the institutionalized elderly. In addition, those very elderly who have survived most of their cohort may be more likely to rate their health status more favorably.

For all age groups 20 to 59 years, a higher percentage of males rate their health as excellent or good than do females. From age 60 on, however, the percentage of females rating their health as excellent or good slightly exceeds that of men of similar age.

TABLE 8.1:   RESPONDENT-ASSESSED HEALTH STATUS AMONG NONINSTITUTIONALIZED
PERSONS 20 YEARS AND OLDER, BY AGE GROUP AND SEX: 1978

Sex and age group	Number (in thousands)	Respondent-assessed health status (percent distribution)		
		Total	Excellent or good	Fair or poor
Both sexes				
20-44 years	76,310	100.0	91.1	8.9
45-64 years	43,403	100.0	78.3	21.7
65-74 years	14,596	100.0	70.2	29.8
75-84 years	6,726	100.0	68.2	31.8
85 years and over	1,466	100.0	71.4	28.6
Male				
20-44 years	36,879	100.0	92.5	7.5
45-64 years	20,734	100.0	79.1	20.9
65-74 years	6,342	100.0	69.7	30.3
75-84 years	2,567	100.0	67.7	32.3
85 years and over	485	100.0	71.0	29.0
Female				
20-44 years	39,429	100.0	89.8	10.2
45-64 years	22,699	100.0	77.5	22.5
65-74 years	8,254	100.0	70.6	29.4
75-84 years	4,159	100.0	68.5	31.5
85 years and over	981	100.0	71.7	28.3

Source: U.S. National Center for Health Statistics, 1983d: Table 1.

ACUTE AND CHRONIC CONDITIONS

The twentieth century has been characterized by "a decline in mortality from infectious disease and acute illness and a corresponding increase in deaths due to chronic disease" (Hickey, 1980, p. 125). Acute conditions, such as injuries, are of relatively short duration and are more or less cured by the intervention of medical attention, the temporary restriction of activity, and the passage of time itself. Although acute conditions occur less frequently with advancing age, recovery time is longer. Chronic conditions such as heart disease, cancer, arthritis, and hypertension, on the other hand, are "common companions of old age" and are seldom cured (Verbrugge, 1983, p. 146). Chronic conditions may have periods of remission but, over time, may also be contributory factors in acute episodes. In the various National Health

TABLE 8.2:   PREVALENCE RATES FOR SELECTED CHRONIC CONDITIONS AMONG NON-
              INSTITUTIONALIZED PERSONS 65 YEARS OLD AND OVER, BY SEX: 1979

(rates per 1,000 persons)

Chronic condition	Male	Female
Heart conditions	265.7	280.6
Coronary heart disease	145.3	96.1
Hypertensive disease	315.0	434.2
Atherosclerosis	121.5	125.0
Chronic bronchitis and emphysema	104.5	76.0
Arthritis	354.6	504.4
Diabetes	73.7	83.9
Visual impairments	119.7	117.6
Hearing impairments	327.2	249.6
Orthopedic impairments	144.8	174.2

Source: U.S. National Center for Health Statistics, 1983e: Table 2.

Interview Surveys, almost all the conditions reported by persons 85 and over are chronic rather than acute. The overwhelming majority of older persons have at least one chronic disease—some 86 percent of the noninstitutionalized population 65 and above according to a recent NHIS. Even this figure is an understatement because some persons "have conditions they do not know about or deliberately fail to report" (U.S. Bureau of the Census, 1984d, p. 74). Multiple chronic conditions are typical of old age and make diagnosis and treatment difficult. Generally a period of poor health, possibly lasting a number of years, precedes death (Hickey, 1980).

Table 8.2 shows prevalence data for selected chronic conditions among noninstitutionalized persons 65 years and over. Arthritis and hypertensive disease were the chronic conditions most frequently reported by both men and women, followed by heart conditions and hearing impairments. Atherosclerosis, diabetes, and visual impairments were reported by males and females at similar rates. Males were much more likely to report chronic bronchitis and emphysema and hearing impairments than were females, while females had markedly higher rates for hypertensive disease, arthritis and orthopedic impairments. Although women reported a slightly higher prevalence of total heart conditions, the major heart condition—coronary heart disease alone—was considerably higher for males. A comparison of chronic conditions among the elderly with those of other age groups indicates that the prevalence of heart conditions, hypertensive disease, diabetes, arthritis and visual and hearing impairments is associated with age for both sexes (U.S. National Center for Health Statistics, 1983e, p. 7).

The high prevalence of chronic conditions among the aged does not necessarily mean an equivalent level of disabling conditions. Three of every ten extreme aged noninstitutionalized persons in the national surveys of 1970 and 1971 were free of chronic conditions that did not allow them to carry on normal activities. Proportionately more men than women reported no such chronic conditions. An opposite direction was found in younger age groups whose male members were more often troubled by chronic problems. It appears that with increasing age more women contract disabling chronic conditions: in the 65–74 age group 47 percent had no disabling chronic conditions; at ages 75–84, the figure fell to 38 percent, and by 85 and over the proportion was only 30 percent. Among men, the proportion problem-free of disabling chronic conditions at ages 65–74 was 44 percent, only a few percentage points less than the women. The proportion, however, fell to one-third at ages 75–84 and remained at that level for those 85 and over. Comparisons by sex may be misleading, as the types of chronic conditions contracted by males more often result in death. These males, therefore, are not as likely to survive to older ages as are women with less severe chronic conditions.

Differences in attitudes and behavior regarding illness are also important factors in explaining sex differentials. If males delay seeking treatment, their conditions may be more advanced before being diagnosed and hence be more life-threatening or limiting than the same conditions in females. That males experience greater severity of chronic conditions is indicated by the fact that their conditions more often result in limitation of activity. In 1970, about 11 percent more males than females were limited in their major activity in both the 65–74 and 75–84 age groups; by age 85 and over, however, the proportions experiencing limitations by sex were nearly equal.

PHYSICIAN VISITS

Approximately one-fourth of persons who were 85 years and older in 1970–71 had not seen a physician in the past 12 months. Women were somewhat more likely than were men to have visited a doctor (Table 8.3). Over 60 percent of each sex had seen a doctor fewer than five times in the past year. The number of physician visits, obviously, corresponds very closely to the number and severity of acute and chronic conditions experienced by each individual. Only 5 percent of men and 7 percent of women had 20 or more visits during the year. Females age 85 and over averaged one more visit per year than males at the same ages.

By 1979–80, the proportion having no visits during the past year fell for every subgroup, with corresponding movement into the 1–4 visit category. The proportion of persons reporting 5–9 annual visits increased slightly. The proportion having ten or more visits actually declined for every age-sex combination. Although the average number of visits per person decreased over the decade in all age and sex categories, females continued to exceed males in average number of visits in each age category. For the period 1979–80, males averaged 4.5 visits, whereas females averaged 5.2 visits. There were few differences at both periods in the pattern of physician visits by age.

LIMITATION OF ACTIVITY

Respondents in the NHIS were asked whether their chronic conditions limited their major activity, referring to their ability to work, keep house, or go to school. Women who have always performed the role of housewife as their primary activity may have little trouble responding to this question, but persons of either sex who have retired may find it difficult to define their major activity. Their inability to work at a job or business may not be due to chronic conditions, but rather to retirement, especially if retirement was mandatory. On the other hand, retired persons may see themselves as able to carry on their major activities if they can take care of themselves and their

TABLE 8.3: PHYSICIAN VISITS IN TWELVE MONTH PERIOD AMONG NONINSTITUTIONALIZED PERSONS 65 YEARS OLD AND OVER, BY AGE GROUP AND SEX: 1970-71 AND 1979-80

Year, sex and age group	Average annual number of persons (in thousands)	Total number of annual visits (in thousands)	Number of visits per person	Number of visits (percent distribution)					
				Total	None	1-4	5-9	10-19	20+
1970-71									
Both sexes									
65 to 74 years	11,944	61,037	5.1	100.0	28.1	40.1	14.7	12.0	5.0
75 to 84 years	6,057	33,692	5.6	100.0	25.0	40.3	15.6	13.6	5.5
85 years and over	1,166	6,713	5.8	100.0	25.9	38.6	15.8	13.7	6.0
Male									
65 to 74 years	5,261	25,674	4.9	100.0	31.1	39.8	13.4	11.1	4.5
75 to 84 years	2,430	11,673	4.8	100.0	28.9	41.4	13.3	12.1	4.2
85 years and over	446	2,259	5.1	100.0	26.6	40.6	15.1	12.7	5.0
Female									
65 to 74 years	6,683	35,363	5.3	100.0	25.7	40.4	15.8	12.7	5.5
75 to 84 years	3,627	22,019	6.1	100.0	22.4	39.5	17.0	14.6	6.4
85 years and over	720	4,454	6.2	100.0	25.4	37.4	16.3	14.3	6.7
1979-80									
Both sexes									
65 to 74 years	15,058	69,494	4.6	100.0	22.3	47.0	15.9	11.2	3.7
75 to 84 years	6,950	34,564	5.0	100.0	19.4	47.1	17.0	12.8	3.7
85 years and over	1,572	7,852	5.0	100.0	20.6	46.6	17.8	11.5	3.4
Male									
65 to 74 years	6,555	27,921	4.3	100.0	25.9	46.0	14.8	10.0	3.3
75 to 84 years	2,616	12,073	4.6	100.0	22.2	47.1	16.2	11.0	3.5
85 years and over	544	2,467	4.5	100.0	23.6	44.4	18.1	11.6	2.2
Female									
65 to 74 years	8,503	41,573	4.9	100.0	19.5	47.7	16.8	12.0	4.0
75 to 84 years	4,334	22,491	5.2	100.0	17.7	47.1	17.4	13.9	3.9
85 years and over	1,028	5,385	5.2	100.0	19.0	47.8	17.7	11.5	4.0

Source: U.S. National Center for Health Statistics, Health Interview Survey, Annual Public Use Tapes.

place of residence and are not restricted in their leisure-time pursuits. The great majority of those 85 and older probably have redefined their major activity to be retirement. But in the case of the younger old, some of whom may still be working, the issue becomes more important. Recognizing the problem with the definition of "work" as the major activity of retired persons, the NHIS questionnaire was changed beginning in 1982. All adults under the age of 70 are now asked about their ability to "work" and all those 60 years and over are asked about their ability to perform "activities" of daily living. As a result, it is expected that the proportion of elderly persons reporting limitation in activity will decrease in the future, both in relation to earlier time periods and in relationship to middle-aged persons, especially among males (Wilson, 1984).

If someone other than the elderly individual is the survey respondent in the household, other discrepancies may also occur in definitions of primary activity. These points should be kept in mind in the discussion which follows.

Throughout the decade 1970–80 approximately one-third of noninstitutionalized persons 85 and older had no activity limitations, another one-third could not perform unaided, and the remaining third were limited in either the amount or kinds of activities they could perform (Table 8.4). There was little difference by sex in the proportion of this age group who were unlimited in their activity. However, a higher proportion of men could not perform without aid. The figure for 1979–80 was 43 percent for men compared to 27 percent for women. Differences by sex were greater at younger ages. The proportion of 65–74 year-old men who could not perform without assistance was five times that of the women; among the 75–84 year-olds, the proportion among men was three times that of the women.

For both sexes, the proportion not limited in their activity decreased sharply with increasing age. Although differences by sex were fairly large at 65–74 and 75–84, by age 85 and over the proportions of men and women who had no activity limitations were nearly equal. This reflects in part the greater survival potential of females, with or without chronic conditions.

Activity limitations can take a number of forms, three of which will be considered here. In order of increasing severity, these are: (1) restricted activity days; (2) bed disability days; and (3) hospital episodes. According to the NHIS, a day of restricted activity is one in which a

TABLE 8.4: LIMITATION OF ACTIVITY AMONG NONINSTITUTIONALIZED PERSONS 65 YEARS OLD AND OVER, BY AGE GROUP AND SEX: 1970-71 AND 1979-80

Year, sex, and age group	Average annual number of persons (in thousands)	Type of limitation (percent distribution)			
		Total	No limitation	Some limitation Limit in amount or kind of acti- vity performed	Cannot perform unaided
1970-71					
Both sexes					
65-74 years	11,950	100.0	63.5	23.7	12.7
75-84 years	6,059	100.0	48.6	30.4	20.9
85 years and over	1,163	100.0	34.1	30.5	35.5
Male					
65-74 years	5,263	100.0	59.4	17.7	22.9
75-84 years	2,432	100.0	43.8	21.6	34.6
85 years and over	445	100.0	35.6	20.8	43.7
Female					
65-74 years	6,687	100.0	66.9	28.5	4.7
75-84 years	3,627	100.0	51.9	36.3	11.7
85 years and over	718	100.0	33.1	36.6	30.4
1979-80					
Both sexes					
65-74 years	15,076	100.0	58.7	27.1	14.2
75-84 years	6,964	100.0	49.7	30.5	19.8
85 years and over	1,576	100.0	34.0	33.4	32.7
Male					
65-74 years	6,562	100.0	54.2	19.9	25.9
75-84 years	2,620	100.0	46.9	19.5	33.6
85 years and over	546	100.0	33.4	23.4	43.2
Female					
65-74 years	8,514	100.0	62.2	32.7	5.1
75-84 years	4,344	100.0	51.4	37.2	11.5
85 years and over	1,030	100.0	34.2	38.6	27.1

Source: U.S. National Center for Health Statistics, Health Interview Survey, Annual Public Use Tapes.

person substantially reduces the amount of activity normal for that day because of a specific condition or injury. Persons 85 and over reported an average of 38 such days in 1970–71. Men reported far fewer days of restricted activity (an average of 26) than did women (an average of 46). Restricted activity days increased with age for women, from an average of 29 days for those 65–74 to 46 days for those 85 and above. For males, however, the number of restricted activity days showed no consistent pattern by age. In 1979–80 both men and women reported an increased number of restricted activity days; the average rose to almost 49 days. The difference between men and women (41.5 for men and 52.8 days for women), however, was less than at the start of the decade.

Bed disability days were defined as those in which the person stayed in bed for all or most of the day because of a specific illness, condition, or injury. All hospital days for in-patients were considered to be days of bed disability, but the statistics also included persons who were bedridden in their homes. Persons 85 and over reported an average of 24 days of bed disability in 1970–71. The extreme elderly women reported 29 days, almost twice as many as their male counterparts (16). As in the case of restricted activity days, the number of bed disability days tended to increase with advancing age for both sexes. For 1979–80 the average number of bed days for persons 85 and over (24.3 days) remained approximately the same as earlier. As with restricted activity days, the difference between men and women diminished (25.9 bed days for men and 21.4 for women).

SHORT-STAY HOSPITAL EPISODES

In 1970–71, only one of every five noninstitutionalized persons 85 and older spent some time in a short-stay hospital within the past year. Data for each of the three major age groups for persons 65 and over indicate there was little difference by sex, although the younger old men were more likely to have experienced one or more hospital episodes (Table 8.5). Differences by age in the proportion hospitalized were relatively small but tended to increase, especially for females. Only about 1 percent of persons in each of the three age groups reported short-stay hospitalization on three or more occasions during the year.

Data for 1979–80 indicate the proportions for those not hospitalized during the past year decreased in each age-sex category (Table 8.5).

TABLE 8.5: SHORT-STAY HOSPITAL EPISODES AMONG NONINSTITUTIONALIZED PERSONS
65 YEARS OLD AND OVER, BY AGE GROUP AND SEX: 1970-71 AND 1979-80

Year, sex and age group	Average annual number of persons (in thousands)	Number of episodes (percent distribution)				
		Total	None	1	2	3 or more
1970-71						
Both sexes						
65-74 years	11,950	100.0	85.4	10.8	2.7	1.1
75-84 years	6,059	100.0	82.3	13.3	3.2	1.2
85 years and over	1,163	100.0	80.0	15.1	3.4	1.5
Male						
65-74 years	5,263	100.0	84.5	11.2	3.1	1.1
75-84 years	2,432	100.0	80.7	14.3	3.6	1.3
85 years and over	445	100.0	80.0	15.4	3.3	1.3
Female						
65-74 years	6,687	100.0	86.1	10.5	2.3	1.1
75-84 years	3,627	100.0	83.3	12.7	3.0	1.1
85 years and over	718	100.0	80.0	15.0	3.4	1.7
1979-80						
Both sexes						
65-74 years	15,076	100.0	83.3	12.6	2.9	1.2
75-84 years	6,964	100.0	79.2	15.4	3.7	1.6
85 years and over	1,576	100.0	77.4	17.0	4.2	1.4
Male						
65-74 years	6,562	100.0	82.4	13.0	3.2	1.3
75-84 years	2,620	100.0	77.8	16.1	4.4	1.6
85 years and over	546	100.0	75.6	19.0	4.3	1.1
Female						
65-74 years	8,514	100.0	84.0	12.2	2.6	1.1
75-84 years	4,344	100.0	80.1	15.0	3.3	1.6
85 years and over	1,030	100.0	78.3	16.0	4.1	1.6

Source: U.S. National Center for Health Statistics, Health Interview Survey, Annual
Public Use Tapes.

The proportions of those in each subgroup who experienced one or more
episodes increased. (The proportion of persons experiencing three or
more hospitalizations remained about one percent.) These changes may
not reflect a deterioration in the health of the elderly, but rather changes
in survival probabilities due to improved medical care and broader

societal changes such as increased coverage by health insurance programs. In addition, the data may be somewhat misleading since NHIS data exclude the hospital experience of persons who died either in the hospital or after being discharged from the hospital prior to the national survey. Also, the institutionalized population was excluded from the survey. For acute care, the institutionalized elderly often use hospital departments of the long-term and custodial institutions in which they reside.

Table 8.6 shows days of hospitalization by sex and age group in 1970–71 and 1979–80 only for those hospitalized at least once during the year preceding the survey. In 1970–71, those experiencing less than five days were the smallest proportion in each age-sex category. The proportion of persons having 20 or more hospital days increased steadily with age, despite the intervention of institutionalization or death.

By 1979–80, greater proportions in each age-sex category had 1–4 days of hospitalization compared to the 1970–71 data, whereas smaller proportions in each subgroup had 20 or more days. As with the other measures of health status discussed in this chapter, however, these statistics may not reflect actual changes in the health status of the elderly. They may be affected by such outside factors as access to medical care and the relative costs of outpatient care, hospitalization, and institutionalization.

The length of hospitalization increases with age. In 1982, persons 85 years and over who had been in a short-stay hospital had an average length of stay of 11.3 days. As shown below, the average length of stay in days increased with advancing age and was slightly higher for elderly women than for elderly men (U.S. National Center for Health Statistics, 1984b, Table 1):

Age group	Male	Female
65–74 years	9.4	9.7
75–84 years	10.1	10.6
85 years and over	10.9	11.5

ABILITY TO FUNCTION AT HOME

Many very elderly persons with chronic health problems need some home care services in order to continue to live in the community rather

TABLE 8.6:   SHORT-STAY HOSPITAL DAYS AMONG NONINSTITUTIONALIZED PERSONS 65 YEARS
OLD AND OVER WITH AT LEAST ONE HOSPITALIZATION EPISODE IN PAST YEAR, BY
AGE GROUP AND SEX: 1970-71 AND 1979-80

Year, sex and age group	Average annual number with episodes (in thousands)	Number of days (percent distribution)				
		Total	1-4	5-9	10-19	20+
1970-71						
Both sexes						
65-74 years	1,729	100.0	18.8	27.9	26.3	27.0
75-84 years	1,068	100.0	16.1	25.8	28.6	29.4
85 years and over	233	100.0	12.7	28.8	22.2	36.3
Male						
65-74 years	803	100.0	17.0	26.9	26.5	29.6
75-84 years	463	100.0	16.5	25.7	27.6	30.2
85 years and over	89	100.0	16.4	24.3	22.6	36.7
Female						
65-74 years	926	100.0	20.4	28.7	26.1	24.8
75-84 years	605	100.0	15.9	26.0	29.4	28.8
85 years and over	144	100.0	10.4	31.6	21.9	36.1
1979-80						
Both sexes						
65-74 years	2,506	100.0	26.1	29.9	24.2	19.9
75-84 years	1,441	100.0	22.2	26.9	28.3	22.6
85 years and over	356	100.0	21.3	28.1	28.5	22.1
Male						
65-74 years	1,152	100.0	25.6	30.2	24.0	20.3
75-84 years	579	100.0	23.6	26.9	29.0	20.5
85 years and over	133	100.0	24.1	33.5	27.4	15.0
Female						
65-74 years	1,354	100.0	26.5	29.6	24.4	19.5
75-84 years	862	100.0	21.3	26.8	27.8	24.0
85 years and over	223	100.0	19.7	24.9	29.1	26.2

Source: U.S. National Center for Health Statistics, Health Interview Survey, Annual
Public Use Tapes.

than in nursing homes or other institutions. Data from the 1982 National Long-Term Care Survey of the noninstitutionalized population 65 years old and over (Table 8.7) indicate that the need for assistance in daily living activities increases sharply with advancing age. Among those aged 65 to 74 years, 14 percent reported the need for assistance in at least one daily living activity. Over half of persons 85 years and

TABLE 8.7:   NEED FOR HOME CARE SERVICES AMONG NONINSTITUTIONALIZED PERSONS
             65 YEARS OLD AND OVER, BY TYPE OF NEED AND AGE GROUP: 1982
             NATIONAL LONG-TERM CARE SURVEY

(percentage of age group)

Type of need	65-74 years	75-79 years	80-84 years	85 years and over
Activities of daily living requiring help:				
Eating	0.9	1.3	2.5	5.3
Bed transfer	2.7	4.1	6.0	10.7
Chair transfer	3.1	4.6	7.1	12.6
Walking inside	5.0	8.0	13.2	23.6
Going outside	7.4	13.0	20.4	35.2
Dressing	2.7	4.1	6.4	11.7
Bathing	4.0	7.2	11.5	20.6
Using bathroom	2.2	3.4	5.6	11.1
Incontinent	4.5	6.1	9.3	14.1
Instrumental activities of daily living requiring help:				
Preparing meals	4.1	7.8	12.4	24.9
Doing laundry	5.9	10.6	17.6	32.9
Light housework	3.8	6.4	10.6	20.9
Grocery shopping	8.3	15.0	24.3	44.6
Managing money	8.3	7.1	11.5	22.6
Taking medicine	2.2	4.7	7.4	15.4
Using telephone	2.7	6.0	10.1	21.2

Source: Hanley, 1984.

over required assistance in at least one such activity. Over one-third of the extreme elderly needed help in going outside, almost one-quarter required assistance for walking inside, and one-fifth needed help bathing. Approximately 10 percent required assistance in such basic physical activities as moving from or to a bed or chair, with dressing or with bathing. Fourteen percent were incontinent. Over 5 percent required assistance with eating. Relatively large proportions of the oldest old required assistance with daily home management activities. Almost one-half needed help with grocery shopping, one-third with doing laundry, and one quarter with meal preparation. The proportions of females among the extreme aged who required assistance were slightly higher in most categories than the proportions for men. For all categories, substantially higher proportions of nonwhites reported the need for assistance than did whites (Hanley, 1984).

Analysis of the Home Care Supplement to the 1979 NHIS indicated a similar increase in functional impairment with increasing age. Data from the 1979 survey indicated that the proportion of persons needing at-home medical or nursing services, including injections, physical therapy and bandage-changing, rose from 1.5 percent of those 65–74 years to 9 percent of persons 85 years and over. Slightly over 1 percent of the young old reported themselves as usually staying in bed as compared with over 5 percent of the extremely old (U.S. National Center for Health Statistics, 1983b, Tables 6 and 11). Clearly the proportion of those aged 85 years and over needing assistance in the various activities of daily living is markedly higher than among those under age 85.

THE INSTITUTIONALIZED VERY OLD

As seen in Chapter 7, the vast majority of the very old who are institutionalized reside in nursing homes or homes for the aged. Residents of homes for the aged are predominantly the old old, female, and white. According to data from the 1980 census (Table 8.8), over one-fifth of the population 85 years and over resided in homes for the aged. The percentage among those 85 years and over (22.2 percent) was more than 3 times that for the next younger age group (75 to 84 years old) and 15 times that of the young old (65 to 74 years). Over one-third (34.2 percent) of all residents of homes for the aged in 1980 were 85 years and older, and more than one-third (35.5 percent) were 75 to 84 years old.

Women are far more likely to be in homes for the aged than are men: 25.4 percent of all women 85 years and older, compared to 15.1 percent of all men. Of the extreme elderly in these homes, almost 80 percent are women. The higher proportion of females is due in part to their longer life expectancy and their increased likelihood of living alone. Whites 85 years and over are twice as likely as nonwhites to reside in homes for the aged (23.2 percent versus 11.9 percent, respectively). Less than 5 percent of very old residents of homes for the aged are nonwhite.

According to the 1977 National Nursing Home Survey (Table 8.9), the most common chronic conditions among very old nursing home

TABLE 8.8:   RESIDENTS OF HOMES FOR THE AGED AMONG PERSONS 65 YEARS OLD AND OVER,
BY AGE GROUP, SEX AND RACE: 1980

Sex and race	Number[a]			Percent distribution of those in homes for aged		
	65 to 74 years	75 to 84 years	85 years and over	65 to 74 years	75 to 84 years	85 years and over
Total in homes for aged	238,962	506,250	487,746	100.0	100.0	100.0
Male	92,176	131,170	100,958	38.6	25.9	20.7
Female	146,786	375,080	386,788	61.4	74.1	79.3
White	214,396	473,957	465,312	89.7	93.6	95.4
Black	20,877	26,282	18,308	8.7	5.2	3.8
Other nonwhite	3,689	6,011	4,126	1.7	1.2	.8
Total number of persons in each age group	15,590,108	7,715,599	2,192,679	---	---	---

Source: U.S. Bureau of the Census, 1984a: Table 266.

a. Based on approximately 19 percent sample.

residents are arteriosclerosis (63 percent), chronic heart trouble (48 percent), senility (40 percent), and for women, arthritis and rheumatism (36 percent). Among those 85 years and older, males are more likely than females to have cancer, heart trouble and chronic respiratory disease. Females have higher rates of hypertension, arthritis and rheumatism, hip fractures, senility and chronic brain syndrome.

Most of the institutionalized very elderly have multiple chronic conditions. But given the vague nature of the latter category and the possible overlap with symptoms of various mental disorders and hardening of the arteries, accurate diagnosis of the multiple chronic problems suffered by nursing home residents (and the extreme elderly in general) is very difficult. Nonetheless, a realistic assessment of health problems among the aged must take account of the multiple conditions which are typical among persons of advanced age. Physical problems, in fact, are not the only reasons for admissions to nursing homes; social and behavioral problems characterize many patients (Hickey, 1980).

As with the noninstitutionalized population, the need for assistance in performing daily living activities increases with age. Almost all of the very elderly residents of nursing homes require some assistance

TABLE 8.9: PREVALENCE RATES FOR SELECTED CHRONIC CONDITIONS AMONG NURSING HOME RESIDENTS 65 YEARS AND OLDER, BY AGE GROUP AND SEX: 1977

(rates per 1,000 residents)

Chronic condition	65 to 74 years			75 to 84 years			85 years and older		
	Total	Male	Female	Total	Male	Female	Total	Male	Female
Arteriosclerosis	329.2	354.2	314.0	535.3	508.7	544.8	632.0	604.9	639.0
Heart trouble	277.2	289.6	269.6	367.9	372.8	366.1	439.3	476.3	429.8
Hypertension	204.6	189.1	214.0	234.9	192.9	249.9	218.2	145.4	236.8
Stroke	227.8	237.0	222.3	187.4	222.9	174.8	131.2	134.7	130.3
Arthritis, rheumatism	161.0	132.2	178.6	236.8	195.8	288.0	336.4	230.9	363.5
Hip fracture	46.8	35.8[a]	53.5	89.0	40.1	106.5	116.5	53.1	132.8
Diabetes	180.9	144.8	203.0	162.7	136.3	172.1	122.2	114.3	124.3
Cancer	52.6	57.4	49.8	53.7	70.8	47.7	52.5	91.8	42.5
Respiratory disease	74.8	128.4	42.1	65.5	130.7	42.2	67.5	133.7	50.6
Senility	219.0	182.1	241.6	366.3	319.9	382.9	421.8	395.7	428.5
Chronic brain syndrome	228.1	221.3	232.3	278.7	286.4	276.0	259.8	217.6	270.6

Source: U.S. National Center for Health Statistics, 1981: Table 8.

a. Figure does not meet NHIS standards of reliability or precision.

TABLE 8.10   FUNCTIONAL STATUS FOR SELECTED ACTIVITIES AMONG NURSING HOME RESIDENTS
65 YEARS AND OLDER, BY AGE GROUP: 1977

(percent distribution)

Functional Status	65 to 74 years	75 to 84 years	85 years and older
Independent in all following activities:	14.0	7.2	4.4
Bathes independently	18.8	11.1	8.3
Walks independently	43.2	33.2	22.5
Dresses independently	38.8	27.5	24.2
Uses toilet independently	53.1	45.7	41.0
No difficulty controlling bowel or bladder	62.4	52.9	47.8
Eats independently	72.9	66.2	63.5
Hearing unimpaired	81.0	71.6	54.9
Vision unimpaired	75.4	67.9	57.2

Source: U.S. National Center for Health Statistics, 1981: Tables 10 and 11.

in such activities (Table 8.10). Less than 5 percent of residents 85 years and older are independent in bathing, dressing, using the toilet, mobility, continence and eating. Over 50 percent have bowel or bladder difficulties; over 50 percent need assistance using toilet facilities. More than 75 percent of the very old nursing home residents cannot dress independently. Almost 80 percent cannot walk independently, and over 90 percent of the very elderly require assistance with bathing.

For chronically ill elderly persons without living relatives to care for them, institutionalization may be inevitable. Thus it is not surprising that most very aged residents of institutions (91 percent compared with 75 percent of the noninstitutionalized population 85 years and over) do not have a living spouse. Some 11 percent of the institutionalized extreme aged have never married compared with 6 percent of their counterparts in the community (U.S. Bureau of the Census, 1980 Public Use Microdata Samples). As the probability of losing one's

TABLE 8.11:   LIVING ARRANGEMENTS PRIOR TO ADMISSION OF NURSING HOME RESIDENTS 85 YEARS
AND OLDER, BY SEX: 1977

| Living arrangements | Number | | | Percent distribution | | |
	Both sexes	Male	Female	Both sexes	Male	Female
All arrangements	449,900	91,700	358,200	100.0	100.0	100.0
Private residence	188,600	36,400	152,100	41.9	39.7	42.5
Alone	71,100	11,100	59,900	15.8	12.1	16.7
Unknown if with others	13,000	2,200	10,800	2.9	2.4	3.0
With others	104,500	23,100	81,400	23.2	25.2	22.7
Immediate family	90,100	20,800	69,300	20.0	22.7	19.3
Another health facility	218,700	46,300	172,300	48.6	50.5	48.1
Another nursing home	57,800	11,100	46,700	12.8	12.1	13.0
General or short-stay hospital	145,400	31,400	114,000	32.3	34.2	31.8
Other	15,500	3,800	11,600	3.5	4.2	3.2
Other arrangements	42,800	9,000	33,800	9.5	9.8	9.4

Source: U.S. National Center for Health Statistics, 1981: Table 2.

spouse and children to death increases with age, so does the probability of becoming a resident of an institution.

Data from the 1977 National Nursing Home Survey (Table 8.11) indicate that approximately one-third of the residents 85 years and older lived alone prior to entering their current nursing home or transferred from another nursing home. Another one-third transferred from a general or short-stay hospital. One-fifth of the very elderly lived with immediate family in a private residence before moving into a nursing home.

Even among the elderly residents of nursing homes, the myth of abandonment by family is not substantiated. Data from the National Nursing Home Survey indicate that over two-thirds of residents 85 years and over received daily or weekly visitors. Of these, more than two-thirds of the visitors were from immediate family, including spouses, children and siblings.

MEDICARE-FINANCED SERVICES

Data on the use of medical services financed under the Medicare health insurance programs provide additional information on the health

TABLE 8.12:   PERSONS SERVED AND REIMBURSEMENTS PER PERSON SERVED AMONG MEDICARE ENROLLEES
65 YEARS OLD AND OVER, BY AGE GROUP AND TYPE OF SERVICE: 1981

Age group	Hospital Insurance				Supplementary Medical Insurance			
	All categories[a]	In-patient	Skilled nursing facility	Home health agency	All categories[a]	Physician and other medical	Out-patient	Home health agency
Persons served per 1,000 enrollees								
65-74 years	203	200	4	21	629	609	268	4
75-84 years	286	278	14	48	714	697	297	10
85 years and over	353	336	30	72	776	758	321	19
Reimbursement per person served								
65-74 years	$3,746	$3,695	$1,601	$767	$595	$510	$231	$520
75-84 years	3,999	3,910	1,496	782	642	560	213	489
85 years and over	4,021	3,935	1,385	768	619	547	178	443

Source: U.S. Health Care Financing Administration, 1983: Tables Q, R and S.

a.   Figures for "all categories" do not equal sum of individual categories because enrollees
may be reimbursed for more than one than one type of service.

status of the elderly. The standard hospital insurance (HI) plan covers
inpatient hospitalization and skilled nursing facility stays. The voluntary supplementary medical insurance (SMI) plan covers physician
services both in and out of hospitals, diagnostic and laboratory procedures, and a variety of outpatient medical needs. Reimbursements
for home health care visits are made under both plans. Neither plan
provides for routine eye and dental care, preventive services, nor long-
term nursing home care. Benefit payments under Medicare have been
made since July 1, 1966.

An examination of 1981 Medicare reimbursements (Table 8.12)
indicates that the proportion of Medicare enrollees receiving HI and
SMI benefits increased with advancing age. For each 1,000 enrollees
age 65 to 74 years, 203 persons received HI benefits, largely for inpatient hospitalization, and 629 persons received SMI benefits, mostly
for physician services. For those enrollees 85 years and over, the proportions receiving HI and SMI benefits were 353 per 1,000 and 776
per 1,000, respectively. Although, at all ages, relatively few persons
received benefits for skilled nursing facility care or for home health

TABLE 8:13: REIMBURSEMENTS PER MEDICARE ENROLLEE FOR PERSONS 65 YEARS OLD AND OVER,
BY AGE GROUP AND TYPE OF SERVICE: 1981[a]

Age group	Hospital Insurance				Supplementary Medical Insurance			
	All categories	In- patient	Skilled nursing facility	Home health agency	All categories	Physician and other medical	Out- patient	Home health agency
65-74 years	$ 701	681	6	15	341	283	56	2
75-84 years	1,091	1,036	20	36	431	367	60	5
85 years and over	1,313	1,223	39	51	423	365	50	7

Source: Calculated from U.S. Health Care Financing Administration, 1983, Section IV: Tables
8 and 11.

a. Reimbursement per person among those ever enrolled in Medicare in 1981.

care services, the proportions did increase with age. Among those age
65 to 74 years, 4 persons per 1,000 enrollees received skilled nursing
facility benefits. For those 85 years and older, the proportion increased
sevenfold, to 30 per 1,000 enrollees. The proportion of those receiving
home health care benefits more than tripled.

The amount of money reimbursed per person served showed no consistent increase with age indicating, perhaps, that similar services are
provided to all elderly Medicare recipients, without major changes in
services provided for the extreme elderly. For some services, in fact,
the reimbursement per person served decreased for the extreme elderly.
The amount of money reimbursed per enrollee, however, did increase
with age, reflecting the increasing proportion, at each older age group,
of enrollees who are served under Medicare (Table 8.13).

For the population 85 years and over, among both whites and nonwhites, a higher proportion of males than females received hospital
insurance benefits, largely for inpatient hospitalization. A larger proportion of females than males, white and nonwhite, received benefits
for physician and other medical services. A higher proportion of females
also received reimbursement for skilled nursing facility care. This reflects differences in marital status and living arrangements between
elderly men and women. With the exception of home health care and
outpatient services, the proportion of whites receiving Medicare-fi-

TABLE 8.14:   PERSONS SERVED AND REIMBURSEMENTS AMONG MEDICARE ENROLLEES 85 YEARS AND OVER,
BY RACE, SEX AND TYPE OF SERVICE: 1981

Race and sex	Hospital Insurance				Supplementary Medical Insurance			
	All categories[a]	In- patient	Skilled nursing facility	Home health agency	All categories[a]	Physician and other medical	Out- patient	Home health agency
Persons served per 1,000 enrollees								
All persons								
Both sexes	353	336	30	72	776	758	321	19
Male	374	359	25	71	751	730	315	18
Female	344	326	33	72	786	769	324	19
White								
Both sexes	359	343	32	71	782	764	322	18
Male	383	369	26	71	760	742	316	18
Female	349	332	34	71	791	774	324	18
Nonwhite								
Both sexes	313	291	15	86	727	696	332	26
Male	308	288	14	80	656	617	321	25
Female	316	293	16	88	760	733	337	27
Reimbursement per person served								
All persons								
Both sexes	$4,021	$3,935	$1,385	$768	$619	547	178	443
Male	4,113	4,047	1,226	751	681	612	182	392
Female	3,979	3,883	1,436	775	595	522	177	442
White								
Both sexes	3,982	3,893	1,370	750	618	548	176	428
Male	4,056	3,989	1,209	731	680	611	179	392
Female	3,948	3,848	1,423	758	594	523	175	442
Nonwhite								
Both sexes	4,552	4,521	1,629	957	643	550	208	594
Male	4,698	4,669	1,634	944	709	616	222	549
Female	4,483	4,450	1,626	963	617	525	202	614

Source: U.S. Health Care Financing Administration, 1983, Section IV: Tables 10 and 12.

a.   Figures for "all categories" do not equal sum of individual categories because enrollees
may be reimbursed for more than one type of service.

nanced services was higher than for nonwhites. Perhaps one of the
most striking differences between whites and nonwhites is for skilled
nursing facility services. The proportion of very elderly nonwhite males
receiving such services was 14 per 1,000 enrollees compared with 26
per 1,000 white male enrollees. For nonwhite and white females the

TABLE 8.15:   USE OF MEDICAID IN TWELVE MONTH PERIOD AMONG NONINSTITUTIONALIZED
               PERSONS 65 YEARS OLD AND OVER, BY AGE GROUP AND SEX: 1980

Sex and age group	Number (in thousands)	Used Medicaid Number (in thousands)	Used Medicaid Percent
Both sexes			
65 to 74 years	15,224	961	6.3
75 to 84 years	7,059	583	8.3
85 years and over	1,607	177	11.0
Male			
65 to 74 years	6,629	328	4.9
75 to 84 years	2,654	171	6.5
85 years and over	554	34	6.1
Female			
65 to 74 years	8,595	634	7.4
75 to 84 years	4,405	412	9.4
85 years and over	1,053	143	13.6

Source: U.S. National Center for Health Statistics, 1980 Health Interview
           Survey, 1980 Public Use Tape.

proportions were 16 and 34 per 1,000 enrollees respectively (Table
8.14). Relatively more nonwhite men and women received home health
care services than did their white counterparts (Table 8.14).

Table 8.15 shows data on the use of Medicaid among the noninstitutionalized elderly in 1980. Not surprisingly, the use of Medicaid
increases with advancing age, especially for women—reflective of both
the increased use of medical facilities and services by the very old and
also of the decline in their income.

CONCLUSION

Research on the health status of the extreme elderly points to one
fundamental and inescapable conclusion—the population of chronically ill elderly people is growing rapidly and will continue to do so
for the foreseeable future. Even if, as Hickey has suggested, individuals
stay healthier until a later point in life and live somewhat longer, they
will "still experience most of the same health problems in advanced
old age as old people do today" (1980, p. 171). Whether most individuals
will indeed stay healthier to a later age than they now do is open to

question, since it depends on a wide array of genetic and environmental influences, all of which interact in ways which are still poorly understood (Stub, 1982). The problem of prediction is compounded by the fact that American society gives little attention to *preventive* care, preferring to concentrate its resources on curative efforts. Furthermore, despite tremendous advances in medicine, the medical profession is ill-equipped to cope with the multiplicity of chronic problems which characterize the extreme elderly (Hickey, 1980).

To date, neither government nor the medical profession nor the public at large have fully recognized or adequately planned for the many economic, social, and ethical dilemmas raised by an aging population. For most individuals, the last years of life are, and will continue to be, threatened with lengthy periods of disability and dependence. Specialized care facilities and the commitment of ever-increasing amounts of scarce resources will be required to meet the growing demands on the health care system. Hence it is crucial that quality-of-life issues be raised and answers to difficult questions attempted. The common assumption that quantity of life can be equated with quality, however valid it may have been in the past, can no longer be accepted uncritically.

9   *Mortality Patterns*

Declining mortality is one of the major factors explaining the unprecedented growth of the elderly population of the United States since 1900. In the early years of this century, when the risk of death from infectious disease was being sharply reduced, declining mortality generally resulted in improved infant survival and increased numbers of youth surviving to adulthood. More recently, decreased mortality among middle-aged and older adults has resulted in relatively more individuals surviving to very old ages. For the first time on record, reductions in mortality among the elderly are as great or greater than reductions among the young.

It is generally agreed among social scientists that "the most comprehensive indicator of patterns of health and disease—and of living standards and societal development as well—is a population's life expectancy at various ages" (Omran, 1977, p. 18). Life expectancy at birth is the most common index of mortality conditions (United Nations, 1982). The expectation of life at birth is computed from age-specific death rates for persons at every age, and this reflects a population's mortality experience at all ages. Table 9.1 shows the tremendous advances in life expectancy at birth achieved in the United States during the course of the twentieth century. Also shown are life expectancy values at ages 30 and 65. During the 80–year period from 1901 to 1981 life expectancy at birth climbed from 47.9 to 70.2 years for males and from 50.9 to 77.8 years for females. For both sexes, most of this increase in aggregate life expectancy occurred in the years before

TABLE 9.1:   EXPECTATION OF LIFE AT BIRTH AND AT AGES 30 AND 65, BY SEX:
1901 TO 1981

Year	Male			Female		
	0	30	65	0	30	65
1901	47.9	34.3	11.3	50.9	35.9	12.0
1911	51.8	35.3	11.5	55.0	37.4	12.2
1921	57.3	38.1	12.2	59.3	39.0	12.8
1931	58.6	37.1	12.0	62.0	39.5	13.1
1941	61.9	38.3	12.2	66.5	41.8	13.8
1951	65.7	39.9	12.8	71.4	44.6	15.2
1961	67.1	40.7	13.1	73.6	46.3	16.1
1971	67.4	40.8	13.1	75.1	47.4	17.1
1981	70.2	42.9	14.2	77.8	49.4	18.6

Source: U.S. Social Security Administration, 1983: Table 5.

1941. From 1901 to 1941, males gained 14.0 years in life expectancy at birth, whereas the gain from 1941 to 1981 was 8.3 years; for females, the increment at birth was 15.6 years in the first half of the period and fell to 11.3 years in the latter half.

In contrast, a male aged 30 had a life expectancy of 34.3 years in 1901, 38.3 years in 1941 and 42.9 years in 1981.Thus slightly more than half of the registered increase in *adult* life expectancy took place in the second half of the period covered. Similarly, the gain in life expectancy of a 30–year-old female between 1901 and 1941--from 35.9 to 41.8 years, was slightly less than that between 1941 and 1981—from 41.8 to 49.4 years.

Compared to the striking gains at younger ages, the changes in life expectancy at age 65 during the first four decades of this century were not impressive. Among men average expectation changed by just under one year between 1901 and 1941 (from 11.3 to 12.2 years); this was equivalent to only about half the gain which occurred between 1941 and 1981—when expectancy advanced by 2 years to 14.2 years. The change in life expectancy among elderly women was more dramatic. A gain of 1.8 years in life expectancy at age 65 (from 12.0 to 13.8 years) between 1901 and 1941 was greatly overshadowed by an advance of almost 5 years in the most recent period—to an average remaining lifetime of 18.6 years.

Progress in the reduction of mortality is most commonly measured in terms of life expectancy at birth. However, this measure is a "capsulized indicator" of progress in the elimination of premature death at all ages (U.S. Bureau of the Census, 1984d). Examination of data on life expectation at birth does not reveal at what ages improvement has occurred over time. It is especially useful to distinguish progress in survival at ages under 65 and ages 65 to 85. Changes in death rates at these ages can be conveniently summarized by computation of life table survival rates between particular ages. Based on the life table for 1900, almost 51 percent of males and 54 percent of females who survived childhood could expect to reach age 65; the life table for 1980 indicates that 72 percent of males and 85 percent of females who reached age 20 could anticipate living to age 65 (Table 9.2). The proportions of males and females surviving from age 65 to age 85 in 1900 were 13 and 15 percent respectively. By 1980 the chance of survival of males from 65 to 85 had almost doubled—to 25 percent, whereas the chance of survival of females to age 85 tripled—to 45 percent. Thus the 1980 life table indicates that women aged 65 had nearly as good a chance of reaching age 85 as women aged 20 had of reaching 65 at the beginning of the century.

The overwhelming share of the progress in survival between ages 65 and 85 among both men and women occurred in the decades following 1940 (Table 9.2). For both sexes the greatest advance occurred in the 1940s and the decade of second greatest improvement was the 1970s.

Causes of the more favorable experience in the post–1940 period may include advances in diagnostic and treatment techniques for major chronic diseases, improvement in economic status among the elderly with the advent of the social security system and the increased availability of medical care following the introduction of new government programs (Medicare and Medicaid).

The fluctuations in improvement in mortality at older ages are also reflected in age-specific death rates. Mortality patterns in the most recent decades have been analyzed in terms of three distinct phases: the years from the Great Depression to 1954, the period 1954 to 1968, and 1968 to the present. The earliest period was one of relatively rapid decline in mortality among the elderly (but not as rapid as change at younger ages), the middle period was a stagnant interlude and the

TABLE 9.2: NUMBER LIVING AT BEGINNING OF AGE PER 100,000 AND PERCENT SURVIVING
            BETWEEN SELECTED AGES, BY SEX, UNITED STATES: 1900 TO 1980

Sex and year	Surviving to exact age (l_x)			Survival ratios (per 100)	
	20	65	85	20 to 65	65 to 85
Male					
1900	73,892	37,319	4,728	50.50	12.67
1910	78,905	41,006	5,274	51.97	12.86
1920	83,560	47,925	6,801	57.35	14.19
1930	88,260	50,518	7,490	57.24	14.83
1940	91,559	55,523	8,287	60.64	14.93
1950	94,805	61,791	11,982	65.18	19.39
1960	95,445	63,798	12,576	66.84	19.71
1970	96,144	64,303	13,513	66.88	21.01
1980	97,270	70,521	17,563	72.50	24.90
Female					
1900	76,557	41,029	6,210	53.59	15.14
1910	81,497	47,594	7,401	58.40	15.55
1920	85,851	50,462	8,227	58.78	16.30
1930	90,222	57,391	10,854	63.61	18.91
1940	93,242	65,419	13,520	70.16	20.67
1950	96,132	74,300	21,199	77.29	28.53
1960	96,737	78,231	25,019	80.87	31.98
1970	97,338	79,680	30,581	81.86	38.38
1980	98,162	83,421	37,593	84.98	45.06

Source: U.S. Social Security Administration, 1983: Tables 3a to 3i.

most recent period one of unprecedented decline in mortality rates at
the oldest ages (see Crimmins, 1981; Rosenwaike et al., 1980; U.S.
Bureau of the Census, 1984d; Wilkin, 1981).

National Center for Health Statistics data (1984a, Table B) show
that in the 65 and over age group (age adjusted by the direct method,
using five age groups), mortality declined at a rate of 1.5 percent per
year from 1940 to 1954. The decline slowed to 0.5 percent from 1955
to 1967 and then increased sharply from 1968 to 1980, reaching an
annual rate of 2.1 percent. In each of these three phases, the rate of
declining mortality was greater among females (with declines of 2.0
percent, 1.0 percent and 2.3 percent respectively) than among males
(whose corresponding rates were 1.1 percent, −0.2 percent and 1.7
percent).

During the latest of these periods, 1968 to 1980, the reductions in mortality among the elderly were almost identical for the three major elderly groups. While the mortality rate decreased by 19.6 percent from 1968 to 1980 for those aged 65–74, and by 19.3 percent for those aged 75–84, the death rate for the 85 and older group declined by 18.4 percent (U.S. National Center for Health Statistics, 1984a, Table A).

Overall, mortality differences between males and females 65 years of age and over have increased steadily over time. In 1940, the age-adjusted death rate for males was 22 percent higher than that for females; by 1960, the difference had increased to 47 percent and by 1970 to 74 percent. The difference had leveled off to 71 percent in 1980 (U.S. National Center for Health Statistics, 1984a, Table 4). However, the increase has been slower for the 85 and over population. The ratio of the male death rate to the female death rate for those 65 and over (based on age-adjusted figures) increased at an annual rate of 0.9 percent in 1940–54, 1.2 percent in 1955–67 and 0.6 percent in 1968–80. In contrast, the ratios for the 85 and over category *declined* during the first period (at an annual rate of 0.2 percent) and then grew at a relatively sluggish rate of 0.9 percent per annum in the first and 0.7 percent per annum in the second of the succeeding periods (U.S. National Center for Health Statistics, 1984a). (The latter figure, nevertheless, was above that of the annual percent change in the mortality sex ratio for the entire 65 and over group.)

National data have consistently indicated that blacks have lower life expectancy than whites. In 1969–71 the expectation of life at birth of black males (60 years) was 7.9 years below that for white males; for black females the expectation of life at birth (68.3 years) was 7.2 years below that for white females (U.S. Department of Health, Education and Welfare, 1979). The difference in life expectancy between the white and black populations had narrowed somewhat by 1982 from the 1969–71 levels. Among the race-sex groups, black males continued to have the lowest life expectancy at birth (64.9 years), followed by white males (71.5 years). Black females (73.5 years) had the largest gain in life expectancy and white females (78.8 years) the smallest gain (U.S. National Center for Health Statistics, 1984c).

Age-adjusted death rates indicate what mortality levels would be if age distributions were identical for each racial group. The age-adjusted death rate of the black population in 1970 was 54 percent higher than that of the white population (U.S. Department of Health, Education and Welfare, 1979). Age-specific death rates for blacks indicate a strik-

TABLE 9.3: DEATH RATES BY RACE, SELECTED AGES: 1980

(Rates per 100,000 population)

Age	Male			Female		
	Black	White	Ratio	Black	White	Ratio
55-59 years	2,457	1,376	1.79	1,306	696	1.88
60-64 years	3,377	2,141	1.58	1,861	1,079	1.72
65-69 years	4,484	3,312	1.35	2,538	1,643	1.54
70-74 years	6,048	5,023	1.20	3,760	2,585	1.45
75-79 years	8,092	7,468	1.08	5,244	4,189	1.25
80-84 years	11,554	11,267	1.03	8,030	7,236	1.11
85 and over	16,099	19,097	0.84	12,367	14,980	0.83

Source: U.S. National Center for Health Statistics, 1983a: Table 1.

ing pattern relative to whites. Beginning in the young adult years, the ratio of black to white death rates decreases with advancing age. Table 9.3 indicates that in 1980 the ratio decreased from 1.79 among males at 55–59 years of age (1.88 among females) to 1.03 at age 80–84 (1.11 among females) and was below 1.00 for the extreme aged. The black-white mortality ratio pattern is a consistent one for both males and females: with advancing age rates for blacks decline relative to those for whites, from a marked excess to a deficit.

The fall in death rates for blacks to a level lower than that for whites at very old ages—termed the mortality crossover—has intrigued a number of social scientists. The hypothesis has been advanced that the most robust blacks survive and that these individuals are hardier than surviving whites (Jackson, 1980; Manton, 1980). A mortality crossover is not without precedent: Nam reports many examples where groups with higher mortality at young ages have lower mortality at older ages, relative to a comparison population at older ages (Nam et al., 1978). As noted in Chapter 2, however, age data on extreme aged blacks is so unreliable that it is questionable to what extent the black-white mortality crossover can be accepted as valid. Age misstatement in particular has been found to be a major or even the sole explanation for such a crossover in rates (U.S. Department of Health, Education and Welfare, 1979; Rosenwaike, 1979).

Table 9.3 indicates that the black-white mortality crossover now occurs in the 85 and over category. In 1959–61, interestingly, the crossover, based on official statistics was at age 75. However, the correction for discrepancies in age reporting made by Kitagawa and Hauser (1973) moved the "crossing" to a higher age so that the nonwhite and white mortality curves did not cross until the 85 and over age category. In effect, the correction of Kitagawa and Hauser may have forecast the eventual results of improvement in accuracy of data sources. This improvement may now be producing a more realistic picture of mortality risks among blacks relative to whites.

The dramatic shift since 1968 in the pattern of mortality for the population 85 and over is clearly reflected in statistics by cause of death. As noted above, the significant decline in mortality among infants and children earlier in the century was due to the control of infectious disease, the primary cause of death at young ages.

Public health victories over infectious disease, however, yielded only modest declines in mortality for the elderly, since infectious disease is not the primary danger facing them. Instead, their ranks are filled with those who survived these diseases in their youth and developed immunity in the process. Among the elderly, it is chronic degenerative diseases which have accounted for a large and growing share of deaths during the twentieth century. In 1900, 38 percent of deaths among the older population were due to these causes (U.S. National Center for Health Statistics, 1982b). In recent decades, three-quarters of all deaths among those 85 and older have been the result of three major causes—heart disease, cerebrovascular disease (stroke) and malignant neoplasms (cancer).

The sharp decline in mortality since 1968 among persons 85 and over is closely tied to recent medical advances—improvements in the treatment of the chronic degenerative diseases which constitute their primary threat. During the period 1968–78 the death rate from two of these leading causes declined among persons 85 and over. The sharpest downturn occurred for cerebrovascular disease; the decline for heart disease was also substantial. However, the death rate for cancer increased, particularly for males (Table 9.4).

The reasons for the major reductions in death rates for the cardiovascular diseases include progress in controlling such risk factors as high saturated fat and cholesterol diets, cigarette smoking and hypertension, as well as positive developments in emergency, acute and long-term care for patients with coronary heart disease and stroke (Stamler, 1978; Soltero, et al., 1978; Kleinman, et al., 1979).

TABLE 9.4:   AVERAGE ANNUAL PERCENT CHANGE IN DEATH RATES FOR MAJOR CAUSES OF DEATH, ALL AGES
AND SELECTED AGES, BY SEX: 1968 TO 1980

Cause of Death (Ninth Revision Classification Numbers)	Male			Female		
	All ages	85-89 years	90-94 years	All ages	85-89 years	90-94 years
All causes	-1.86	-1.48	-1.48	-2.27	-2.29	-1.86
Heart disease (390-398, 402, 404-429)	-2.22	-1.73	-1.47	-2.55	-2.23	-1.56
Malignant neoplasms (140-209)	.79	1.77	2.01	.22	.27	.73
Vascular diseases (400-401, 403, 430-458, 582-583,587)	-4.67	-4.32	-4.22	-4.79	-4.33	-3.83
Violence (E800-E989)	-1.72	-3.09	-3.21	-2.39	-5.50	-5.84
Respiratory disease (460-519)	-1.60	1.11	.32	-2.19	-1.34	-1.38
Congenital malformations and diseases of infancy (740-778)	-5.25	-5.24	2.53	-4.66	-.23	3.64
Digestive disease (520-570, 572-579)	-3.10	-1.25	-.57	-2.47	-.62	.25
Diabetes mellitus (250)	-2.84	-2.43	-.39	-3.88	-2.13	.08
Cirrhosis of liver (571)	-1.11	-.70	-2.19	-1.59	-.82	-1.32
All other causes	-.34	1.19	1.21	-.15	2.51	2.59

Source: U.S. Social Security Administration, 1983: Table 1.

The rise in mortality from cancer (which at some sites has a very long latency period) is generally due to increased environmental exposures and particularly reflects the marked increase in the proportion of the population who have been smokers since the first few decades of the present century when the recent aged commenced the smoking habit. Although death rates due to cancer increased, the percent of the population that smokes has decreased in recent years. Had the number of smokers not decreased, cancer rates might have increased at a faster pace.

A cautionary note must be introduced into any discussion of trends in causes of death over time. That is, the introduction of a new revision of the International Classification of Diseases (ICD) every decade can

TABLE 9.5: PERCENT OF TOTAL DEATHS OF PERSONS 85 YEARS AND OVER FOR LEADING
CAUSES OF DEATH, BY SEX: 1939-41 TO 1979-81

Cause of death	1939-41	1949-51	1959-61	1969-71	1979-81
Both sexes					
All causes	100.00	100.00	100.00	100.00	100.00
Diseases of heart	36.28	45.10	50.18	48.30	48.67
Cerebrovascular diseases	11.14	14.76	18.74	18.33	14.41
Malignant neoplasms	5.91	7.27	7.46	8.05	10.13
Pneumonia and influenza	8.45	4.60	5.10	5.08	5.25
Atherosclerosis	6.59	8.53	7.20	5.40	4.13
Accidents	5.89	4.97	3.18	2.44	1.82
Diabetes mellitus	0.92	0.75	0.90	1.40	1.40
Symptoms and ill-defined	6.59	0.91	0.70	0.73	1.07
All other causes	18.23	13.11	6.54	10.27	13.13
Male					
All causes	100.00	100.00	100.00	100.00	100.00
Diseases of heart	35.86	44.70	49.18	47.34	46.51
Cerebrovascular diseases	10.59	13.84	17.29	16.18	11.74
Malignant neoplasms	6.11	7.89	8.51	9.64	12.81
Pneumonia and influenza	8.37	4.65	5.39	5.48	5.82
Atherosclerosis	6.81	8.43	6.83	4.87	3.54
Accidents	14.44	4.00	2.80	2.45	2.01
Diabetes mellitus	0.87	0.66	0.79	1.21	1.15
Symptoms and ill-defined	6.36	1.04	0.81	0.82	1.10
All other causes	20.59	14.79	8.40	12.01	15.31
Female					
All causes	100.00	100.00	100.00	100.00	100.00
Diseases of heart	36.62	45.43	50.72	48.92	49.87
Cerebrovascular diseases	11.60	15.48	19.77	19.70	15.89
Malignant neoplasms	5.74	6.79	6.71	7.04	8.64
Pneumonia and influenza	8.51	4.56	4.90	4.82	4.93
Atherosclerosis	6.41	8.60	7.46	5.74	4.46
Accidents	7.07	5.73	3.45	2.44	1.71
Diabetes mellitus	0.96	0.82	0.97	1.52	1.54
Symptoms and ill-defined	6.77	0.81	0.63	0.68	1.05
All other causes	16.32	11.78	5.39	9.14	11.91

Source: U.S. National Center for Health Statistics, Vital Statistics of the
United States, Annual, Vol. II - Mortality.

TABLE 9.6:   PERCENT OF TOTAL DEATHS OF WHITES AND NONWHITES 85 YEARS AND OVER
FOR LEADING CAUSES OF DEATH: 1939-41 TO 1979-81

Cause of death	1939-41	1949-51	1959-61	1969-71	1979-81
White					
All causes	100.00	100.00	100.00	100.00	100.00
Diseases of heart	37.12	45.44	50.42	48.50	48.96
Cerebrovascular diseases	11.17	14.78	18.73	18.33	14.41
Malignant neoplasms	6.12	7.39	7.48	8.01	10.03
Pneumonia and influenza	8.50	4.55	5.10	5.11	5.32
Atherosclerosis	6.77	8.68	7.28	5.48	4.18
Accidents	6.11	5.08	3.23	2.46	1.80
Diabetes mellitus	0.95	0.75	0.89	1.39	1.36
Symptoms and ill-defined	5.31	0.63	0.52	0.58	0.94
All other causes	17.95	12.70	6.35	10.14	12.99
Nonwhite					
All causes	100.00	100.00	100.00	100.00	100.00
Diseases of heart	25.13	39.24	45.58	44.98	44.43
Cerebrovascular diseases	10.86	14.35	18.73	18.32	14.32
Malignant neoplasms	3.06	5.27	7.11	8.74	11.58
Pneumonia and influenza	7.70	5.46	5.11	4.70	4.22
Atherosclerosis	4.18	5.89	5.68	4.08	3.33
Accidents	2.98	3.04	2.33	2.12	2.00
Diabetes mellitus	0.57	0.64	0.93	1.63	2.06
Symptoms and ill-defined	23.59	5.72	3.96	3.32	2.99
All other causes	21.93	20.39	10.57	12.11	15.07

Source: See source for Table 9.5

produce a break in the continuity of mortality statistics for particular causes due to shifts in classification. Although comparability ratios that measure the aggregate change produced between revisions are available, they may not take account of the possibility that individual age-sex groups, such as the extreme elderly, may be differentially affected by the changes (U.S. National Center for Health Statistics, 1975; Halliday and Anderson, 1977). Deaths in Tables 9.5 through 9.9 for 1979–81 are classified according to the Ninth Revision of the International Classification of Diseases (ICD) using comparable ICD codes

TABLE 9.7:   DEATH RATES AMONG PERSONS 85 YEARS AND OVER FOR SELECTED CAUSES,
              BY SEX: 1949-51 TO 1979-81

(Deaths per 100,000 population)

Cause of death	1949-51	1959-61	1969-71	1979-81
Both sexes				
All causes	20,193	19,663	17,900	15,612
Diseases of heart	9,108	9,866	8,646	7,599
Cerebrovascular diseases	2,980	3,685	3,281	2,249
Malignant neoplasms	1,469	1,466	1,441	1,582
Pneumonia and influenza	929	1,003	909	819
Atherosclerosis	1,722	1,415	967	644
Accidents	1,004	625	437	284
Male				
All causes	21,803	21,008	20,079	18,342
Diseases of heart	9,745	10,331	9,505	8,532
Cerebrovascular diseases	3,017	3,632	3,249	2,154
Malignant neoplasms	1,720	1,788	1,936	2,350
Pneumonia and influenza	1,014	1,132	1,101	1,067
Atherosclerosis	1,839	1,435	977	648
Accidents	873	588	491	369
Female				
All causes	19,093	18,804	16,739	14,419
Diseases of heart	8,674	9,537	8,188	7,191
Cerebrovascular diseases	2,956	3,718	3,297	2,291
Malignant neoplasms	1,297	1,261	1,178	1,246
Pneumonia and influenza	871	921	807	711
Atherosclerosis	1,642	1,402	961	643
Accidents	1,094	649	409	246

Source: See source for Table 9.5.

from earlier revisions for earlier years (World Health Organization, 1977).

In Table 9.5, which shows the percent of all deaths accounted for by seven leading causes among the 85 and over group between 1939–41 and 1979–81, still another factor is at play. With improvements in diagnostic techniques over time, the share of deaths attributed to the

TABLE 9.8:   DEATH RATES OF WHITES AND NONWHITES 85 YEARS AND OVER FOR LEADING
             CAUSES OF DEATH: 1949-51 TO 1979-81

(Deaths   per 100,000 population)

Cause of death	1949-51	1959-61	1969-71	1979-81
White				
All causes	20,716	20,172	18,393	15,861
Diseases of heart	9,414	10,170	8,921	7,766
Cerebrovascular diseases	3,062	3,779	3,371	2,286
Malignant neoplasms	1,531	1,508	1,473	1,591
Pneumonia and influenza	943	1,029	939	843
Atherosclerosis	1,798	1,468	1,008	664
Accidents	1,052	651	453	286
Nonwhite				
All causes	14,068	13,666	12,453	12,750
Diseases of heart	5,520	6,229	5,601	5,666
Cerebrovascular diseases	2,019	2,560	2,282	1,825
Malignant neoplasms	741	971	1,088	1,477
Pneumonia and influenza	768	698	585	538
Atherosclerosis	828	776	508	425
Accidents	428	319	264	255

Sources: Computed from sources for Tables 3.1 and 9.5.

very vague category, "symptoms and ill-defined conditions," has greatly diminished. Inevitably, this in turn accounts for corresponding increases in the numbers of deaths assigned to more specific categories. The substantial increases between 1939–41 and 1949–51 in the percentages of deaths attributed to heart disease, cerebrovascular disease and cancer are in part due to this artifact. At the same time, however, deaths attributed to pneumonia and influenza dropped sharply, although the decline has not continued. On the other hand, the relative decline in deaths due to accidents has been a continuing one.

Historically, major differences have existed in the classification of cause of death by race. Some of the difference undoubtedly is artifactual and reflects errors in diagnosis which result from differences in the quantity and quality of medical care. Table 9.6 indicates that at every time period much higher proportions of deaths among very aged nonwhites were coded to "symptoms and ill-defined conditions" than was true among whites. The discrepancy was especially great in 1939–41 when almost one-fourth of all deaths among nonwhites 85 and older were coded to the vague category, "symptoms," compared with only 5 percent of deaths of very old whites.

Because of these classification problems, meaningful trend patterns in death rates by cause can be shown only for the years after World War II. Table 9.7 indicates that a rise in death rates for heart disease and stroke among the very elderly took place between 1949–51 and 1959–61 among both males and females and that subsequently sharp decreases have occurred. The death rate for cancer among males 85 and over has increased each decade; among females the pattern has been irregular. The pneumonia and influenza category has not shown much pattern, but has moved up in rank from the sixth to the fourth leading cause of death among the extreme aged as rates for two other leading causes, atherosclerosis (arteriosclerosis) and accidents, have sharply declined (Table 9.7).

In general, trends for the leading causes of death among whites and nonwhites 85 and over have been similar (Table 9.8). One exception has been the somewhat steeper increase in the death rate for cancer for nonwhites which was low relative to the rates for whites in the past, perhaps due to age misstatement among the former. Thus the apparent extremely large increase in cancer mortality for nonwhites between 1969–71 and 1979–81 may be partly a statistical artifact.

For many countries, including the United States, mortality statistics are shown for an open-ended final age group consisting of persons 85 years and over. In part this classification is historic, originating from an era when relatively few deaths occurred in the last group; hence its open-ended feature was of little consequence in the past. In part the classification has also been a practical one stemming from a belief that ages reported for the extreme elderly tended to be less reliable than those for younger persons, making detailed breakouts spurious.

The official vital statistics volumes for the United States have shown detailed characteristics by age group for decedents 85 years of age and over, but death rates for those groups have rarely been produced. In order to examine whether causes of death change in importance with increasing age over 85, examination of selected statistics may be of interest. Table 9.9 indicates that (except for 1949–51) there has been little difference by five-year age group in the proportion of deaths due

TABLE 9.9:   PERCENT OF TOTAL DEATHS OF PERSONS 85 YEARS AND OVER, BY AGE,
             FOR LEADING CAUSES OF DEATH: 1949-51 TO 1979-81

Causes of death and period	85-89 years	90-94 years	95-99 years	100 years and over
1949-51				
All causes	100.00	100.00	100.00	100.00
Diseases of heart	45.88	44.24	42.27	34.97
Cerebrovascular diseases	15.53	13.70	11.60	10.13
Malignant neoplasms	8.19	5.77	4.45	3.10
Pneumonia and influenza	4.18	5.16	6.10	8.19
Atherosclerosis	7.46	10.33	12.27	10.38
Accidents	4.70	5.55	5.52	4.64
Diabetes mellitus	0.91	0.48	0.26	0.21
Symptoms and ill-defined	0.76	0.95	1.71	4.50
All other causes	12.39	13.82	15.82	23.88
1959-61				
All causes	100.00	100.00	100.00	100.00
Diseases of heart	49.98	50.77	48.03	47.84
Cerebrovascular diseases	19.07	18.32	17.48	16.42
Malignant neoplasms	8.52	5.86	4.13	2.76
Pneumonia and influenza	4.61	5.67	7.09	8.77
Atherosclerosis	6.14	8.66	11.01	11.49
Accidents	3.04	3.43	3.57	3.10
Diabetes mellitus	1.04	0.68	0.35	0.34
Symptoms and ill-defined	0.64	0.72	1.01	2.49
All other causes	6.96	5.89	7.36	6.79
1969-71				
All causes	100.00	100.00	100.00	100.00
Diseases of heart	47.91	48.96	49.21	47.77
Cerebrovascular diseases	18.37	18.53	17.79	14.83
Malignant neoplasms	9.29	6.39	4.51	3.13
Pneumonia and influenza	4.59	5.61	6.72	8.51
Atherosclerosis	4.51	6.46	8.23	10.29
Accidents	2.38	2.54	2.67	2.31
Diabetes mellitus	1.65	1.05	0.71	0.57
Symptoms and ill-defined	0.70	0.73	0.93	1.84
All other causes	10.60	9.73	9.23	10.75
1979-81				
All causes	100.00	100.00	100.00	100.00
Diseases of heart	47.55	49.82	51.06	52.19
Cerebrovascular diseases	14.31	14.71	14.35	12.59
Malignant neoplasms	12.00	8.37	5.76	3.38
Pneumonia and influenza	4.69	5.73	6.59	7.82
Atherosclerosis	3.31	4.77	6.29	8.22
Accidents	1.83	1.81	1.80	1.62
Diabetes mellitus	1.60	1.23	0.94	0.69
Symptoms and ill-defined	0.92	1.12	1.49	2.89
All other causes	13.80	12.45	11.71	10.60

Source: See source for Table 9.5.

to heart disease. Regardless of age, close to half of all deaths have been attributed to this cause. On the other hand, the percentage of deaths due to stroke has generally declined with advancing age. The age pattern for cancer is much more striking: in general the relative share of deaths assigned to this cause has fallen by about two-thirds between ages 85–89 and 100 plus. Just the opposite pattern is seen for the percentage of deaths due to pneumonia and influenza and to atherosclerosis; with each advance in age the percentage of deaths attributable to each of these causes shows an increase.

Using mortality statistics by age to produce estimates of the death rates for age components of the 85 and over population is a precarious undertaking. Until the advent of Medicare (with its detailed statistics of the elderly population) age breakdowns of the extreme aged population were available only in the decennial census. Thus only for the period around the census date could any type of meaningful rates be calculated. Table 9.10 shows death rates for five-year age groups computed from national statistics of deaths and decennial census populations. Increments in death rates between ages 90–94 and 95–99 in the 1949–51 period for every subgroup shown appear unreasonably small (or non-existent); the same is true for nonwhites in 1959–61. This is likely to be an artifact of sampling variation since both the 1950 and 1960 statistics were based on samples of the full count. Similarly, comparison of white-nonwhite patterns may be misleading due to the likelihood of extensive misreporting among the latter (Chapter 2). The main conclusion to be drawn from Table 9.10 is that for those age groups where figures are most reliable—85–89 years and 90–94 years—the pattern of mortality has been strongly downward, particularly among women.

It is of interest to note that for five-year age groups culminating with 85 and over, little difference was observed in death rate changes based on Medicare data or NCHS data between 1968 and 1980 (U.S. National Center for Health Statistics, 1984a, Table N). The availability of Medicare, however, has made it possible for analysts of mortality at the oldest ages to study the subject with greater reliability than previously. Using deaths and populations obtained from the same source, Medicare, permits the elimination of errors due to noncomparability of numerator and denominator—as in the traditional published NCHS rates which use population estimates prepared by the Bureau of the Census (Wilkin, 1981).

TABLE 9.10:   DEATH RATES OF PERSONS 85 YEARS AND OVER, BY AGE, RACE AND SEX:
1939-41 TO 1979-81

(Deaths per 1,000 population)

Race, sex, and period	85-89 years	90-94 years	95-99 years	100 years and over
Total				
1939-41	209.1	285.9	321.1	320.0
1949-51	181.1	258.0	272.9	319.3
1959-61	171.4	269.3	318.5	-
1969-71	156.6	224.2	256.3	-
1979-81	133.0	194.5	254.5	-
Male				
1939-41	222.3	301.0	320.0	322.4
1949-51	199.5	275.0	273.4	321.0
1959-61	187.8	284.1	324.1	-
1969-71	182.2	242.7	267.6	-
1979-81	164.4	223.6	272.1	-
Female				
1939-41	198.8	275.8	321.8	318.3
1949-51	168.2	247.3	272.6	318.2
1959-61	162.6	260.7	315.6	-
1969-71	142.5	215.0	251.3	-
1979-81	118.6	182.8	248.1	-
White				
1939-41	214.7	300.4	358.2	399.2
1949-51	185.0	267.4	306.5	401.3
1959-61	175.5	277.3	343.3	-
1969-71	160.6	232.8	271.8	-
1979-81	134.5	199.0	265.6	-
Nonwhite				
1939-41	140.7	182.2	206.0	270.7
1949-51	124.8	155.7	144.0	252.6
1959-61	118.5	176.5	175.2	-
1969-71	108.5	136.8	154.7	-
1979-81	114.2	143.7	171.2	-

Sources: Computed from data in U.S. National Center for Health Statistics, Vital
Statistics of the United States, Annual, Vol. II - Mortality, Tables
3.2, 3.3 and 3.4 and U.S. Bureau of the Census, 1953a: Table 94.

Medicare population counts are not without their flaws, however.
Knowledgeable actuaries believe that data from the program are of
"acceptable reliability up to around ages 90 or 95 and to gradually lose
their reliability as age increases." The major reason for the problems

TABLE 9.11   DEATH RATES OF PERSONS 85 YEARS AND OVER, BASED ON MEDICARE ENROLLMENT
POPULATIONS, BY AGE AND SEX: 1969-71 AND 1979-81

| Age and sex | 1969-71 | | 1979-81 | | Percent |
	Medicare population[a] (in thousands)	Death rate (per 1,000 population)	Medicare population[a] (in thousands)	Death rate (per 1,000 population)	change 1969-71 to 1979-81
Total					
85-89 years	1,021	156.0	1,571	128.6	-17.6
90-94 years	294	238.5	547	197.9	-17.0
95-99 years	56	334.6	121	275.1	-17.8
100 and over	7	442.9	23	259.2	-41.5
Male					
85-89 years	359	183.6	487	161.0	-12.3
90-94 years	93	269.7	153	232.3	-13.9
95-99 years	16	362.8	31	307.7	-15.2
100 and over	2	503.1	6	240.8	-52.1
Females					
85-89 years	662	141.1	1,084	114.1	-19.1
90-94 years	201	224.1	394	184.5	-17.7
95-99 years	39	323.0	90	264.0	-18.3
100 and over	5	422.3	17	265.7	-37.1

Sources: Computed from data in U.S. National Center for Health Statistics, Vital
Statistics of the United States, Annual, (Vol. II. Mortality) and U.S. Social
Security Administration, Job 5234, Actuarial Enrollment Data, Table 10
(unpublished).

a. Figure for January 1 of middle year.   Persons over 114 years in unpublished
tabulations have been excluded.

at the oldest ages are "consistent bias in the statement of age and ...
spurious data in the tape files," perhaps due to duplication or to in-
complete reporting of deaths (Bayo and Faber, 1983).

Despite potential deficiencies in both numerators and denominators,
death rates using published vital statistics as numerators and Medicare
enrollments as denominators have been prepared in Table 9.11 as alternatives to those shown in Table 9.10 for the two most recent time
periods. It may be significant that the percentage declines in the 1970
to 1980 decade were approximately the same—about 17 or 18 percent
for the total population in each of the three age groups: 85–89 years,
90–94 years, and 95–99 years. The much larger decline shown for
centenarians appears implausible. It is not likely that persons in the

very oldest age group in 1979–81 had lower mortality than those 95–99 years of age.

Bayo and Faber (1983) have recently looked closely at the "enigma in the United States" of mortality at very advanced ages. After careful examination of available evidence, they conclude that, as it does in European countries, mortality "increases continuously to the end of the life span" (p. 15). Their findings are based on study of two separate actual cohorts as well as a simulated cohort. The first consisted of "charter old-age insurance beneficiaries" of the Social Security program (persons born in 1872 to 1875) who started receiving Social Security program monthly retirement payments in January 1940, a group for whom "vigorous proof of age was required for entitlement to benefits" (p. 2).

The second group consisted of insured Medicare enrollees from the same cohorts (birth years of 1872 to 1875) who also received benefits from Social Security or the Railroad Retirement System based on covered earnings "because, in most cases, these individuals had to prove their ages" (p. 9). For comparison, the mortality of a synthetic cohort born in 1873–75 was calculated using deaths based on NCHS data. As expected, the more presumably reliable the age of the group studied, the steeper the mortality curve with advancing age. For example, males 100 years of age among the charter old-age insurance beneficiaries had a graduated death rate of 372 per 1,000 (the cohort size was quite small, however); whereas those among the insured Medicare enrollees (a fairly sizable cohort) had a rate of 348 and those from the vital statistics cohort, a rate of 323. Approximately corresponding differences were also observed among female cohorts (Bayo and Faber, 1983).

Although the long-term trend in the death rate for the extreme aged has been downward, the pattern from year to year is not a smooth one, exhibiting marked fluctuations at times. These are most prominent in years of epidemic influenza. The annual death rates since 1940 for the very old population are shown in Table 9.12 and Figure 9.1. The unusually low rate in 1954—not reached again until sixteen years later, in 1970—is notable. The lowest level of mortality among the extreme aged recorded thus far occurred in 1979, a year free of influenza epidemics (U.S. National Center for Health Statistics, 1984c).

The increases in mortality in 1980 (based on final data) and 1981 (based on provisional data) led some observers to question whether the period of rapidly declining adult mortality in the United States was

TABLE 9.12: DEATH RATES AMONG PERSONS 85 AND OVER, BY SEX: 1940 TO 1980

(Deaths per 1,000 population)

Year	Both sexes	Male	Female
1940	235.7	246.4	227.6
1941	218.7	231.9	208.8
1942	211.1	222.1	202.9
1943	230.3	242.6	221.2
1944	215.3	225.5	207.8
1945	209.6	220.7	201.3
1946	210.6	221.1	203.0
1947	216.9	229.3	207.2
1948	213.2	226.4	203.1
1949	203.2	215.0	194.4
1950	202.0	216.4	191.9
1951	197.6	208.2	190.1
1952	190.6	196.7	186.1
1953	191.9	199.2	186.6
1954	181.6	187.4	177.4
1955	189.8	195.9	185.5
1956	192.3	200.5	186.6
1957	197.9	207.3	191.5
1958	198.0	208.3	191.0
1959	194.2	205.4	186.8
1960	198.6	211.9	190.1
1961	196.3	210.8	186.9
1962	204.9	222.5	194.0
1963	209.9	229.4	197.9
1964	199.2	216.4	189.1
1965	200.7	220.8	189.0
1966	199.8	220.1	188.5
1967	192.2	213.4	180.4
1968	195.8	217.3	184.3
1969	188.2	208.8	177.1
1970	175.4	197.7	163.5
1971	175.7	199.0	163.5
1972	175.4	198.2	163.8
1973	176.8	200.7	164.8
1974	169.0	192.8	157.2
1975	156.6	181.3	144.5
1976	160.6	186.7	148.3
1977	153.7	180.7	141.3
1978	154.8	182.1	142.5
1979	149.6	176.0	137.9
1980	159.8	188.0	147.5

Source: U.S. National Center for Health Statistics, 1984a: Tables 1 to 3.

FIGURE 9.1: DEATH RATES FOR THE MALE AND FEMALE POPULATIONS
AGED 85 AND OVER: 1940–1980

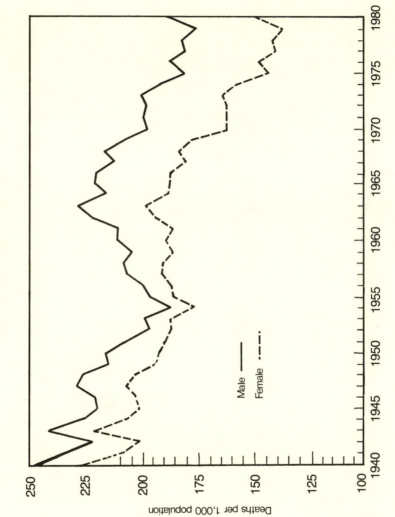

Source: Table 9.12.

coming to an end (Cooper et al., 1983). However, both the age-adjusted death rate and nearly all age-specific rates again fell to record lows by 1982. Final data for 1982 indicate that the death rate for persons 85 and over was 150.5 per 1,000 population (U.S. National Center for Health Statistics, 1984c), approximately one-half of 1 percent above the low level achieved in 1979.

What are the prospects for continuing mortality declines among the elderly? Experience has shown that efforts to estimate future death rates for the oldest age groups typically underestimated them, with mortality experts concurring that death rates were at an "irreducible minimum" in the absence of dramatic advances in medicine (Crimmins, 1981). Thus the extrapolation of base-year mortality figures yielded death rates that were higher than those actually achieved by the year in question. Life expectancy at the older ages has also been increasing rapidly, and there is "no evidence that we are approaching a biological maximum to the life span" with current mortality levels (Crimmins, 1983, p. 14). Thus, although it is unlikely that the primary "killer" diseases at the older ages will be eliminated in the foreseeable future, gains in prevention and treatment are likely to have an impact on death rates and life expectancy:

Life-style changes made to prevent cardiovascular disease should continue to take place, and those that have already occurred may have more effect after a longer period of time. Diffusion of current medical techniques can still cause substantial mortality decline in this area.... More universal diagnosis and treatment of [hypertension] should continue to decrease cardiovascular mortality for years to come (Crimmins, 1981, p. 248).

Diseases such as diabetes, influenza and pneumonia, and kidney diseases "will probably also continue to decline at their current rate, as advances are made in [their] treatment and prevention" (Crimmins, 1981, p. 249). There is considerable disagreement among experts about the outlook for cancer death rates, however. Most "do not predict significant decreases for cancer death rates in the near future because comparatively little is known about its causes and prevention. Even as cancer treatment is developed it is possible that cancer death rates may not decline and could increase as exposure to carcinogenic substances is increased" (Crimmins, 1981, p. 249).

But the effects of lower death rates for specific diseases will be tempered by the fact that risks of death are competing:

Multiple causes are often involved in the event of death; with the elimination of one cause, the other(s) may account for death with only a short lag. . . . If deaths from a particular cause (e.g., cancer) were eliminated or sharply reduced, those saved would immediately be subject to death from other causes (e.g., diseases of the heart) and, as a result, the rates from these other causes would tend to rise, particularly if the average age of death from the two cause categories is close (U.S. Bureau of the Census, 1984d, p. 53).

Differences in death rates and life expectancy between men and women have been widening over time. According to Verbrugge (1983, p. 145) the gap will continue to increase, "but at a declining rate. In other words, the biggest gains for women compared with men have already occurred, and future gains will be smaller." The reasons for such differences are largely unknown: "they emerge from some combination of genetic risks for each sex, from risks acquired during life, and from attitudes that influence symptom perception and curative behavior" (Verbrugge, 1983, p. 139). The effects of changes in life style and health-related behavior on the gap between the sexes cannot be foreseen.

As to the black-white mortality "crossover," its elimination or postponement may mean "an increase in the health disadvantage of older blacks compared to older whites in the future." The reasoning behind this seeming paradox is that "more of the less 'robust' blacks will be surviving to advanced ages due to better medical care" (Markides, 1983, p. 129). Markides notes further that "this increase in the black disadvantage is likely to be greatest after age 75" (p. 129).

In summary, the potential exists for dramatic new developments in death rates and life expectancy at the oldest ages. It remains to be seen, however, whether the co-existence of declining mortality with increasing morbidity at the older ages recently observed by Verbrugge (1984) will be exacerbated or whether scientific achievements will indeed result in more *disease-free* years of life as opposed to more years per se.

10 International Comparisons

The ongoing demographic changes affecting the extreme elderly and their place in society in the United States is typical of other industrialized nations. Cross-national data comparisons therefore provide useful parallels in considering the likely future trends that may be pertinent to the U.S. experience. The short-term prospects for declines in mortality might be foreshadowed by the experience of countries which already have lower mortality. Sweden and Japan, for example, now have lower mortality rates than the U.S., and the nature of such declines may provide some guidance in estimating the short-term prospects for lower mortality in the U.S.

Recent data analysis has "shown that the 75 and over population is the most rapidly increasing proportion of the population in the majority of urbanized industrialized countries" (Beattie, 1976, p. 639). Data available for those 85 and over show an equally dramatic increase has been observed (Figure 10.1). More than a decade ago a *World Health Statistics* report concluded that, because of achievements in the social and medical fields, increased numbers of persons were living out their natural life span. In a 1982 World Health Organization report, it was observed that in the past only a minority reached old age; however, in the future, in an expanding number of countries, only a minority will fail to do so (Macfadyen, 1982).

To date the population 80 years of age and over appears to be the oldest group for which data have appeared in United Nations publications. In the absence of comparable data limited to those 85 years

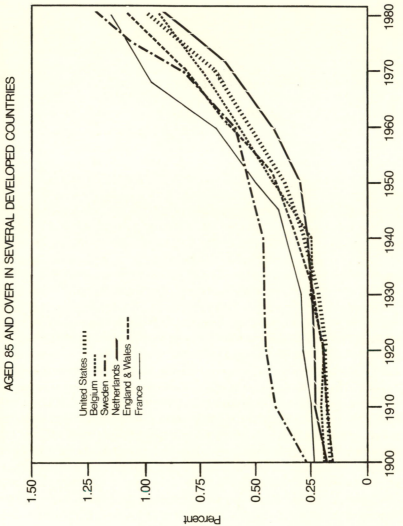

FIGURE 10.1: THE INCREASING PROPORTION OF THE TOTAL POPULATION AGED 85 AND OVER IN SEVERAL DEVELOPED COUNTRIES

United States ▪▪▪▪▪
Belgium ▪▪▪▪▪▪▪
Sweden ▪ ▪ ▪ ▪
Netherlands ▬▬▬
England & Wales ▬ ▬ ▬
France ▬▬▬▬

Percent

1.50 1.25 1.00 0.75 0.50 0.25 0

1900 1910 1920 1930 1940 1950 1960 1970 1980

Sources: Table 1.1; Keyfitz and Flieger, 1968; United Nations, Demographic Yearbook, various years.

and over some statistics for this age group are given. The UN has estimated the world population of those aged 80 years and older will increase dramatically over the 40–year span from 1980 to 2020. This population group is projected to nearly triple in size, increasing from 35 million in 1980 to 101 million in 2020. At present, approximately three-fifths of those aged 80 years and over live in industrialized countries, in comparison with two-fifths in less developed regions. Recent UN projections indicate that by 2020 this situation will reverse, and the majority of the world's extreme aged population will be found in developing countries (Siegel and Hoover, 1982). The projected large increases in both the number and the proportion of those aged 80 years and over result from: 1) declining fertility rates which reduce the proportions at the youngest ages and 2) declining mortality rates which increase the chances of survival for the elderly, thereby enabling a larger proportion to reach extreme ages.

EXTREME AGED PERCENTAGES IN SELECTED COUNTRIES

In comparing the proportion of the population aged 85 years and over for 20 countries (Table 10.1), a wide range of values is evident: from 0.1 percent in China to 1.2 percent in Sweden. Generally, the proportion of the aged population in each country has largely been determined by the population's history of fertility and to some extent, its migration history. In the more industrialized countries, fertility declines have been underway longer. As a result, the proportions of old persons are generally much higher. This is evident in the experience of such countries as France, England and Wales, and Sweden. As early as 1950, more than 10 percent of their total populations were aged 65 years and over (Laslett, 1976). Obviously, over time this affects the proportionate size of the population aged 85 years and over. In 1980 these countries had among the highest percentages of persons in the extreme ages. The comparatively low percentages of those aged 85 and over in Japan and Poland, on the other hand, reflect the relatively late fertility declines in both of these countries. The moderately low ratios in Canada and Australia are probably due to the very substantial levels of migration into these countries during the post-World War II period.

China, the world's most populous nation, is the only developing country included in Table 10.1 since its data for the population aged 85 and

TABLE 10.1:   PROPORTION OF THE POPULATION 85 YEARS OLD AND OVER AND SEX RATIO
OF THE EXTREME ELDERLY POPULATION, 20 COUNTRIES ABOUT 1981[a]

Country	Percent aged 85+	Males per 100 females 85+
Argentina	0.46	52.3
Australia	0.68	37.5
Austria	0.92	36.3
Canada	0.78	50.8
China	0.13	44.5
Denmark	1.13	50.2
France	1.14	31.3
German Democratic Republic	0.87	36.7
German Federal Republic	0.91	35.8
Hungary	0.64	41.8
Italy	0.83	43.9
Japan	0.48	48.3
Netherlands	0.91	53.0
Norway	1.15	52.3
Poland	0.48	36.3
Romania	0.37	55.7
Sweden	1.22	49.2
Switzerland	1.00	41.7
United Kingdom	1.08	30.6
United States	1.03	42.6

Sources: Coale, 1984; United Nations, 1982 Demographic Yearbook.

a. Data are based on censuses or estimates in 1980, 1981 or 1982.

over are extraordinarily accurate. This is due in part to a cultural emphasis on astrology which requires knowledge of birth year, as well as the reliability of the 1982 census which was conducted with meticulous care, according to recent analyses (Banister, 1984; Coale, 1984). On the other hand, India, the world's second most populous country, has been omitted since the quality of its data for the very old is poor. According to the Census Actuary, "age returns after 60 are wholly unreliable except for reflecting 10 yearly group-totals" (Jain, 1980).

Data from other developing countries have not been used because the reported proportion aged 85 years and over is usually grossly exaggerated by age misstatement. This and other errors in age reporting are common in such populations because of low levels of education and lack of adequate birth registration systems in the past (Ewbank, 1981). Exaggeration of age by persons over 50 is particularly prevalent in those countries where status increases with age. Since status often increases with age, and, since persons in ill health often look older than they actually are, exaggeration of age is quite common in many populations in Africa, Asia and Latin America. In some instances, excessive age exaggeration has led to extravagant claims for the longevity of certain populations. For example, a careful study in an area of Ecuador reputed to have an unusually large population of extreme aged found that of 23 reported centenarians, none was actually over 100 and their average age was only 86 years (Mazess and Forman, 1979).

Finally, it is most unlikely that populations in developing countries have high proportions of the extreme aged since the proportion of elderly persons is largely determined by the fertility rate. Populations with high fertility tend to have a young age distribution since there are many children for each parent and many parents for each grandparent. For example, if over a period of several decades a population were to have a life expectancy of 75 years and the total fertility rate (the sum of the age-specific birth rates over all ages of the childbearing period) were five births per woman, only about 0.8 percent of this population would be aged 80 and over. Although many developing countries have much higher total fertility rates, none have life expectancies of 75 years. It can therefore be concluded that their proportion of those 80 years and over will not exceed 0.8 percent and that the percentage of those 85 years and over will be even smaller.

The sex ratio of the populations over age 85 in these 20 countries also is presented in Table 10.1. In all of these populations, there are two or three times as many women over age 85 as there are men (i.e., ratios ranging from 31 to 56 males per 100 females). In this regard the United States is typical of developed countries despite an unusually large sex differential in mortality at the oldest ages.

It is of interest to note that the United States, which ranked fourth in world population in 1980, nevertheless ranked first in numbers of persons 85 years and over, with 2,240,000 extreme aged residents. China, which contained 22 percent of the globe's inhabitants in 1980 (Demeny, 1984), had about 1,340,000 persons 85 years and above, according to its 1982 census statistics which are regarded as "surprisingly precise" (Coale, 1984). Although India, the second most populous nation, has 15 percent of the world population (Demeny, 1984), statistics from its census in 1981 relevant to the extreme aged cannot be considered reliable. Presumably the number of oldest old in India is substantially smaller than the number in China, probably less than one million.

The Soviet Union was third in world population in 1980 with about 6 percent of the total. Unfortunately, as of 1984, the Central Statistical Administration has failed to publish any age data from the January 1979 census of the Soviet Union (Feshbach, 1984). Data from the 1970 census of the U.S.S.R. indicated there were then 2,894,000 persons recorded as aged 80 years or older (Chebotarev and Sachuk, 1980). This figure was equivalent to 78 percent of the total in the U.S. population at this age during the same time period (U.S. Bureau of the Census, 1982a). As a crude measure, it can be assumed that in 1980 the number of persons 85 years and over in the U.S.S.R. may have roughly been three-fourths that in the U.S., or about 1.7 million persons.

The increase in the number of aging persons in the world reflects, as in the U.S., increases in life expectancy as well as reductions over time in fertility. Sharp differences have remained between longevity rates in what the United Nations and others have called the more developed countries (developed regions) and the less developed countries (developing regions). In developing countries the average life expectation or years of life at birth of men and women is 15 to 20 years less (54 and 56 years) than that of their counterparts in developed countries (68 to 76 years) (U.S. Senate, Special Committee on Aging, 1983).

The biological "limits" of longevity have been approached more closely in the more developed regions than in the less developed regions; consequently a greater share of persons at the extreme ages among the elderly are found in the countries in these regions (Siegel and Hoover, 1982). Persons 80 years and over were estimated by the United Nations at 1.7 percent of the total population in the more developed regions in 1975, and this percentage is expected to grow to 2.6 percent by 2000. According to UN projections, during this same quarter century the proportion of those 80 years and over will increase from 0.4 percent of the overall population of the world's less developed regions to 0.6 percent (Grinblat, 1982).

Projections by the United Nations indicate that some of these countries will experience a substantial increase in the proportion of their extreme elderly populations. In Sweden, for example, the proportion over age 80 is projected to increase from 1.5 percent of the population in 1980 to 4.2 percent in 2010. One of the most dramatic increases is projected for Japan where the proportion over age 80 is expected to increase from 1.3 percent in 1980 to 3.2 percent in 2010. The implications of these increases for health care, retirement benefits and pension funds, and family living arrangements will have a dramatic impact on all of the developed countries.

Demographers have demonstrated that initial declines in mortality actually lead to a younger population, because these declines were most pronounced among infants and children. Fertility reductions, however, result in lower proportions of children, thereby increasing the proportions of the population at older ages. "When mortality rate declines at younger ages reach low levels, so as to ensure high survival through childhood and the active adult ages, it is clear that further reductions can only occur at older ages" (Myers, 1983, p. 7).

In the two decade period from 1961 to 1981 the more developed countries have experienced some striking changes in life expectancy. In Eastern Europe life expectancy (for both sexes combined) has remained about the same (at 71 years), whereas in the U.S.S.R. a decline of about two years (from 71 to 69 years) has been reported (Bourgeois-Pichat, 1983). But in the majority of the industrialized countries (including Western Europe and English-speaking non-European countries) life expectancy has increased by about 2.5 years (to 73.5 years). Of particular interest is Japan where life expectancy advanced by fully 7 years (to 76 years) during the period 1961 to 1981, reaching a level surpassing that of other industrialized nations (Bourgeois-Pichat, 1983).

Mortality trends in many developed countries indicate recent sharp declines at older ages that will lead to higher life expectancy levels than previously anticipated. Moreover, recent population projections also indicate that future proportions of older persons will be higher than previously projected (Myers, 1983, p.8).

As Myers points out, "Whereas population aging, as measured by the proportion at older ages, increased very slowly for most Western nations, the potential for larger and more rapid increases (if fertility falls precipitously) is seemingly high for many of today's developing countries" (Myers, p.10). The aging of the older population, as seen in the United States is characteristic of many countries, with growth rates at the very advanced ages greater than at any other age intervals. Moreover, the sex ratio of the total aged population has not only been below unity but also has tended to increase with age. Sex ratios among both developed and developing countries have declined for the most part (Myers, 1983).

MORTALITY DIFFERENTIALS

Although the proportion over age 65 can increase substantially because of declines in fertility, the population over age 85 is increasing rapidly in large part because of declines in mortality among the aged. Table 10.2 presents data on life expectancy at ages 75, 85 and 95 for a variety of countries. In some of the most developed countries of Western Europe, life expectancy at age 85 ranges from 4.7 to 4.9 years for men and 5.6 to 5.8 for women. In all but one of the countries shown, life expectancy for women exceeds that for men by 0.8 to 1.0 years. Although life expectancies for U.S. males and females are comparable with those in other developed countries, the female advantage in life expectancy at age 85 is unusually high, 1.4 years.

Table 10.3 shows the causes of death of persons over age 65 in the United States as compared to their counterparts in Japan and England and Wales. The mortality advantage enjoyed by the elderly in Japan is largely due to substantially lower mortality from diseases of the circulatory system. Their extremely low mortality rate due to ischemic heart disease is counterbalanced by higher rates attributed to cerebrovascular causes. Diseases of the circulatory system are 25 percent lower among the elderly in Japan than in the United States.

The difference between the United States and England and Wales is especially apparent in the higher rates for pneumonia and influenza (1.5 deaths per 1,000 population for the U.S. versus 6.8 for England and Wales). Notable exceptions to the higher mortality rates among the elderly in England and Wales for most categories include "all other" causes of death (including accidents) and "ill-defined conditions."

MARITAL STATUS

Significant sex differentials in mortality among the elderly create an imbalance between the numbers of males and females, thereby resulting in a large population of unmarried elderly women. Table 6.1 showed that among the extreme elderly in the U.S. in 1980, 48 percent of the men were currently married, but only 8 percent of women were married. This differential is due not only to the relative shortage of

TABLE 10.2:   EXPECTATIONS OF LIFE FOR MEN AND WOMEN AT SPECIFIED AGES, SELECTED
               COUNTRIES

Country and year			Age 75	Age 85	Age 95[a]
Australia	1979	Male	8.3	4.5	---
		Female	10.7	5.4	---
China	1964-1982	Male	6.2	3.0	---
		Female	7.4	3.8	---
Japan	1982-1983	Male	8.9	4.6	2.0
		Female	10.9	5.4	2.1
Netherlands	1976-1980	Male	8.4	4.8	2.8
		Female	10.7	5.6	3.0
Sweden	1982	Male	8.6	4.7	2.3
		Female	10.9	5.6	2.6
United States	1980	Male	8.8	5.0	---
		Female	11.5	6.4	---
Female advantage in life expectancy					
Australia	1979		2.4	0.9	---
China	1964-1982		1.2	0.8	---
Japan	1982-1983		2.1	0.8	0.1
Netherlands	1976-1982		2.3	0.8	0.2
Sweden	1982		2.4	1.0	0.3
United States	1980		2.7	1.4	---

Sources: Coale, 1984; Ishikawa, 1984; Sweden, 1982 Befolkningsförändringar;
           United Nations, 1982 Demographic Yearbook; U.S. National Center for
           Health Statistics, 1984d.

a.   Data not available for Australia, China and United States.

men over age 85, but also, as noted in Chapter 6, to the fact that men
generally marry younger women.

Table 10.4 presents data on the marital status of the extreme elderly
in France and in Great Britain. The distributions for those over age
85 are very similar to those for the U.S. Among French men, 45 percent
are currently married and 49 percent are widowed; among the French

TABLE 10.3: CAUSES OF DEATH OF THE POPULATION 65 YEARS OLD AND OVER,
THREE COUNTRIES

Cause	U.S. 1979	Japan 1979	England and Wales 1978
	Percentage of deaths		
Total, all causes	100.0	100.0	100.0
Malignant neoplasms	19.5	19.3	21.2
Hypertensive disease	1.9	3.1	1.2
Ischemic heart disease	33.8	7.4	26.3
Cerebrovascular disease	11.4	27.5	14.5
Other diseases of the circulatory system	12.7	12.4	11.8
Pneumonia and influenza	2.9	5.0	11.2
Bronchitis, emphysema, asthma	1.1	2.1	4.6
Ill-defined conditions	1.0	6.4	0.3
All other causes	15.7	16.8	8.9
	Death rates at age 65+ (per 1,000 population)		
Total, all causes	51.6	45.7	61.1
Malignant neoplasms	10.1	8.8	12.9
Hypertensive disease	1.0	1.4	.7
Ischemic heart disease	17.4	3.4	16.1
Cerebrovascular disease	5.9	12.6	8.9
Other diseases of the circulatory system	6.5	5.7	7.2
Pneumonia and influenza	1.5	2.3	6.8
Bronchitis, emphysema, asthma	0.6	1.0	2.8
Ill-defined conditions	0.5	2.9	0.2
All other causes	8.1	7.7	5.4

Sources: United Nations, 1980 Demographic Yearbook: Table 33; U.S. National
Center for Health Statistics, 1982a.

TABLE 10.4: MARITAL STATUS OF THE POPULATION 85 YEARS OLD AND OVER, FRANCE, 1975, AND GREAT BRITAIN, 1981

Country, sex and marital status	85-89 years	90-94 years	95 years and over[a]	Total 85 years and over[a]
France	Percent distribution			
Male:				
Total	100.0	100.0	100.0	100.0
Single	5.9	6.4	5.4	6.0
Married	48.9	33.3	25.3	44.7
Widowed	44.4	59.5	68.9	48.5
Divorced	0.9	0.8	0.4	0.8
Female:				
Total	100.0	100.0	100.0	100.0
Single	10.7	10.5	11.3	10.7
Married	7.4	3.3	2.5	6.2
Widowed	80.2	84.8	85.1	81.6
Divorced	1.6	1.4	1.1	1.5
	Number of males per 100 females in each category			
Total	37	31	25	35
Single	20	19	12	20
Married	244	310	254	252
Widowed	21	22	20	21
Divorced	20	18	10	19
Great Britain	Percent distribution			
Male:				
Total	100.0	100.0	100.0	100.0
Single	6.8	7.1	12.1	7.0
Married	42.0	29.4	23.0	38.6
Widowed	50.6	63.0	63.6	53.7
Divorced	0.6	0.5	1.1	0.6
Female:				
Total	100.0	100.0	100.0	100.0
Single	15.7	16.1	17.2	15.9
Married	8.4	4.6	4.0	7.2
Widowed	75.3	78.9	78.3	76.3
Divorced	1.8	1.7	2.8	0.6
	Number of males per 100 females in each category			
Total	33	26	22	31
Single	14	11	15	14
Married	165	165	127	163
Widowed	22	21	18	22
Divorced	34	28	41	33

Sources: Parant, 1978; United Kingdom, 1983.

a. For France, excludes the small number of persons 100 years and older.

women only 6 percent are married and 82 percent are widowed. The proportions single (i.e., never married) and divorced are very low in France as in the U.S.

The French and British data make it possible to examine changes in marital status between ages 85 and 100. Since mortality rates are high among the extreme elderly, any data for those over age 85 are largely determined by the characteristics of those aged 85–89 since those over age 90 are so few in number. In the European countries the distribution of women by marital status does not change substantially between ages 85 and 100. It is obvious that the most likely change of status at these ages is from married to widowed, and, since only 7.4 percent in France (and 8.4 percent in Britain) are still married at ages 85–89, there are few whose status is apt to change.

The experience of aged men is quite different. Since almost half of all men are still married at 85–89, many are at risk of a status change. In fact, by age 95–99 only 23–25 percent of the men are still married and almost 70 percent are widowed. There is, therefore, a substantial difference in marital status distribution between men aged 85–89 and those aged 95–99. It is interesting to note that the number of males per 100 females in each marital status category changes very little between ages 85 and 100 (Table 10.4). In fact the sex ratio of the married population aged 95–99 is almost identical to that at age 85–89, remaining at about 250 males per 100 females in France and about 160 males per 100 females in Britain. Similarly, the sex ratio of the widowed stays quite constant at about 21 males per 100 females throughout these ages in both countries.

Table 10.5 presents data on the marital status of the extreme elderly in Sweden for the years 1940, 1960 and 1978, as well as in England and Wales over a roughly similar period. Sweden shows a very different pattern from both France and the U.S. In 1978 only 26 percent of men over age 85 were currently married as opposed to 48 percent in the U.S. and 45 percent in France. (The percent married in England and Wales was intermediate—38 percent). Among the women over age 85 in Sweden, 21 percent were never married, as opposed to only 8 percent in the U.S. and 11 percent in France. (Again, England and Wales was intermediate, with 15 percent).

These differences are due to the extreme marriage patterns in Sweden during the late nineteenth and early twentieth centuries. At the turn of the century, Sweden presented an extreme example of the

TABLE 10.5:   PERCENT DISTRIBUTION OF THE POPULATION 85 YEARS AND OVER, BY
              MARITAL STATUS, SWEDEN: 1940, 1960, 1978 AND ENGLAND AND WALES:
              1931, 1961, 1981

Country, sex and marital status	Years		
Sweden	1940	1960	1978
Male:			
Total	100.0	100.0	100.0
Single	10.8	9.5	11.2
Married	18.7	18.5	26.2
Widowed	70.2	70.6	60.8
Divorced	0.3	1.3	1.8
Female:			
Total	100.0	100.0	100.0
Single	17.0	21.1	21.4
Married	7.0	4.5	4.4
Widowed	75.4	72.6	71.3
Divorced	0.6	1.8	2.9
England and Wales	1931	1961	1981
Male:			
Total	100.0	100.0	100.0
Single	5.6	7.3	6.8
Married	26.8	33.7	38.6
Widowed	67.6	58.9	54.0
Divorced	0.1	0.1	0.6
Female:			
Total	100.0	100.0	100.0
Single	14.2	17.2	15.2
Married	6.1	7.1	7.4
Widowed	79.6	75.6	76.9
Divorced	0.0	0.1	0.6

Sources: Sweden, 1978 Befolkningsförändringar; United Kingdom, 1982.

TABLE 10.6:   AGE OF SPOUSES FOR PERSONS MARRYING AT AGE 65 YEARS OLD AND OVER,
FOUR COUNTRIES

Country and year		Age of brides marrying men age 65 and over			Age of grooms marrying women age 65 or over			Grooms 65+ per 100 brides 65+
		<55	55-64	65+	<55	55-64	65+	
		Percent distribution			Percent distribution			
France	1981	17.6	13.5	68.9	4.7	15.5	79.8	218
Japan	1981	36.6	45.1	18.3	3.2	10.5	86.3	472
Sweden	1981	19.3	32.0	38.5	5.4	19.7	72.1	187
U.S.	1979	17.6	33.8	48.6	2.8	14.3	82.9	171

Sources: United Nations, 1982 Demographic Yearbook: Table 29.

marriage pattern then common in Northwestern Europe. This was characterized by very late age at first marriage among women and a large proportion of women who never married (Davis, 1984). The data in Table 10.5 show that the proportion remaining single among Swedish women over age 85 years has been constant at about 21 percent in recent years. The relatively low proportion of Swedish men over age 85 who are currently married is probably a result of lower remarriage rates among widowers in Sweden than in the United States and France.

In future decades Sweden will come to resemble the United States and France in at least one respect: the proportion never married among women over age 85 will decline substantially. Because of changes in the marriage patterns in Sweden between 1925 and 1940, the proportion never married among women drops from about 19 percent for those aged over 85 in 1978 to 7 percent for those aged 40–49. Therefore during the next 40 years there will be a decline in the proportion never married among extreme elderly women in Sweden.

Table 10.6 provides data on the ages of spouses of persons who marry after age 65 in France, Japan, Sweden and the United States. In France, Sweden and the United States, about twice as many men marry over age 65 than do women. This is due to the fact that there is a relative shortage of widowed and divorced men in this age group relative to the number of marriageable women. However, men over age 65 who do marry tend to marry younger women. In Sweden, only 38 percent of all men who marry at age 65 or over married women in the same age group. On the other hand, 72 percent of the women who marry at age 65 or above married men in this age group. In France the data show smaller differences in the ages of the new spouses of the elderly. About 69 percent of the brides of men over age 65 and 80 percent of the grooms of women over age 65 were over age 65.

The situation in Japan is even more extreme than the other three populations. Almost five times (4.7) as many men over age 65 marry than do women and only 18 percent of the men over 65 who married took brides in the same age group. However, statistics on marriages of women over age 65 are comparable to those in the other populations, 86 percent are to men over age 65.

It can therefore be concluded that the substantial differences between the marital statuses of the sexes over age 85 observed in disparate countries are due to both the unusual sex ratios among the elderly (two or three women for each man) and to the tendency of elderly men to choose brides who are ten or more years younger than themselves.

LIVING ARRANGEMENTS

Myers recently provided a valuable review of efforts that have been made in several developed countries, such as France, Canada and Australia to provide reports on the characteristics of the older population, which include such factors as age, sex, marital status, geographic distribution, and family and household status. But he has concluded that "it is fair to say that few coordinated efforts have been made to systematically collect or present data on important characteristics of the aged population for a wide range of the world's countries. The data presented in *Demographic Yearbooks* for example, are limited by age detail, lack of cross-classifications, timeliness, and coverage of important information. The absence of systematic data has hampered comparative studies in which characteristic patterns at different levels of development and overall population aging can be examined" (Myers, 1983, p.22).

Living arrangement patterns have profound implications for the life conditions of the oldest old and are greatly influenced by marital status, housing availability, income and the household preferences of individuals. "There is a clear need for development of richer and more extensive crossnational data on living arrangements, especially in light of its importance on support systems, both private (family) and public. An additional dimension is the extent of institutionalization of older persons, its determinants and the range of alternatives" (Myers, 1983, p.24).

An important element of the life conditions of older persons is the characteristics of the family and household structure. Most developed countries exhibit a general trend "toward increasingly independent living, especially for females, and a sharp decline in both males and females living in a household with relatives" (Myers and Nathanson, 1982, p. 231). While available crossnational data do not indicate the extent to which older persons reside in households with their children, this family structure appears to be more common in Asian countries such as India, than in other regions for which data are extant. Whereas, only small minorities of aged married persons in the United States and in Western Europe live together with married sons or daughters, a quite different pattern appears to hold in Asia. In Japan 75 percent of all persons 65 years or above lived with their married children in 1975, down somewhat from the level of 85 percent in 1965, but still extremely high by Western standards (Yuzawa, 1977). A recent report from China indicates most old people are rural residents who usually live with their children and grandchildren. Childless elders may live with relatives or friends. A small number of government-run retirement homes provide for those elders with no one to care for them. China has no nursing homes. The seriously ill either receive home care by local medical workers or are treated in chronic disease hospitals (with patients of all ages) (Lewis, 1982).

LABOR FORCE PARTICIPATION

Table 10.7 presents data on labor force participation rates for the population over age 75 in seven developed contries. (Data for persons 85 years and over are rarely available.) In most of the countries shown, the proportions economically active are below 8 percent for men and below 3 percent for women. The one exception is Japan where 24 percent of the men and 5.5 percent of the women report that they are still economically active. These unusually high rates reflect the fact that the modernization of Japan's economy is much more recent than that of the other countries shown in Table 10.7. The shift of a large pro-

TABLE 10.7:   LABOR FORCE PARTICIPATION RATES OF PERSONS 75 YEARS AND OVER, BY
SEX, SELECTED COUNTRIES

(Percent of old old in labor force)

Country and year		Males	Females
Denmark	1970	5.8	1.5
Finland	1975	4.9	0.9
German Federal Republic	1970	7.5	2.6
Japan	1975	24.4	5.5
Norway	1970	3.0	0.4
New Zealand	1976	4.9	0.7
Sweden	1975	2.3	0.5

Sources: United Nations, 1979 Demographic Yearbook: Table 36.

portion of the country's labor force from traditional activities such as agriculture, small manufacture and small trade to large scale industry and commerce generally occurs by recruiting new labor force entrants into the new industries. Therefore the type of work done by the aged is apt to reflect the economic structure of their early working years rather than the current structure.

The higher labor force participation rates for those over age 75 in Japan reflect their employment in the more traditional sectors such as agriculture and the small scale retail and service sectors. For example, among employed persons in Japan over the age of 65, 35 percent were in agriculture and 15 percent were in manufacturing. For the similar group in Sweden, 26 percent were in agriculture and 20 percent were in manufacturing. Since those in agriculture (especially in small scale agriculture) are apt to continue reporting themselves as economically active at older ages, the higher proportion in agriculture among the elderly in Japan leads to lower rates of retirement from employment.

The data presented indicate that aggregate employment activity rates have diminished among the aged as a concomitant of industrialization. As Myers points out, in-depth studies of the sources of income of the elderly that have replaced their employment income "are still extremely rare, but are of considerable importance for both more and less developed countries" (Myers, 1983, p. 24).

SUMMARY

The United States is not the only country experiencing an increase in the proportion of its population that is over 85. Neither is it the only country facing the need for social and economic changes to accommodate this increased population. Most industrialized countries in Western Europe now have about 1 percent of their population over age 85, and many will see this proportion double in the next 30 years.

It is not simply the size of the population over age 85 nor the proportion in this age group that puts strains on society. This population has living arrangements and health problems which distinguish it from most of the rest of the population. For example, among the extreme elderly, there are about two or three women for each man, and a substantial proportion of women in this age group are not currently married. These factors have important implications for the living arrangements for the extreme elderly. Since few are currently married and since extended households are becoming less common in most countries, there is a need for new living arrangements for the very old.

As noted earlier, a substantial share of the extreme elderly are institutionalized. Unfortunately, "little information of a comparative nature is available on the characteristics of the institutionalized in different countries" (Siegel and Hoover, 1982, p. 161). However, as in the United States, in many industrialized countries the growth of private nursing homes for the aged has been explosive. In some of the more developed countries, alternatives to nursing homes such as sheltered or group housing, apartments for the elderly and home health visitors have been developed extensively.

High mortality rates and high morbidity rates make the health needs of the extreme elderly far outweigh their fraction of the population. The provision of these health services and the increased life expectancies at retirement ages have profound implications for national and private mechanisms for providing health and retirement benefits in many countries.

Although most developing countries are experiencing the same general trends as the United States, there are subtle differences that deserve greater attention. For example, the higher labor force participation rates among persons over age 75 in Japan may provide some clues to dealing with some of the economic and social adjustments that come with old age. Although much of the higher rate in Japan is probably due to the recent occupational changes in that country, their experience with continuing employment into old age may provide valuable lessons for other countries.

11 Projections

Projections of the future growth of the extreme elderly population are primarily important for two reasons. First is the need for planning, especially of health facilities, in order to cope with what Maddox (1982) has called the "geriatric imperative." The close association between aging and increasing risks of morbidity and functional impairments necessitates that appropriate institutional and manpower arrangements be designed to ease the transition to an older population. The elderly, especially the very old, require a disproportionate share of the nation's medical resources and institutional care. Gauging their needs is a critical first step in planning for the future.

The enormous and unprecedented costs entailed by an aging population, in the face of limited resources, imply that political as well as social and economic trade-offs between competing demands are inevitable. The unavoidable issues of aging are problems no longer consignable to a vague future date. Because population trends and composition both affect and are affected by nondemographic factors in ways that are not yet well understood (United Nations, 1973), the need for close attention to the prospects for future growth of the elderly is even more compelling.

The second reason why projections of the elderly component of the population are important is closely related to planning needs. That is, such estimates provide a clearer understanding of the effects of demographic factors (in this case primarily future reductions in death rates at the oldest ages) on age-sex structure, population size, dependency ratios and other characteristics. Projections "provide quantitative measures of the potentialities of the present demographic situation and of the demographic processes which are under way and those which are foreseen in the light of present experience" (United Nations, 1973, p. 557).

Traditionally, attention has been directed to the *proportions* of elderly persons within populations—that is, the number of aged persons *relative to* younger groups. But this narrow focus "tends to divert attention from the serious implications of growth in absolute numbers" that has been occurring in recent decades (Binstock, Chow, and Schulz, 1982, p. ii). Moreover, the socioeconomic characteristics of the very old, even more than their numbers or proportion of the total population, have significant implications for planning. In this sense, the *consequences* of growth are more important than the determinants, and planning efforts must be "population responsive" rather than "population influencing" (Myers, 1982, p.3). It is increasingly important to recognize that the oldest segment of the population does not exist in isolation from the rest of the society. All segments are intricately interrelated, and the well-being of each is closely tied to, and often dependent on, the numbers, characteristics and behavior of the others. To take an obvious illustration, the welfare of the elderly is clearly influenced by the continued willingness of younger generations to finance their support through the tax structure. Considerable national attention in recent years has been devoted to the inadequacies of Social Security and Medicare in particular, and projections of the future size and composition of the elderly population indicate that concerns about increased taxes are not unwarranted.

Projections are important tools for planning and policy studies but they are inherently inaccurate (Stoto, 1983). Projections necessitate "assumptions as to the frequency and magnitude of essentially unpredictable events as well as affirmations of faith concerning the nature of the political, social, and economic life of the future" (United Nations, 1973, p. 562). Projections are not predictions, and hence the effects of alternative assumptions on the results must be considered. The discussion in this chapter will be confined to the two most widely used sets of projections—those devised by the Bureau of the Census and by the Social Security Administration. Since the two series rely on somewhat different assumptions and have a different analytical intent, both their underlying rationales and the effects of alternative assumptions on the numbers generated will be reviewed.

Although the precise numbers of future elderly vary based on the assumptions used in the calculations, the *trends* are unmistakable, and it is certain that the size of the elderly population will increase dramatically in years to come. The demographic implications of those trends and numbers form the central interest of this chapter, whereas the closing chapter will focus on broader implications, primarily economic.

Before proceeding, it is important to point out the paucity of research efforts on the "frail elderly," those dependent and needing help in performing everyday tasks, who are disproportionately found among the oldest of the old. Streib (1983) has referred to this group as "the excluded twenty percent" and has indicated how researchers have inadvertently concentrated their attention on "the rational, functioning older person—the healthier, more active, more vocal elderly" (p. 41). The frail elderly, in contrast, are much more difficult to study, yet they are "the most vulnerable group and have the greatest need for supportive services" (p. 41) and their numbers are increasing rapidly. Furthermore, many of them "do not live with kin and have minimal family support systems. Thus, outside agencies must become involved in the provision of maintenance and supportive services" (Streib, 1983, p. 43). The frail elderly are also disproportionately represented in institutions. Thus, the frail elderly will be dependent on society for their most basic needs, and this final stage of dependency seems inescapable for the majority of those who survive to extreme old age (Neugarten, 1978).

PROJECTIONS: BACKGROUND AND ACCURACY

There is ample precedent for poor marksmanship in projecting the elderly population. Dorn (1950) reviewed the various projections of the U.S. population made in the 1930s and early 1940s and found that demographers consistently underestimated the effects of scientific developments on lowering mortality rates. Myers found the official national projections of numbers of older persons made in the post-World War II period equally disappointing, noting that the underestimates in the forecasts were attributable "primarily to shortcomings in projecting mortality trends for the older ages" and that "the experience of other developed countries has been no more successful in forecasting mortality trends and in capturing the growth of the elderly population" (1978, p. 441). Mortality consistently played a minor role in past projections:

In addition to being based on pessimistic views about future mortality improvement, fertility rather than mortality projection has been emphasized in past national population projections. Through the 1970's population projections for the U.S. were made assuming three different fertility projections but only one mortality projection (Crimmins, 1983, p. 16).

Estimates of the future size of the elderly population have thus been typically understated.

In 1970, the Commission on Population Growth and the American Future was charged by the President and Congress with formulating policy designed to deal with "the pervasive impact of population growth on every facet of American Life." The Commission enlisted a corps of leading scientists for its research efforts. Its final report concluded that, "while the entire population 65 years old and over will rise 43 percent between 1970 and the year 2000, persons 75 to 84 will increase by 65 percent, and those 85 years and over by 52 percent" (Commission, 1972, p. 66). Since all persons who will be 65 years and over well into the next century were already alive in 1970, these projections of growth relied on assumptions about mortality rates. The 1980 census count of the population 85 and over—2.24 million—was 59 percent above the 1970 figure, (Table 1.2) compared to the 52 percent increase estimated by the Commission by the year 2000. The Commission's severe underestimate of the growth of the extreme aged thus was apparent within one decade.

Another series of projections prepared by the Bureau of the Census started with the estimated population distribution in 1974 and assumed a general decline in death rates in future years. In the 25–year span, 1975 to 2000, the population 85 and over was projected to grow by almost 77 percent, to 3.2 million (U.S. Bureau of the Census, 1975). But within two years of its publication, these projections were obsolete and a new series was issued. The updated series was required, the Bureau indicated, "to reflect the recent decline in age-specific death rates in the middle and older adult ages and recent research on future trends in mortality" (U.S. Bureau of the Census, 1977, p. 1). The revised series showed the 85 and over population reaching nearly 3.8 million in the year 2000, a figure 17 percent above that published two years earlier. Some observers were not convinced that even the new series adequately portrayed future growth, and their reservations were confirmed by the most recent group of projections, issued in preliminary form late in 1982 (U.S. Bureau of the Census, 1982b). A somewhat revised version was published in full detail in 1984. According to the preliminary set of figures, the size of the population 85 and older in the year 2000 (middle series) was projected to exceed 5.1 million persons, (U.S. Bureau of the Census, 1982b) well above the 3.2 million estimated in 1975. The revised projection for the population 85 years and over is only slightly smaller: 4.9 million (U.S. Bureau of the Census, 1984c). As Myers has noted, it is clear that reductions in mortality among the aged in recent years have not been fully appreciated by projection-makers, with the result that the number of aged persons has been repeatedly underestimated. He concluded that careful attention to mortality trends and bolder forecasts of future reductions in death rates for the elderly were indispensable (Myers, 1978). But it is clear that even with the bolder and better assumptions now being made, projections are not predictions. The Social Security Administration, in introducing its most recent series of projections, has noted the many uncertainties in forecasting future mortality trends:

Future improvements in mortality will depend upon such factors as the development and application of new diagnostic, surgical, and life-sustaining techniques, the presence of environmental pollutants, improvements in exercise and nutrition, the incidence of violence, the isolation and treatment of causes of disease, the emergence of new forms of disease, improvements in prenatal care, the incidence of abortion, the prevalence of cigarette smoking, the misuse of drugs (including alcohol), the extent to which people assume responsibility for their own health, and changes in our conception of the value of life (1984, p. 7).

Even in light of this impressive list of unknowns, projecting future mortality trends has generally been viewed as easier than forecasting trends in fertility. The need for frequent updating of the estimates and ever-more-refined assumptions, as well as a cautious approach to their use, will not soon be outgrown. The longer the projection period, of course, the more unreliable the results.

ASSUMPTIONS AND THEIR EFFECTS

There are three major assumptions underlying the three series of population projections (Alternatives I, II and III) constructed by the Office of the Actuary of the Social Security Administration (SSA). Using Bureau of the Census population estimates for July 1, 1982, (with some slight modifications) as a base and adjusting for net census undercount, plus adding in residents of Puerto Rico and U.S. possessions as well as American citizens living abroad, the SSA projection-makers then assumed, first, that mortality improvements would continue to shift from infectious to degenerative diseases and that death rates by age and sex would continue to decline for most causes. They assumed that:

In Alternative I, the ultimate rates of improvement were the same for males and females. In Alternatives II and III, the ultimate rates of improvement for some of the causes were assumed to be higher for women than for men. Thus, the gap between male and female mortality is assumed to continue to widen, but at a decreased rate as women become increasingly subject to many of the same environmental hazards and social pressures that affect men (U.S. Social Security Administration, 1984, p. 8).

For the middle series of projections (Alternative II), a set of "ultimate annual improvements" for each age group, sex and cause of death was postulated based on past trends and central death rates for 1982.

Central death rates were projected by age group, sex, and cause of death from their estimated 1982 levels by applying annual percentage improvements. The annual improvements applied to obtain the 1983 levels were 50 percent, 100 percent, and 150 percent of the average annual improvements for 1968–1980 for Alternatives I, II, and III, respectively. The assumed annual improvements applied during 1983–2008 were calculated by a logarithmic formula designed to gradually transform the improvement applied to obtain the 1983 levels into the postulated ultimate annual improvements. The ultimate improvements were assumed to apply during 2008–2080 (U.S. Social Security Administration, 1984, pp. 8–9).

In regard to fertility, the SSA assumed an intermediate total fertility rate of 2.0 children per woman as the most likely course of future fertility trends in the United States. Alternatives I and III used ultimate total fertility rates of 2.3 and 1.6 children per woman, respectively. As with the mortality assumptions, those relating to fertility were also based on past and current experience. But since all native-born individuals who will reach age 65 by 2045 or age 85 by 2065 had already been born by 1980, the fertility assumptions are relatively unimportant before those dates, affecting mainly the *proportion* of young versus older persons in the society rather than the *number* of older people per se.

The third major assumption made by the SSA was that an annual net immigration of 400,000 persons—the yearly average since about 1965—would continue into the future according to Alternative II. Alternatives I and III assumed an annual net immigration of 500,000 and 300,000 respectively (U.S. Social Security Administration, 1984). All three alternatives assumed no future net *illegal* immigration.

Unlike the Bureau of the Census, the SSA was interested in projecting numbers of persons by marital status, as well as by age and sex, since the marital status composition of the population is relevant to projecting future benefits requirements. Hence distributions by age, sex and marital status are available in the SSA projections only. The Bureau of the Census, however, has constructed estimates by race, whereas the SSA did not.

The most recent projections made by the Bureau of the Census (1984c) used the following assumptions: (1) mortality: for each of the three series, death rates were assumed to decline steadily, producing a range of total life expectancy at birth in the year 2080 of 77.4 (high mortality assumption) to 85.9 with low mortality. "The middle assumption is consistent with projections done by the Social Security Administration in which rapid declines in mortality rates were projected to the year 2005," after which rates fell more slowly (U.S. Bureau of the Census, 1984c, pp. 1–2); (2) fertility: the middle series assumed an average of 1.9 births per woman, compared to the SSA intermediate assumption of 2.0. The high and low fertility assumptions made by the Bureau were 2.3 and 1.6 births per woman, the same as the SSA figures for the high and low alternatives respectively; (3) net immigration: the Bureau of the Census projections used varying assumptions about net immigration, ranging from a low of 250,000 per year to a high of 750,000 per year. This compared with assumptions of 300,000 to 500,000 in the SSA series. The rationale for this wide range was "uncertainty as to the future course of refugee movements, possible changes in immigration legislation over the next 100 years, and the lack of adequate data on the legal flows of emigrants from the United States as well as the flows of undocumented aliens into and out of the United States" (U.S. Bureau of the Census, 1984c, p. 2). The middle series assumption of 450,000 is somewhat higher than the 400,000 used for the Alternative II series of SSA projections.

RESULTS OF PROJECTIONS

What do the projections indicate about the future size (relative and absolute) and structure of the elderly population? First, the absolute size of both the population over 65 and that over 85 will increase considerably according to all three alternatives postulated by the Social Security Administration in its most recent report (Table 11.1). Even with the highest set of estimated death rates (Alternative I), the size of the extreme elderly population will nearly double by the year 2000 and increase more than four-fold by 2040. The intermediate (Alternative II) estimate shows a population 85 and over of 13.1 million by 2040, compared to the 2.4 million estimated for 1980, or more than a five-fold increase. Using the lowest mortality assumption (Alternative III, in which annual improvements in central death rates are set at twice the Alternative II improvements) would produce a 2040 population of almost 18 million people age 85 or older, or over one-third more than the result using the intermediate assumption.

The population of women 85 and over is expected to grow faster than that of men, as the sex differential in mortality continues to widen (but at a lower rate than in previous decades) in the remainder of this century but at a slower rate in the next. The number of males 85 and over will not quite double by the year 2000 according to the intermediate projection, whereas the number of females will more than double. By 2040, Alternative II estimates show a population of about 4.0 million males in this age range, or somewhat close to the 3.8 million extreme elderly females forecast for the year 2000, forty years earlier. Projected sex ratios, however, vary about a narrow range, averaging close to 40 males for every 100 females for each date shown, but with a slight tendency to rise over time. The fact that this imbalance between the sexes will prevail indefinitely "has an important bearing on the provision of care and attention to females, who are often widowed

TABLE 11.1:   EFFECTS OF ALTERNATIVE ASSUMPTIONS IN SOCIAL SECURITY ADMINISTRATION
PROJECTIONS OF SIZE OF POPULATION 85 YEARS OLD AND OVER, BY SEX:
1980 TO 2040[a]

(in thousands)

Sex and alternative assumptions	1980	1990	2000	2020	2040
Both Sexes					
Alternative I	2,393	3,435	4,574	5,734	10,137
Alternative II	2,393	3,563	5,161	7,142	13,084
Alternative III	2,393	3,686	5,744	9,020	17,941
Male					
Alternative I	714	936	1,212	1,544	2,926
Alternative II	714	973	1,388	2,003	3,984
Alternative III	714	1,011	1,569	2,672	5,970
Female					
Alternative I	1,678	2,501	3,362	4,189	7,211
Alternative II	1,678	2,590	3,773	5,139	9,101
Alternative III	1,678	2,677	4,175	6,347	11,971

Source: U.S. Social Security Administration, 1984.

a.   Social Security data include Puerto Rico, and U.S. citizens living abroad and,
therefore, are slightly larger than data for the United States as prepared by
the Bureau of the Census.

and lack financial resources that might have been accrued from paid
employment during their life times" (Myers, 1982, p. 28).

The most recent Bureau of the Census middle series projections of
the elderly population by age, sex and race for selected dates up to
2050 are shown in Table 11.2. (Distributions by race are not prepared
by the Social Security Administration.) Growth in percentage terms
for the total, white, and nonwhite populations, always using the 1982
figures as the base, appears in Table 11.3. For each date shown, the
nonwhite total population is growing faster than the white, due to its
higher fertility rates. The size of the nonwhite population will more
than double by the year 2050; during the same interval the white
population will increase by only 20 percent. In fact, after reaching a

TABLE 11.2: PROJECTIONS OF SIZE OF THE POPULATION 65 YEARS OLD AND OVER AND 85 YEARS OLD AND OVER, BY RACE AND SEX, BUREAU OF THE CENSUS (MIDDLE SERIES): 1982 TO 2050

(in thousands)

Year and age	Total			White			Nonwhite		
	Both sexes	Male	Female	Both sexes	Male	Female	Both sexes	Male	Female
1982									
65 years and over	26,824	10,778	16,045	24,293	9,746	14,547	2,531	1,032	1,498
85 years and over	2,445	722	1,722	2,248	657	1,590	197	65	132
1990									
65 years and over	31,697	12,638	19,059	28,597	11,439	17,156	3,100	1,199	1,903
85 years and over	3,313	919	2,393	3,019	828	2,190	294	91	203
2000									
65 years and over	34,921	13,763	21,159	31,126	12,382	18,744	3,795	1,381	2,415
85 years and over	4,926	1,350	3,576	4,444	1,217	3,227	482	133	349
2025									
65 years and over	58,771	24,479	34,292	50,217	21,192	29,025	8,554	3,287	5,267
85 years and over	7,452	2,082	5,370	6,483	1,841	4,642	969	241	728
2050									
65 years and over	67,412	27,477	39,935	54,543	22,433	32,111	12,869	5,044	7,824
85 years and over	16,034	4,786	11,247	13,371	4,046	9,326	2,663	740	1,921

Source: U.S. Bureau of the Census, 1984c.

TABLE 11.3: PROJECTED PERCENTAGE INCREASES OVER 1982 BASE POPULATION FOR THE TOTAL POPULATION AND SELECTED OLDER AGE CATEGORIES, BY RACE AND SEX, BUREAU OF THE CENSUS (MIDDLE SERIES): 1990 TO 2050

Year and age	Total			White			Nonwhite		
	Both sexes	Male	Female	Both sexes	Male	Female	Both sexes	Male	Female
1990									
Total	7.6	7.6	7.6	6.3	6.2	6.2	15.7	15.6	15.9
65 years and over	18.2	17.3	18.8	17.7	17.4	17.9	22.5	16.2	27.0
85 years and over	35.5	27.3	39.0	34.3	26.0	37.7	49.2	40.0	53.8
2000									
Total	15.5	15.5	15.4	12.2	12.3	12.2	34.9	34.7	35.1
65 years and over	30.2	27.7	31.9	28.1	27.0	28.9	49.9	33.8	61.2
85 years and over	101.5	87.0	107.7	97.7	85.2	103.0	144.7	104.6	164.4
2025									
Total	29.9	29.7	30.0	21.3	21.3	21.3	80.6	80.5	80.6
65 years and over	119.1	127.1	113.7	106.7	117.4	99.5	238.0	218.5	251.5
85 years and over	204.8	188.4	211.8	188.4	180.2	191.9	391.9	270.8	451.5
2050									
Total	33.4	32.3	34.4	20.1	19.2	21.0	112.0	111.5	112.5
65 years and over	151.3	154.9	148.9	124.5	130.2	120.7	408.5	388.8	422.3
85 years and over	555.8	562.9	553.1	494.8	515.8	486.5	1251.8	1038.5	1355.3

Source: U.S. Bureau of the Census, 1984c.

TABLE 11.4:   COMPARISON OF PROJECTIONS OF SIZE OF THE POPULATION 65 YEARS OLD AND OVER
AND 85 YEARS AND OVER, SOCIAL SECURITY ADMINISTRATION AND BUREAU OF THE
CENSUS: 1990 TO 2050
(in thousands)

Year	Bureau of the Census (Middle Series)			Social Security Administration (Alternative II)		
	65 years old and over	85 years old and over		65 years old and over	85 years old and over	
		Number	Percent of persons 65+		Number	Percent of persons 65+
1990	31,697	3,313	10.5	32,570	3,563	10.9
2000	34,921	4,926	14.1	36,184	5,161	14.3
2020	51,422	7,081	13.8	53,273	7,142	13.4
2040	66,988	12,834	19.2	68,847	13,084	19.0
2050	67,412	16,034	23.8	NA	NA	NA

Source: U.S. Social Security Administration, 1984; U.S. Bureau of the Census, 1984c.

peak of 241 million in 2030, the white population is expected to cease
growing (U.S. Bureau of the Census, 1984c, Table 6). For both races
at every date, the age segment 65 and older is growing considerably
faster than the total population, and the growth of the 85 and older
group is even more dramatic. The very large percentage increases
shown for the nonwhite elderly reflect the relatively small base numbers for this group as well as the cumulative effects of assumed birth,
death, and immigration rates. For both racial categories, the number
of elderly women will increase faster than the number of men through
the year 2000. Slightly larger percentage increases are reported for
white men than for white women after this date.

Some idea of the differences between the SSA and Bureau of the
Census projections can be obtained from Table 11.4. The two sets of
figures are relatively close in 1990 and 2000, and the SSA intermediate
projection of 7.1 million persons 85 and over in 2020 is almost identical
with the figure that results from the Bureau of the Census middle
series for 2020.

The proportion of the total population which is over 65 will increase
from 11.6 percent in 1982 to 13.0 percent in 2000 and then, with the

aging of the baby boom generation, will jump to 19.5 percent by 2025 and nearly 22 percent in 2050, according to Bureau of the Census middle series projections (Table 11.5). The proportion of whites 65 and over will be somewhat greater than for nonwhites—by 2050, 18 percent of nonwhites will be over 65 compared to nearly 23 percent of whites, reflecting the higher fertility of the former group.

The aging of the elderly segment is also made clear by the projections shown in Table 11.5. Those 85 and over as a proportion of the group 65 and over will increase from the current 9.1 percent to almost 13 percent by 2025; then, as the baby boom generation reaches extreme old age, the ratio 85+/65+ will nearly double by 2050, to almost 24 percent, or approximately one in four of those 65 and over. For non-whites, the ratio 85+/65+ will be smaller than that for whites only.

The future age composition of the population 85 years and over also has been estimated by the Social Security Administration and the Census Bureau. Between 1980 and 2020, according to the SSA inter-mediate model, growth percentages are projected to mount with in-creasing age. During this four decade span it is estimated that the number of persons 85–89 years old will double, the number 90–94 years old will almost quadruple, and the number 95 years and over will increase eightfold (Table 11.6). After 2020, as a result of entry into extreme old age of the post-World War II baby boom cohorts, the pattern of increase will reverse. Between 2020 and 2040 the youngest members of the 85 and over population are expected to grow more rapidly than the oldest members. The proportion of the extreme aged population that is 95 and over is projected to climb from 6 percent of the total in 1980 to 17 percent in 2020 and then to fall somewhat to about 14 percent in 2040 (Table 11.6).

The Census Bureau series of projections for five-year age groups among the extreme elderly also shows the population 95 and over increasing absolutely and proportionally to 2020 and then declining proportionally to 2040 (Table 11.7). However, by 2050 the percentage aged 95 and over would again increase—to almost 21 percent of the extreme aged population. By that date the number of persons aged 95–99 years would be almost as large as the current population 85–89 years of age and the number of centenarians would be well above the present nonagenarian population.

All recent projections postulate sizable declines in death rates at older ages and concomitant increases in life expectancy. As Table 11.8

TABLE 11.5: PROJECTED PERCENT OF ELDERLY IN THE POPULATION, BY SELECTED AGE CATEGORIES, RACE AND SEX, BUREAU OF THE CENSUS (MIDDLE SERIES): 1982 TO 2050

Year and age category	Total			White			Nonwhite		
	Both sexes	Male	Female	Both sexes	Male	Female	Both sexes	Male	Female
1982									
Persons 65+ as % of total	11.6	9.5	13.5	12.2	10.1	14.3	7.5	6.4	8.5
Persons 85+ as % of total	1.1	0.6	1.4	1.1	0.7	1.6	0.6	0.4	0.8
Persons 85+ as % of persons 65+	9.1	6.7	10.7	9.3	6.7	10.9	7.8	6.3	8.8
1990									
Persons 65+ as % of total	12.7	10.4	14.9	13.6	11.1	15.9	8.0	6.5	9.4
Persons 85+ as % of total	1.3	0.8	1.9	1.4	0.8	2.0	0.8	0.5	1.0
Persons 85+ as % of persons 65+	10.5	7.3	12.6	10.6	7.2	12.8	9.5	7.6	10.7
2000									
Persons 65+ as % of total	13.0	10.5	15.4	14.0	11.4	16.5	8.4	6.4	10.2
Persons 85+ as % of total	1.8	1.0	2.6	2.0	1.1	2.8	1.1	0.6	1.5
Persons 85+ as % of persons 65+	14.1	9.8	16.9	14.3	9.8	17.2	12.7	9.6	14.5
2025									
Persons 65+ as % of total	19.5	16.7	22.1	20.9	18.0	23.6	14.1	11.4	16.6
Persons 85+ as % of total	2.5	1.4	3.5	2.7	1.6	3.8	1.6	0.8	2.3
Persons 85+ as % of persons 65+	12.7	8.5	15.7	12.9	8.7	16.0	11.3	7.3	13.8
2050									
Persons 65+ as % of total	21.8	18.4	25.0	22.9	19.4	26.1	18.0	14.9	21.0
Persons 85+ as % of total	5.2	3.2	7.0	5.6	3.5	7.6	3.7	2.2	5.2
Persons 85+ as % of persons 65+	23.8	17.4	28.2	24.5	18.0	29.0	20.7	14.7	24.5

Source: U.S. Bureau of the Census, 1984c.

TABLE 11.6:   PROJECTIONS OF SIZE OF THE POPULATION 85 YEARS OLD AND OVER, BY SEX
AND AGE GROUP, SOCIAL SECURITY ADMINISTRATION (ALTERNATIVE II):   1980
TO 2040

(in thousands)

Sex and age	1980	1990	2000	2020	2040
Both sexes					
Total	2,393	3,563	5,161	7,142	13,084
85-89 years	1,662	2,338	3,159	3,744	7,382
90-94 years	579	922	1,453	2,193	3,887
95 years and over	152	303	554	1,205	1,815
Male					
Total	714	973	1,388	2,003	3,984
85-89 years	514	679	927	1,187	2,472
90-94 years	161	228	351	571	1,100
95 years and over	39	66	110	245	412
Female					
Total	1,678	2,590	3,362	5,139	9,101
85-89 years	1,148	1,658	2,227	2,557	4,910
90-94 years	417	694	1,102	1,622	2,788
95 years and over	113	238	444	960	1,403

Source: U.S. Social Security Administration, 1984.

makes clear, the range in projected death rates for persons in age
groups 85 to 94 years for selected dates in the future, according to the
patterns of mortality decline assumed by the Social Security Administration, is very broad. This was done deliberately because future
events influencing death rates are subject to considerable uncertainty
and the projection-makers wished to encompass a variety of possibilities.

According to the SSA projections, the range in life expectancy at
birth in the year 2000 under the three alternatives (Table 11.9) will
be from 72.1 to 75.2 years for males and from 79.5 to 82.7 years for
females. By 2040, the range between the alternatives will be 6.3 years
for males (from 73.3 to 79.6 years) and will be slightly greater for
females—from 80.7 to 87.4 or a difference of 6.7 years. (See Figures
11.1 and 11.2.) The range in life expectancy shown in the high, middle,
and low series of projections produced by the Bureau of the Census is
similarly broad. The wide range of values shown in both Table 11.8
and Table 11.9 underscores the need for a cautious approach to the use
of projections. Although every effort is made to ensure that the un-

TABLE 11.7:   PROJECTIONS OF SIZE OF THE POPULATION 85 YEARS OLD AND OVER, BY SEX
AND AGE GROUP, BUREAU OF THE CENSUS (MIDDLE SERIES):   1982 TO 2050

(in thousands)

Sex and age	1982	1990	2000	2020	2040	2050
Both Sexes						
Total	2,445	3,313	4,926	7,081	12,834	16,034
85-89 years	1,637	2,157	3,025	3,587	7,012	7,829
90-94 years	620	849	1,355	2,158	3,777	4,915
95-99 years	155	253	438	975	1,448	2,261
100 years and over	32	54	108	361	597	1,029
Male						
Total	722	919	1,350	1,942	3,804	4,786
85-89 years	503	642	907	1,121	2,319	2,649
90-94 years	169	211	335	555	1,047	1,405
95-99 years	41	55	90	206	333	541
100 years and over	9	11	18	60	105	191
Female						
Total	1,722	2,393	3,576	5,139	9,030	11,247
85-89 years	1,134	1,515	2,118	2,466	4,693	5,179
90-94 years	450	638	1,020	1,603	2,730	3,510
95-99 years	114	198	348	769	1,115	1,720
100 years and over	24	42	90	301	492	838

Source: U.S. Bureau of the Census, 1984c.

derlying assumptions are realistic and that the range of projections encompasses the most likely future course of population change, projections are still educated guesses with a wide margin for error.

In view of the poor record of estimating future mortality levels of past "official" projections, it is pertinent to consider the opinions of some of the scholars who have carefully examined future life expectation. Collins and McMillan (1982) have recently constructed a combined age, period and cohort model for predicting future levels of mortality based on the inclusion of past mortality levels of each age group both by calendar year and by year of birth. Their model indicates that by the year 2000 the life expectancy at birth of U.S. females will be 85.6 years. This projection is more than four years greater than the

TABLE 11.8: PROJECTED CENTRAL DEATH RATES FOR THE POPULATION 85 TO 89 YEARS
AND 90 TO 94 YEARS, BY SEX, SOCIAL SECURITY ADMINISTRATION
ALTERNATIVE ASSUMPTIONS: 1982 TO 2040

(Deaths per 100,000 population)

Age group, sex, and alternative assumptions	1982	1990	2000	2020	2040
85 to 89 years					
Male					
Alternative I	15,841	15,511	15,177	14,292	13,494
Alternative II	15,841	14,489	13,507	12,301	11,252
Alternative III	15,841	13,554	11,973	10,009	8,411
Female					
Alternative I	11,221	10,495	9,832	9,127	8,518
Alternative II	11,221	9,614	8,477	7,544	6,756
Alternative III	11,221	8,823	7,313	5,957	4,896
90 to 94 years					
Male					
Alternative I	22,589	21,984	21,364	20,012	18,799
Alternative II	22,589	20,651	19,160	17,339	15,767
Alternative III	22,589	19,432	17,166	14,363	12,083
Female					
Alternative I	17,759	16,903	16,051	14,837	13,776
Alternative II	17,759	15,696	14,091	12,476	11,112
Alternative III	17,759	14,597	12,370	10,103	8,321

Source: U.S. Social Security Administration, 1984: Tables 7a-7c.

medium assumptions of either the Social Security Administration or
the Census Bureau. On the other hand, Keyfitz (1978) sees a barrier
now set at an expectation of life of about 80 years that is an "intrinsic
ceiling" that must be raised. A wisely cautious view, perhaps the majority consensus at present, is taken by Rice and Feldman (1983) who
observe that the SSA projected mortality trends "appear reasonable,
but our understanding of the dynamics of mortality rates is, at best
rather poor ... we cannot anticipate with any assurance when the next
alteration in course will take place" (p. 390).

Despite the current consensus among projection-makers that death
rates for the elderly, especially those in extreme old age, will continue
to decline, unpredictable events, such as life style changes, may operate

TABLE 11.9: PROJECTED LIFE EXPECTANCY (IN YEARS) AT BIRTH AND AT AGE 65, BY SEX, SOCIAL SECURITY ADMINISTRATION ALTERNATIVE ASSUMPTIONS: 1980 TO 2040

Sex and year	Birth			Age 65		
	Alternative I	Alternative II	Alternative III	Alternative I	Alternative II	Alternative III
Male						
1980	69.9	69.9	69.9	14.0	14.0	14.0
1990	71.4	72.4	73.4	14.5	15.1	15.6
2000	72.1	73.7	75.2	14.8	15.7	16.6
2020	72.7	74.7	77.4	15.2	16.4	18.2
2040	73.3	75.7	79.6	15.6	17.1	19.9
Female						
1980	77.5	77.5	77.5	18.4	18.4	18.4
1990	78.9	79.9	80.8	19.2	19.8	20.5
2000	79.5	81.1	82.7	19.5	20.7	21.8
2020	80.1	82.3	85.1	20.1	21.6	23.7
2040	80.7	83.4	87.4	20.6	22.5	25.5

Source: U.S. Social Security Administration, 1984.

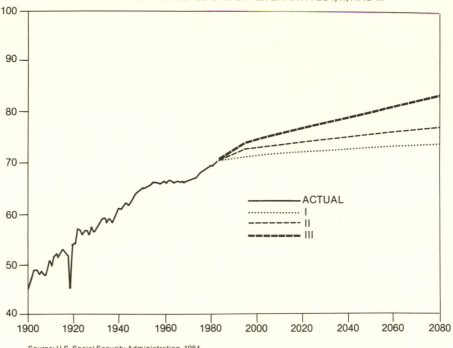

FIGURE 11.1: MALE LIFE EXPECTANCY (IN YEARS), 1900-2080
ACTUAL AND AS PROJECTED UNDER ALTERNATIVES I, II, AND III

Source: U.S. Social Security Administration, 1984.

to prevent death rates from falling further. The behavioral component in health and illness, in particular, is becoming more important as the cause of death structure continues to shift from infectious to chronic diseases. This is one reason why the gap in mortality between the sexes will probably continue to widen despite changes in the life style of women, especially increasing labor force participation, which may operate in the opposite direction (Verbrugge, 1983).

The outlook for morbidity rates closely correlates with mortality trends. Recent work by Verbrugge (1984) suggests that declining death rates will be accompanied by increasing sickness rates, as scientific advances allow the postponement of death but fail to yield actual cures for chronic, degenerative diseases. Although "individuals in the future

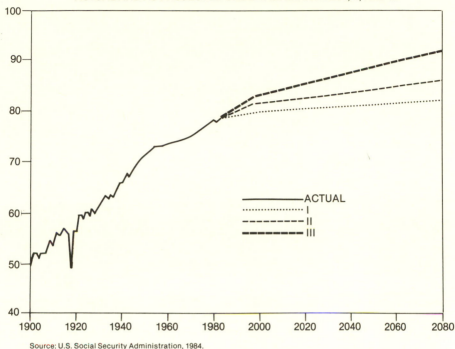

FIGURE 11.2: FEMALE LIFE EXPECTANCY (IN YEARS), 1900-2080:
ACTUAL AND AS PROJECTED UNDER ALTERNATIVES I, II, AND III

Source: U.S. Social Security Administration, 1984.

will generally live five to ten years longer [and] stay healthier until later in life, [they will] still experience most of the same health problems in advanced old age as old people do today" (Hickey, 1980, p. 171).

Foreign-born elderly are now overwhelmingly of European origin. This factor too is due to change in future years, since a repetition of the large-scale immigration movements from Europe which occurred in the late nineteenth and early twentieth centuries is unlikely. As early as the 1960s, in fact, the number of immigrants from Latin America already exceeded the number coming from Europe. The immigrant group in the future is likely to be largely Latin American or Asian. Population composition by race is presented in Table 11.10 for the period 1982 to 2050. The proportion white is slated to decline consist-

TABLE 11.10: PROJECTED POPULATION COMPOSITION, BY RACE, BUREAU OF THE CENSUS
              (MIDDLE SERIES): 1982 TO 2050

(percent distribution)

| Year | Total | White | Nonwhite | Black | |
				Percent of total population	Percent of nonwhite population
1982	100.0	85.6	14.4	12.0	82.9
1990	100.0	84.4	15.6	12.6	80.8
2000	100.0	83.1	16.9	13.3	78.9
2010	100.0	81.7	18.3	14.1	77.4
2030	100.0	79.3	20.7	15.6	75.4
2050	100.0	77.0	23.0	16.9	73.5

Source: U.S. Bureau of the Census, 1984c.

ently over time, from its present 85.6 percent of the total to a low of
77.0 percent by 2050. Both the proportion nonwhite and the proportion
black will increase, with the latter changing from 12 percent of the
total to nearly 17 percent by 2050. At least one in five persons in the
general population will be classified as nonwhite by the year 2030,
compared to about one in seven today. Interestingly, the ratio of blacks
to all nonwhites is also projected to decline.

Differences in death rates by sex and the projected continued widening of sex differentials in expectation of life will continue to affect
the distribution of the elderly population by marital status, as has been
the case in the past. The Social Security Administration, taking past
and current experience into consideration, has postulated future marital status distributions by age and sex. According to Table 11.11, the
proportion married of the extreme aged will remain relatively stable
for both sexes through 2040, whereas the proportion widowed will fall
due to declining death rates. The percentage divorced will increase by
sixfold among women. The end result of the various trends is that one
in every two men will be currently married at age 85, but only one in
seven women will be so classified.

TABLE 11.11:   PROJECTED MARITAL STATUS OF THE POPULATION 85 YEARS OLD AND OVER,
BY SEX, SOCIAL SECURITY ADMINISTRATION (ALTERNATIVE II): 1980
TO 2040
(percent distribution)

Year	Total	Single	Married	Widowed	Divorced
Male					
1980	100.0	4.4	41.7	51.8	2.2
1990	100.0	3.1	48.8	45.3	2.8
2000	100.0	3.4	51.9	41.1	3.6
2020	100.0	3.4	51.9	40.1	4.6
2040	100.0	7.3	52.3	35.2	5.1
Female					
1980	100.0	6.3	13.8	77.7	2.4
1990	100.0	6.1	10.7	81.0	2.2
2000	100.0	5.4	11.2	78.3	5.1
2020	100.0	4.0	11.5	74.2	10.3
2040	100.0	7.2	13.8	63.9	15.1

Source: U.S. Social Security Administration, 1984.

Marital status, especially for women, is closely related to their income prospects in later life, and elderly widows suffer disproportionately from poverty. One recent study, taking account of recent changes
in women's labor force activity, relative earnings, pension systems,
and projections of the marital status, age, and sex distribution of the
elderly population, has concluded that "in the absence of policy change,
current poverty trends among aged women will continue into the future" (Warlick, 1983, p. 36).

The numbers of future elderly (since they have already been born)
may be forecast based on relatively simple mortality assumptions, but
projections of the conditions of their lives rest on a wide array of intermediate developments, subject to rapid change as political, economic, technological and social circumstances themselves change. How
the growing numbers of the elderly will fare in the final phases of life

is in many respects an open question. Present and future generations of the elderly are "pioneers" in the sense that there are no precedents to guide their future behavior or expectations (Stub, 1982). Appropriate roles for individuals who may survive in reasonably good health for 20 to 40 years past the traditional retirement age, or about one-third of their life span, have yet to be developed. An even greater lack is the absence of meaningful activity or even the expectation of activity on the part of the "frail elderly." Given the extraordinary demands which these individuals are likely to make on society in their last years, questions of what positive contributions they can and should make to society will certainly be raised in coming years. The answers, and how the extreme elderly fare based on societal choices, will reveal much about the American system of values.

What will dependency ratios look like in years to come, according to the projection-makers? Each of the three SSA alternative projections foresees an increase in the aged dependency ratio (ADR), defined as the ratio of persons 65 and over to those aged 20–64, at least to the year 2040 (Table 11.12). According to the SSA:

A sharp increase in the aged dependency ratio shortly after the turn of the century appears certain, as the baby-boom generation attains age 65 while the baby-bust generation attains age 20. The magnitude of the increase, however, will depend upon future mortality improvements among the aged and future fertility rates. Even under optimistic assumptions, however, the aged dependency ratio will increase almost 70 percent by the year 2030 (1984, p. 16).

According to the Social Security Administration, however, increases in the aged dependency ratio may be offset by changes in the total dependency ratio (the number of persons 65 and over plus those under 20 relative to the group aged 20–64):

Under all three alternatives, the total dependency ratio is projected to decrease ... until shortly after the turn of the century, reflecting both the small number of children resulting from the low fertility rates experienced since 1970 and projected to be experienced in the near future, and the slow growth in the aged population resulting from the low fertility rates experienced during the 1930's. The existence of this extremely favorable demographic composition is often overlooked because of the attention given to the financial problems expected

TABLE 11.12: EFFECTS OF ALTERNATIVE ASSUMPTIONS ON PROPORTION ELDERLY, AGED DEPENDENCY
RATIO, AND TOTAL DEPENDENCY RATIO, SOCIAL SECURITY ADMINISTRATION: 1980
TO 2040

Year and alternative assumptions	Age group as percent of US total population		Persons 85+ as percent of persons 65+	Dependency ratio	
	65+	85+		Total	Aged
1980					
Alternative I	11.2	1.0	9.1	.756	.196
Alternative II	11.2	1.0	9.1	.756	.196
Alternative III	11.2	1.0	9.1	.756	.196
2000					
Alternative I	12.3	1.6	13.2	.707	.211
Alternative II	13.0	1.9	14.3	.691	.221
Alternative III	13.8	2.1	15.3	.665	.230
2020					
Alternative I	15.3	1.8	11.5	.784	.272
Alternative II	17.3	2.3	13.4	.744	.301
Alternative III	20.1	3.1	15.6	.694	.341
2040					
Alternative I	17.1	2.8	16.2	.855	.317
Alternative II	21.1	4.0	19.0	.843	.390
Alternative III	27.9	6.3	22.8	.862	.520

Source: U.S. Social Security Administration, 1984.

when the baby-boom generation begins to attain retirement age (1984, pp. 16–17).

Projected values of the total dependency ratio in 2040 range roughly from 12 to 14 percent higher than the 1980 value.

This view may be overly optimistic, however, since it seems to assume that the *costs* of supporting an elderly person from retirement to death are the same as for a child from birth to labor force entry; there is too little evidence available on this question to date to warrant such an assumption. Increasing numbers and proportions of elderly, the fact that the elderly group is itself aging, and the changing characteristics of the oldest segments of the population all have important implications for numerous facets of American life. Several of the more important ramifications of our aging society will be discussed in the concluding chapter.

12 Overview

Population growth is a phenomenon that in the United States in recent decades has generally been associated with an increase in fertility. The post-World War II "baby boom" caused a new surge in the annual birth and growth rates in the United States. By its very nature, an increase in the birth rate attracts considerable attention. Population cohorts of increased size create demand for additional hospital maternity wards, school buildings, housing, and other consumer goods and services.

Population growth through decreased mortality, however, may not attract as much attention. This type of population increment tends to occur more slowly and often is distributed over a number of age groups, further lessening its visibility. When mortality rates decline in a segment of the population that has had relatively stable rates and when these declines are most pronounced in a seldom studied age group, the result is a population expansion that is barely noticed.

Although it is still not widely recognized, persons 85 years and over—the oldest old—currently constitute the most rapidly growing portion of the American population. This is true for most other industrialized nations as well. Between 1960 and 1980, the oldest old increased by 141 percent in the United States, a rate far in excess of that of all persons 65 years and over (54 percent), or that of the total population (26 percent). This rapid growth of the extreme elderly is not new. In the previous 20–year span, 1940–1960, this group grew just as rapidly, by 154 percent. What is new is the fact that the sheer number of persons 85 and over is now of sufficient magnitude to have a major impact on the health care and social service systems. Furthermore, unless there are unprecedented reversals in the long-term pattern of mortality decline, the extreme elderly will continue to show highly disproportionate advances in number in the foreseeable future. The growth of the very old merits careful consideration.

Historically, the number of persons 85 years and over has been greater at each census because successive population cohorts were larger in childhood than previous ones. (At the same time declining fertility was contributing to relatively higher proportions at the elderly ages). Mortality decline has been an important phenomenon throughout the twentieth century. Until the period around World War II, this decline was concentrated in infancy and childhood, resulting in absolute increases in the number of young people in the population. Since at least 1940, however, the major reason for the spectacular increase in the number of oldest old has been declining mortality. In recent decades, death rate declines at the older ages have been as large or larger than those at younger ages, resulting in unprecedented numbers of persons reaching extreme old age (U.S. National Center for Health Statistics, 1984a; Crimmins, 1981; Rosenwaike, et al., 1980). A sharp downturn in mortality from cardiovascular disease is largely responsible for declining death rates. Projections of continuing declines in mortality among the aged are a major factor in accounting for the large increases anticipated in the future size of the oldest old population.

The Bureau of the Census (1984c) in its most recent series of projections, shows an increase of 117 percent in the number of oldest old between 1980 and 2000 and another increase of 44 percent between 2000 and 2020, based on its "middle" assumptions regarding mortality. In actual numbers, the population 85 years and over would advance from 2.3 million in 1980 to 4.9 million by 2000 and to over 7.1 million by 2020. The number of oldest old will experience a further dramatic surge when baby boom cohorts reach advanced ages; by 2040 the population 85 years or older is expected to reach almost 13 million. Thus the age distribution of the population in the future will be dramatically different from that of the past and present.

The demographic analysis of population subgroups among the elderly is a relatively new phenomenon. The elderly are now recognized as an extremely diverse group, spanning a 30–to–35 year age range (Soldo, 1980). This large group is no longer viewed as homogeneous in social, physical and cultural characteristics, but is acknowledged to be composed of very dissimilar populations. Among the new designations for subpopulations among the aged, the most popular are the "young old" and the "old old." Like the term "elderly" itself, definitions of the latter population vary. These include persons 75 years and over (Neugarten, 1974; Streib, 1983), 80 years and over (Siegel and Hoover, 1982), and 85 years and over, termed the "extreme aged" (Lopez and Hanada, 1982). Any definition is arbitrary. Neugarten's distinction (1982) between young old and old old, however is not based solely, or even primarily, on chronological age but rather on health status and social characteristics. Streib's description of the "frail elderly" (1983) takes account of both age and ability to function independently. Both researchers have recognized that although age and functional condition overlap to a considerable extent in a population, there are many exceptions among individuals.

The definition used here for the oldest old is the population aged 85 and over. The rationale for this choice is twofold: first, demographic statistics are conventionally published in five-year age categories. When a terminal age group such as 75 + or 85 + is used, a pure age criterion is employed, with no attention to functional condition. On the other hand, more than any other age group, it is the population aged 85 and above that most resembles the traditional image of an old age linked to frailty and dependence, illness and death. The characteristics of this population differ markedly in many respects from those of the younger old. Hence equating the oldest old as a functional category with the population 85 and over as a statistical artifact serves as a convenient tool and facilitates comparisons with other published data.

Many in the gerontological community are aware of the present and future importance of the extreme aged in American society, yet data on the demographic characteristics of this population remain relatively undeveloped and sometimes unavailable. Information about both the size and the socioeconomic characteristics of a population is essential to understanding its conditions of life. Published U.S. census data on our oldest citizens are limited and have been available only for the aggregate group 85 years and over, with no further subdivision by age. Surprisingly, perhaps, the published reports of the 1980 census contain even fewer cross-tabulations on the social and economic characteristics of this population than did the 1970 reports. The 1970 census, for example, provided information on labor force status and on migration for persons 85 years and over, whereas the maximum age category for which data were presented in 1980 was 75 years and over. At both censuses the highest age category presenting education level and income statistics was 75 years and over. However, data showing living arrangements and marital status of those 85 years and over were provided in both 1970 and 1980.

The lack of published data, however, does not preclude detailed study of the demographic characteristics of the oldest old. For recent censuses, there exists an alternative means of studying those characteristics of a population not available from published sources. The Census Bureau has realized that many in the research community (now with access to increasingly sophisticated computer technology) have found the published census reports inadequate for their particular purposes. Accordingly, sample tapes from the 1970 and 1980 census basic record files (coded so as to preclude breach of confidentiality rules) have been made available which permit individual researchers freedom to retabulate or manipulate data for a small sample of those enumerated to their own specifications. The public use microdata samples of the decennial censuses of population and housing provide social scientists with a valuable resource for examining various cross-classifications of personal characteristics that would not otherwise be available. In order to produce a comprehensive portrait of the extreme elderly, public use samples of the 1970 and 1980 censuses have been extensively utilized in this monograph.

Referring to the population over age 65 as a whole, Pampel (1981, p. 155) observed "little support for arguments that the aged suffer in contemporary society because of loss of extended family ties, isolation of parents from their adult children, and complete dependence of aged persons on government services and housing." Indications are, however, that the oldest old population may not fit Pampel's generalizations very well and may, in fact, suffer disproportionately from the losses and dependent status he mentions. Comparison of the characteristics of the population 85 and over with those of the youngest group of older persons, those 65 to 69 years of age, can enable us to determine how distinctly different the oldest old population is from the younger aged.

Perhaps the most unique feature of the extreme elderly is the relative numbers of males and females. Reductions in mortality over the years have benefited females substantially more than males. At every age, male mortality exceeds female mortality. At the older ages, where death rates are highest, the sex ratio (the number of males per 100 females) has shown the greatest imbalances, "and these imbalances have increased as the male-female gap in mortality has widened" (Davis and van den Oever, 1982, p. 500). A revolutionary imbalance of the sexes has occurred at the oldest ages. The 1980 census indicated that there were 80 males for every 100 females at ages 65–69 years, but only 44 men for every 100 women at ages 85 years and over.

The very pronounced differences in the marital status distribution of elderly males and females are largely explained by the imbalances in the sex ratio, but other factors are also important, namely the tendency for men to marry women some years younger than themselves and the greater likelihood of remarriage for males. The data in Table 12.1 show that almost half (48 percent) of all men 85 years and over enumerated in 1980 were currently married compared to only 1 of every 12 women. The oldest old of both sexes were much less likely to be currently married than the young old. A majority (55 percent) of women aged 65–69 years, for example, were married, as were 4 out of 5 men. The vast majority (82 percent) of extreme elderly women in 1980 were widowed, compared with only about one-third of those in the age group 65–69 years. (About 6 percent of 85 and over males and 8 percent of females had never married.) Young old males were rarely widowed (7 percent), although this status was common among the oldest old (44 percent).

Marital status variations are important in accounting for differences in living arrangements of older men and women. Because males are much more likely to be married than are females they are more likely to live in a family setting. A majority of all males 85 years and older (59 percent) live in families compared with only approximately one-third of females (37 percent) in this age group. By contrast, two-thirds (67 percent) of all females aged 65–69 years live in families, as do the overwhelming share (85 percent) of all males (Table 12.1).

In 1980 almost 36 percent of all women 85 years old and over lived in single-person households, or in households with only nonrelatives present, substantially more than the 29 percent recorded in 1970. Myers and Nathanson (1982, p. 227) observe that "this trend toward independent living, which is shared by males to a lesser extent, has persisted over several decades and appears to be characteristic of many developed countries." Concomitant with this trend toward independent living, there has been a sharp decline in the numbers of both elderly

TABLE 12.1: SELECTED CHARACTERISTICS OF THE "YOUNG OLD" AND "OLDEST OLD": 1970 AND
1980

Population characteristics	1970		1980	
	65-69 Years	85+ Years	65-69 Years	85+ Years
Sex ratio: (males per 100 females)	80.7	53.3	80.0	43.7
Percent currently married:				
Males	80.6	42.4	83.0	48.4
Females	52.0	9.9	54.8	8.4
Percent widowed:				
Males	8.8	47.0	7.3	43.8
Females	36.5	79.0	33.8	81.8
Percent in families:				
Males	83.9	60.4	85.4	58.9
Females	67.2	47.9	66.8	36.7
Percent living in households alone or with nonrelatives:				
Males	13.8	24.2	12.9	24.1
Females	30.5	29.0	31.5	35.6
Percent in institutions:				
Males	1.8	14.3	1.4	16.1
Females	1.6	21.9	1.3	26.3
Education:				
% high school graduates	30.5	23.0	45.1	30.0
% 8+ years of school	70.9	60.1	81.2	66.6
Race and nativity:				
% black	9.0	7.6	8.8	7.1
% foreign born	12.8	18.6	7.8	18.6
Percent in labor force:				
Males	39.0	6.8	29.2	4.2
Females	17.2	3.4	15.0	1.5
Percent below poverty level:	21.6	37.1	11.6	21.3
Median income previous year:				
Males	$3,616	$1,668	$8,584	$4,797
Females	$1,558	$1,171	$3,819	$3,284

Source: U.S. Bureau of the Census (1970 and 1980 censuses and public use microdata
samples).

males and females who live in a household with relatives (usually their children) other than a spouse.

Another significant trend is the increasing proportion of extreme elderly, particularly women, residing in institutions. Table 12.1 indicates that the percentage of all women 85 years of age and over living in nursing homes and other long-term care facilities climbed from 22 percent in 1970 to 26 percent in 1980. During the same period the percentage of men increased from 14 to 16 percent. In sharp contrast, less than 2 percent of all persons aged 65–69 years required institutionalization in 1970 and the proportion declined by 1980.

The oldest old differ in a number of other demographic characteristics from the young old. The foreign born constitute almost 19 percent of the total U.S. population aged 85 and over, but represent about 8 percent of the young old. Blacks, on the other hand, account for almost 9 percent of the U.S. population aged 65–69 years, but are only about 7 percent of the oldest old.

Long-term trends which continued during the 1970s included advances in the educational status of older persons (as better educated cohorts replaced less well educated ones) and declines in labor force participation due to Social Security and pension benefits that enabled more persons to retire at earlier ages. Approximately 30 percent of all young old (65–69 years) men and women in 1970 had at least a high school education; by 1980 the figure was 45 percent. The percentage of oldest old who had completed high school was considerably smaller – 23 percent in 1970 and 30 percent in 1980. In 1980, 29 percent of males 65–69 years old were working or looking for work. For males 85 and over the comparable figure was 4 percent, down from almost 7 percent a decade earlier. Labor force participation among women was about half that for men among all categories of old people (Table 12.1).

In 1970 the incidence of poverty among Americans 65 years of age and older was double the national incidence. Since the late 1960s, as a result of "the enactment of large increases in benefits and a cost-of-living escalator clause for the Social Security program, the increasing coverage of older persons under a variety of public and private pension plans, and the implementation of new income support programs, such as SSI [Supplemental Security Income], Medicare, Medicaid and property tax relief", the relative economic situation of the older population improved dramatically (Fowles, 1983). This remarkable change meant that in 1982 the percentage of persons living in poverty in the 65 +

age group was almost identical to that of the national average (Preston, 1984). The oldest old also have experienced an overall decline in poverty in recent years but continue to have a high poverty rate relative to younger persons. According to the 1970 census, about 37 percent of persons 85 years and over had incomes below the federal government's poverty index; this fell substantially (to 21 percent) by 1980. At the same time, about 12 percent of all persons aged 65 to 69 years had incomes below the official poverty threshold.

A dramatic increase in the risk of dying occurs with advancing age. Males aged 85 and over exhibit a five-fold increase in mortality compared with men two decades younger. Among women there is an eight-fold increase in mortality between the ages of 65–69 and 85 and over. With advancing age the excess mortality of males relative to females declines. Among persons 65–69 years of age the death rate for men is twice that for women, but for the extreme aged the excess has been reduced to somewhat over one and one-quarter times (U.S. National Center for Health Statistics, 1984c).

The health of the elderly population is of considerable interest to demographers. Siegel (1980a, p. 351) has emphasized that "there are important interrelations between the health of older persons and demographic changes." Anticipated demographic changes are certain to affect the demand for health care and the provision of health services. Recent projections made by the Social Security Administration (1983) indicate that today's adults have an excellent chance of joining the very old in the future. According to the Administration's projected U.S. life table (which assumes a moderate level of mortality decline in the future), one of four males who will be 60 years of age by the end of this decade can expect to reach age 85. For females, the proportion will be almost one in two.

The attainment of extreme old age is frequently accompanied by a multiplicity of chronic health problems. When chronic disability occurs the oldest old either need assistance with the tasks of daily living in order to continue living in their community setting or must enter a nursing home or other institution. Data from the 1979 National Health Interview Survey and from the 1977 National Nursing Home Survey (U.S. National Center for Health Statistics, 1979, 1981, 1983b) indicate that the need for help rises very sharply with age. A basic physical activity, such as walking, may be used as an example. Only about 1 in 20 of those aged 65–74 years—institutionalized or noninstitutionalized—need assistance in walking, compared with about 4 in 10 of those 85 or over. About 3 out of 4 of the extreme elderly living in institutions and 1 out of 4 of the noninstitutionalized need assistance walking. More than 70 percent of those 85 and over require assistance in connection with some of their normal daily activities, whereas only 10 percent of those 65–74 are in this category (Johnston and Hoover, 1982, p. 209). A very substantial proportion of the very old thus need another person's help in order to carry out simple everyday activities. This stronger likelihood of dependency is a distinguishing feature of the oldest old as a group. Hospital utilization also increases significantly with age. In the 65–74 age group there are 306 hospital stays per 1,000 persons; the figure jumps to 507 per 1,000 for those 85 years and above. In addition, the latter individuals remain in the hospital longer and have more surgery. Of those 65–74 years of age, only 1 in 100 is a nursing home resident; for ages 85 and over, the ratio is more than 1 in 5.

In profile, the fastest growing segment of the population consists of persons over age 85. The majority of these individuals are white and female, better educated and with a higher income than past cohorts of this age. Most are widowed and live alone. Yet, demographic statistics, dealing as they do with purely quantitative information, present only a partial view of the complex social issues raised in connection with the extreme elderly population. The aging of the elderly population, accompanied by changes in their social and economic characteristics, has profound implications for society as well as for the individuals themselves. In particular, "because there is such a high correlation between advanced age and increased functional disabilities, the U.S. can expect an intensified demand for health and social services, especially for costly long-term care, and a greater strain on government and fiscal resources" (Barberis, 1981). The coexistence of declining mortality with increasing morbidity now being documented by researchers (Verbrugge, 1984) reflects the growing capability of the health care system to facilitate the survival of even those persons with severe chronic disorders into extreme old age. But the enormous costs of medical care cannot be borne by individuals living on limited post-retirement income and assets. Hence the quantity and quality of life in extreme old age are broad-ranging social problems. More and more the government is being viewed as the agent responsible for the financial needs of the aged (Jackson, 1980). The likelihood of a decline in the proportion of elderly persons who have living relatives will also "necessitate a greater role of government in the support of the elderly, particularly in providing health and other services" (Siegel, 1980b). At the same time, rising levels of income and education among the elderly imply a demand for more and better health care and other programs tailored to their needs, as well as a greater ability to seek out such services.

Neglected by demographers for many years, the oldest old can no longer be ignored. As noted in this monograph, this is a population subgroup whose spectacular growth, unique characteristics and unprecedented need for social services are certain to bring about broad changes in American life in the coming decades.

13 Implications

Of the many social, economic, political and other changes entailed by an aging population, this chapter will focus on the economic, health care, and social service factors. Current and potential sources of support for the extreme elderly in particular will also be discussed. Emphasis will be on the costs and needs of this population as opposed to the very different costs and needs of younger old people. The intention is not to offer solutions but to illustrate the complexities of the issues and to point out the unprecedented nature of the problems and the paucity of reliable data on which to base policy decisions. The chapter concludes with an assessment of the future prospects of the aged.

Twenty-five percent of the federal budget now goes to programs for the aged, and current demographic trends point to sizable increases by the year 2010, when the baby boom generation reaches age 65. Binstock (1981) has estimated that benefits for the aged could consume more than 40 percent of the federal budget by early in the next century. However, such an increase would merely maintain *current* benefit levels, already considered inadequate by many, and would not finance additional programs or expand existing ones. Although government spending on programs for the aged will increase in dollar amounts, it will only give the same (or even reduced) benefits to more people. Schulz (1980, introd.) suggests that *preserving* the progress made thus far will be a major challenge for the future. According to Petri (1982), many politicians now favor reductions in old-age benefits, especially through increases in retirement age; perhaps the major reason for this cautious approach to government spending is the widespread belief that "long-term projections of the United States social security system now indicate that the system will not be able to deliver the benefits that are now legislated without very large increases in future tax rates" (p. 86). While delaying the retirement age may remove some of the young old from benefit programs, it will not lessen the economic demands made by the extreme elderly who, because of their infirmities, will be unable to work.

The single overriding factor in the economic needs of the elderly is the cost of health care. Projected changes in the size and composition of the elderly population are much easier to predict than trends in ill health and infirmity among the old. Rice and Feldman (1983) note that there may be an increasing number of individuals with chronic functional limitations, an increasing number of individuals who remain in good health until death, and a decreasing number of individuals with only a moderate degree of infirmity. "What effect this would have on the prevalence of morbidity would, of course, depend on the relative magnitudes of the various changes. Unfortunately, our current knowledge of the natural history of most conditions is rather meager and we have little systematic information about terminal illnesses" (p.391).

At present, "the elderly are the major consumers of a runaway product in the market place," since their health care costs are "disproportionate to both their income levels and their overall numbers in the population" (Hickey, 1980, p. 146). This high usage is likely to continue at least in the near future. In the next few decades the average educational level of cohorts reaching ages 85 years and over will be higher than in the past, and the more highly educated tend to live longer, be in better health but, relative to their health status, use more medical care than the less educated (Rice and Feldman, 1983). Within the elderly segment, the extreme elderly require the greatest number of per capita health dollars; the aging of the elderly population implies that ever greater amounts of money must be expended on their needs. From 1978 to 2025, the costs of Medicare and Medicaid are projected to increase, in real terms, more than ten times, or twice as fast as increases in Social Security (Schulz, 1980, p. 194). These trends augur well neither for the individual, who is expected to finance up to half of his or her own medical costs through private health insurance or other means, nor for society at large, which must finance the other half as well as take over when individual resources are exhausted.

The elderly currently pay approximately 30 percent of their health care costs out-of-pocket. This proportion is likely to increase in future years, as more limitations are placed on government-financed insurance program payments and as higher coinsurance payments are required of the elderly. Because changes in the Social Security benefit formula will yield less generous cost-of-living increases in the future, many of the elderly may have diminished financial resources relative to the increased medical expenses they will be expected to assume (Binstock, 1983b).

There are three major categories of financial support for the elderly: the individual's own resources, those of the family and, finally, the government. For the individual, "income support in retirement [is] based primarily on work and is thus affected by the time-limited nature of a person's employment and earnings history" (Giele, 1982, p. 45). But some groups fare worse than others on this criterion—women, minorities, the less educated, the handicapped, those who worked only part-time or in low-skilled jobs accumulate little or no pension benefits. For women in particular, the majority of the oldest population and the bulk of the elderly poor, Warlick (1983) has considered income and work trends as well as demographic projections to conclude that, in the absence of deliberate policy intervention, future cohorts of women will experience no absolute improvement in their income status in old age. She notes that "poverty statistics suggest that for a woman not to ponder her future economic circumstances with caution, and in some cases despair, is to defy the hard facts of economic reality" (1983, p. 35).

Even if individuals cannot rely solely on their own resources throughout their retirement years, their families are available to help when needed. This is a common view and under the current administration in Washington family assistance is being looked to increasingly as government tries to cut costs. "Numerous studies have shown that health, income, and relations with family and friends are consistent predictors of life satisfaction or morale among the aged" (Markides, 1983, p. 119). The family is typically viewed as the institution best suited to support the elderly in noneconomic ways and perhaps save economically as well by delaying or avoiding institutionalization (Arling and McAuley, 1983).

Broad social trends seem to militate against family care-giving. With urbanization and industrialization families began "to lose control over those material resources, especially land and agricultural production, that were traditionally used to employ, support, and sustain the aged" (Giele, 1982, p. 44). The family's capacity to provide care is also said to be limited by the geographic distance that often exists between parents and children, a physical distancing that may produce psychological and social distance as well (Sclar, 1980, p. 31). Morris (1980, p. 125) maintains that "there is no indication that, on average, family willingness to maintain bonds of affection with their elders has declined. What is changed is the absolute situation that the family confronts." Families today have fewer children, are subject to divorce more frequently, and women—who traditionally have cared for frail elderly parents—are often involved in careers outside the home, thus diminishing the chances that extreme aged parents will be able to depend on their adult children for everyday assistance. This implies a need for the development of alternative sources of services for the oldest old. Such services might take the form of visiting homemakers, the expansion of delivered meals programs, respite programs, adult day care, and other approaches to long-term care. Because of the "medical model" of the Medicare and Medicaid programs, many of the costs of these "social" continuum of care alternatives are neither reimbursed nor adequately funded (Binstock, 1983b).

Not only has it become increasingly difficult for families, even if they are willing, to provide support for the elderly, but the alternative of nonfamily support, especially institutionalization, continues to be viewed very negatively by both the elderly themselves and their relatives. Yet, for those 85 and over, whether suffering from a variety of chronic conditions, or lacking relatives able and willing to assist them, or unable to live independently for financial reasons, dependence on the impersonal services of strangers seems unavoidable. If current patterns of use continue, nursing home care will be required for a substantial portion of the oldest old. In 1980, 1.5 million elderly persons were nursing home residents and this is projected to increase to 5.2 million by 2040, a 250 percent increase. For the population aged 85 and above, a 400 percent increase is predicted. In 1980, 37 percent of all nursing home residents were 85 or above; by 2040, this is projected to increase to 56 percent. Commenting on these figures, Rice and Feldman (1983) note that the expansion of the extreme aged population has had a greater impact on nursing home residence than on days of hospital care or physician visits.

The question of how much support the family *should* provide to the elderly, or how much families *could* realistically provide, is far from settled. Morris (1980, p. 126) points out the need to identify "the minimum social expectation of family responsibility and obligation before social provision is activated." But Arling and McAuley indicate the complexities of these issues: "Families should not be expected to deny themselves food and shelter in order to contribute to care for the older person. Should they, however, defer college education for their children, limit their residential mobility, or substantially reduce the savings and investments which help ensure their own finanicial position in old age?" (1983, p. 306). Furthermore, who is to make such decisions and on what basis, and who is to enforce them once they are made? What of those needy elderly who have no living relatives? For those with family help available, how much is enough?

For the very old declining health and perhaps the need for expensive institutional care, combined with the inevitable falling off in personal and family resources, imply an ever-greater dependence on public support. Even if they have delayed retirement, chances seem good that survival to advanced old age will have diminished any savings they brought to retirement, and death or sickness will have reduced the number of relatives able to provide assistance as well as their ability to do so. It must be recognized that resources, regardless of the source, are scarce. Demands, on the other hand, even when they are equally valid and compelling, are unlimited. Hence difficult choices are often necessary—for individuals, for families and for governments.

In an imperfect world, such choices are not always wise or equitable, but they must nonetheless be made. Given limited resources, the elderly cannot and should not be entirely dependent on government for their needs, but the trend in recent decades has been in that direction. There are compelling reasons to expect that such trends may be halted or reversed. Political decisions and social values, both subject to rapid change as other circumstances change, will affect the level and types of support available to the elderly in general and the more needy oldest old in particular. Future gains for the elderly, or even the preservation of current programs, may be closely tied to the performance of the economy. The still widespread belief that pensions, Social Security and Medicare benefits are all rewards for previous service is likely to become increasingly strained as the costs of such programs mount and ever-greater sacrifices on the part of younger generations become necessary. It seems inevitable that values and expectations regarding old age and aging will in the future, as they have in the past, be tempered by perceived demographic and fiscal realities.

Hospital cost containment legislation is likely as health care expenditures continue to rise at a faster rate than the cost of other goods and services. Binstock (1983b) foresees one of the most likely cost containment policies will be the rationing of health care on a cost/benefit analysis basis using the criteria of chronological old age; on this basis the delivery of expensive, highly technical procedures would tip in favor of younger persons. He also envisions the possibility of a two-class health care system in which extraordinary and costly medical procedures will be available only for patients able to pay for them from their personal resources, a situation that may negatively affect the very old disproportionately.

The reduction of disease and death rates is and has been a universal aim of governments. It has long been acceptable public policy to attempt to influence birth rates and migration rates in order to control population size and composition, but efforts to manipulate death rates to achieve the same aims are never seriously considered. But if the goal of mortality reduction is to improve the quality of life, rather than to merely prolong it, the medical advances of the twentieth century must be considered in a new light. That is, until recently there was no perceived contradiction between the dual aims of reducing the incidence of death and disease on the one hand and improving the quality of life on the other. Now, however, quite obviously there *are* contradictions.

It is important to reiterate the general neglect of the oldest old in research on old age and aging, and the effect of this neglect on public policy. The "important value premises that have structured policy for the 'young-old'—those that stress maximization of the older person's rights to make choices about the future—may raise serious conflicts when one considers the issues confronting the frail elderly" and the extremely aged (Orbach, 1983, p. 25). It should be clear from earlier chapters in this monograph that the oldest old differ in many critical respects, such as income and health care requirements, from the younger old; the particular characteristics of the former necessitate that most will be dependent on society for their basic needs in extreme old age.

This dependent status in the final years of life is unlikely to vanish in the foreseeable future, despite declines in death rates, favorable trends in educational levels and lifetime earnings, and possibly later retirement. Those final years promise to be the most costly years of an individual's lifetime, years in which the quality of life may be questionable for many and in which the individual's ability to be self-reliant and make decisions about his or her future will be severely constrained. Society in general and taxpayers in particular are likely to ask what is to be gained from efforts to prolong life under such circumstances. The other side of the coin is what is to be sacrificed in pursuit of doubtful gains? Thus questions about the allocation of scarce resources will, as always, be in the forefront of decision-making.

In addition to the equitable allocation of scarce resources, another major consideration in assessing the future prospects of the oldest old is the fact that it is largely younger generations of workers who ultimately finance the broad spectrum of social programs supporting them. They do so at some sacrifice of current living standards, both in anticipation of their own old age and because the elderly have generally been viewed as deserving of benefits. The oldest old present a greater dilemma—what sacrifices should be required, and what will be tolerated, to support the frail elderly over years of extraordinarily expensive medical and other forms of basic maintenance care, when, at the end, there is no prospect of their becoming either productive citizens or merely self-supporting? Here the contrast between supporting the very old and supporting dependent children becomes clear—the latter have prospects of joining the labor force and producing, as well as consuming, once their education is complete; the former look forward only to increasing debility and death. As an aging population makes ever-greater demands on the nation's resources it is inevitable that serious issues of equity between generations, the value of life and the social utility of continuous postponement of death from chronic, incurable disease (as opposed to prolongation of healthy, active life) will be raised.

What then is the outlook for the extreme elderly? It seems safe to offer the following observations, given demographic, political, and economic realities and their trends over time:

1. Prior to the twentieth century, old age and aging were not viewed as problems to be solved. It is the unprecedented changes in the numbers and proportions of the elderly and their characteristics, behavior and expectations that turned aging into the dilemma it has now become and that will force modification of values and attitudes as well. History illustrates the inevitability of change; hence we can anticipate that

the rationale for continuing to finance expensive programs for *all* elderly, regardless of their needs or prospects, and possibly at the expense of neglecting other important social goals, will be closely scrutinized in coming years. The prevailing views, in fact, are already beginning to be challenged (Neugarten, 1982; Binstock, 1983a; Brodsky, 1983).

2. Compared to trying to predict future attitudes and values regarding old age, aging and the support of the elderly, the demographic trends are straightforward and reliable. There will be sizable increases in the numbers and proportion of the very old, who include the most dependent and needy groups. These changes will be accompanied by a declining ratio of producers to consumers. At the same time, "the extraordinary demands and pressures for health and related social services experienced in recent years as a result of demographic factors are likely to continue in the future" (U.S. National Center for Health Statistics, 1983c, p. 10). Rapid cost increases for medical care, on the other hand, show no sign of abating. Declines in family size, combined with increasing pressure on family resources as the aged live longer and require more care, will necessitate that outside agencies assume primary responsibility for the provision of services to the oldest old, whose children, in any case, frequently will be over 65 and perhaps retired, poor and suffering severe health problems themselves (Streib, 1983). If current patterns of use continue, the demand for nursing home care in particular is bound to grow considerably, with the increase being greatest at ages 85 and above (U.S. National Center for Health Statistics, 1983c). All these changes will occur even if there are no further improvements in mortality at the older ages and even if rates of utilization of medical resources remain stable:

If the constant mortality assumption is taken as a "minimum impact" projection, some increases would still occur in the number of people with limitation of activity, the number of hospital days, the number of nursing home residents, and corresponding costs. Under the declining mortality assumption there would be an even greater level of disability and dependence, and the costs associated with providing health care for an increasingly elderly population would be correspondingly higher (U.S. National Center for Health Statistics, 1983c, p. 25).

Moreover, even when in the best of health, the very old will still need a wide range of supportive services (U.S. National Center for Health Statistics, 1983c).

3. For the extreme elderly it is unlikely that either the individuals themselves or their families can be expected to provide the wide range of supportive services that will be required. The resources of the extreme aged themselves may run out long before they reach age 85, many of the oldest old have no relatives to turn to, and family resources too can be quickly exhausted. Clearly, outside agencies will have to assume primary responsibility at some point. Increasing individual responsibility for health, with the emphasis on prevention of chronic illness, will help to minimize or at least postpone the final stage of dependency, but is unlikely to eliminate it. On the other hand, the increasing educational attainment of generations reaching old age may produce a *greater* demand for health services (Rice and Feldman, 1983).

4. Our society is beginning to recognize that "mere survival is an insufficient objective" (Frankfather, et al., 1981, p. 102). A long life is not necessarily synonymous with a good or desirable life, as philosopher Daniel Callahan points out:

Until some good reasons have been presented why a longer life *per se* is good as distinguished from a long life where the evils of life have been . . . minimized, there is no public policy case to be made for the investment of so much as one cent in efforts to extend life for its own sake (cited in Menzel, 1983, p. 187).

In the first century B.C. Cicero wrote with absolute clarity about the limits to respect for old age: "Old age is honored only on condition that it defends itself, maintains its rights, is subservient to no one, and to the last breath rules over its own domain" (cited in Fischer, 1977, p. 14). Traditional societies, in spite of their apparent brutality toward the frail aged left to die, exhibited "a combination of realism, respect, and even affection for the aged who were so treated . . . [but] developed societies have yet to resolve such issues with the degree of moral clarity and ethical consistency that emerged under harsher conditions." (Giele, 1982, p. 56). To enhance life so long as that is possible and then to accept the inevitable with grace and dignity may be a difficult and yet distant goal, but nonetheless a worthy one.

References

Arling, Greg, and William J. McAuley. 1983. The Feasibility of Public Payments to Family Caregiving. The Gerontologist 23:300–306.

Banister, Judith. 1984. An Analysis of Recent Data on the Population of China. Population and Development Review 10:241–247.

Barberis, Mary. 1981. America's Elderly: Policy Implications. Population Bulletin, Vol. 35, No. 4 (Policy Supplement). Washington, D.C.: Population Reference Bureau.

Bayo, Francisco R. 1972. Mortality of the Aged. Transactions of the Society of Actuaries 24:1–24.

Bayo, Francisco R., and Joseph F. Faber. 1983. Mortality Experience Around Age 100. Transactions of the Society of Actuaries 35 (in press).

Beattie, Walter M., Jr. 1976. Aging and the Social Services. In Robert H. Binstock and Ethel Shanas (eds.), Handbook of Aging and the Social Sciences. New York: Van Nostrand Reinhold Company, pp. 619–642.

Biggar, Jeanne C. 1980. Who Moved among the Elderly, 1965–70: A Comparison of Types of Older Movers. Research on Aging 2:73–91.

Binstock, Robert H. 1981. Federal Policy Toward the Aged: Its Inadequacies and Its Politics. In Harold J. Wershow (ed.), Controversial Issues in Gerontology. New York: Springer Publishing Co., Inc., pp. 153–163.

———. 1983a. The Aged as Scapegoat. The Gerontologist 23:136–143.

———. 1983b. Health Care of the Aging: Trends, Dilemmas, and Prospects for the Year 2000. Paper presented at International Symposium convened by Texas Research Institute of Mental Sciences, Houston, Texas, October.

Binstock, Robert H., Wing-Sun Chow, and James H. Schulz (eds.) 1982. International Perspectives on Aging: Population and Policy Challenges. New York: United Nations Fund for Population Activities.

Bourgeois-Pichat, Jean. 1983. La Mortalité dans les Pays Industrialisés de 1960 à 1980. Futuribles, No. 67:63–74.

Bowerman, W.G. 1939. Centenarians. Transactions, Actuarial Society of America 40:360–378.

Brodsky, David. 1983. Future Policy Directions. In William P. Browne and Laura Katz Olson (eds.), Aging and Public Policy: The Politics of Growing Old in America. Westport, CT: Greenwood Press, pp. 221–238.

Chebotarev, Dmitri F., and Nina N. Sachuk. 1980. Union of Soviet Socialist Republics. In Erdman Palmore (ed.), International Handbook on Aging. Westport, CT: Greenwood Press, pp. 400–417.

Cherlin, Andrew. 1983. A Sense of History: Recent Research on Aging and the Family. In Matilda White Riley, Beth B. Hess and Kathleen Bond (eds.), Aging in Society: Selected Reviews of Recent Research. Hillsdale, NJ: Lawrence Erlbaum Associates, pp. 5–23.

Coale, Ansley. 1984. Rapid Population Change in China, 1952–1982. National Academy of Sciences. Washington, D.C.: National Academy Press.

Collins, Glen. 1984. Increasing Numbers of Aged Return North from Florida. New York Times. March 15.

Collins, James J., and David B. McMillan. 1982. A Method for Estimating Future Mortality Levels: The United States, 1985 to 2000. Paper presented at meeting of the Population Association of America.

Commission on Population Growth and the American Future. 1972. Population and the American Future. Washington, D.C.: U.S. Government Printing Office.

Cooper, Richard, Robert Cohen, and Abas Amiry. 1983. Is the Period of Rapidly Declining Adult Mortality in the United States Coming to an End? American Journal of Public Health 73:1091–1093.

Crimmins, Eileen M. 1981. The Changing Pattern of American Mortality Decline, 1940–77, and Its Implications for the Future. Population and Development Review 7:229–254.

———. 1983. Recent and Prospective Trends in Old Age Mortality. Paper presented at Annual Meetings of American Association for the Advancement of Science, Detroit, MI, May.

Davis, Karen. 1975. Equal Treatment and Unequal Benefits: The Medicare Program. Milbank Memorial Fund Quarterly 53:449–488.

Davis, Kingsley. 1984. Wives and Work: The Sex Role Revolution and Its Consequences. Population and Development Review 10:397–417.

Davis, Kingsley, and Pietronella van den Oever. 1982. Demographic Foundations of New Sex Roles. Population and Development Review 8:495–511.

Deimling, Gary T. 1982. Macro- and Microlevel Age Service Planning and the 1980 Census. The Gerontologist 22:151–152.

Demeny, Paul. 1984. A Perspective on Long-Term Population Growth. Population and Development Review 10:103–126.

Dorn, Harold F. 1950. Pitfalls in Population Forecasts and Projections. Journal of the American Statistical Association 45:311–334.

Dowd, James J., and Vern L. Bengtson. 1981. Aging in Minority Populations: An Examination of the Double Jeopardy Hypothesis. *In* Cary S. Kart and Barbara B. Manard (eds.), Aging in America: Readings in Social Gerontology (2nd ed.). Sherman Oaks, CA: Alfred Publishing Company, Inc., pp. 348–365.

Eisdorfer, Carl. 1975. Some Variables Relating to Longevity in Humans. *In* Adrian M. Ostfeld and Don C. Gibson (eds.), Epidemiology of Aging. U.S. Department of Health, Education and Welfare. Washington, D.C.: U.S. Government Printing Office, pp. 97–107.

Espenshade, Thomas J., and Rachel Eisenberg Braun. 1983. Economic Aspects of an Aging Population and the Material Well-Being of Older Persons. *In* Matilda White Riley, Beth B. Hess and Kathleen Bond (eds.), Aging in Society: Selected Reviews of Recent Research. Hillsdale, NJ: Lawrence Erlbaum Associates, pp. 25–51.

Ewbank, Douglas C. 1981. Age Misreporting and Age-Selective Underenumeration: Sources, Patterns and Consequences for Demographic Analysis. National Academy of Sciences. Washington, D.C.: National Academy Press.

Feshbach, Murray. 1984. On Infant Mortality in the Soviet Union: A Comment. Population and Development Review 10:87–90.

Fischer, David H. 1977. Growing Old in America. New York: Oxford University Press.

Fowles, Donald. 1983. The Changing Older Population. Aging 339:6–11.

Frankfather, Dwight L., Michael J. Smith, and Francis G. Caro. 1981.Family Care of the Elderly: Public Initiatives and Private Obligations. Lexington, MA: D.C. Heath.

Giele, Janet Zollinger. 1982. Family and Social Networks. *In* Robert H. Binstock, Wing-Sun Chow and James H. Schulz (eds.), International Perspectives on Aging: Population and Policy Challenges. New York: United Nations Fund for Population Activities, pp. 41–74.

Glick, Paul C. 1979. The Future Marital Status and Living Arrangements of the Elderly. The Gerontologist 19:301–309.

Grinblat, Joseph. 1982. Aging in the World: Demographic Determinants, Past Trends and Long-Term Perspectives to 2075. World Health Statistics Quarterly 35:124–132.

Halliday, M. L., and T. W. Anderson. 1977.Adjustment Factors in Mortality Statistics. Journal of the American Medical Association 238:2025–2026.

Hanley, R. 1984. Results from the 1982 Long-Term Care Survey: Age, Ethnicity and Gender Differences in Daily Activity Limitations among Elderly in the Community. Paper presented at Annual Meeting of Gerontological Society of America, San Antonio, Texas, November.

Heaton, Tim. 1983. Recent Trends in Geographical Distribution of the Elderly Population. *In* Matilda W. Riley, Beth B. Hess and Kathleen Bond (eds.), Aging in Society: Selected Reviews of Recent Research. Hillsdale, NJ: Lawrence Erlbaum Associates, pp. 95–113.

Heaton, Tim, William B. Clifford, and Glenn V. Fuguitt. 1980. Changing Patterns of Retirement Migration: Movement Between Metropolitan and Nonmetropolitan Areas. Research on Aging 2: 93–104.

Hendricks, Jon, and C. Davis Hendricks. 1977. Aging in Mass Society: Myths and Realities. Cambridge, MA: Winthrop.

Hermalin, Albert I. 1966. The Effect of Changes in Mortality Rates on Population and Age Distribution in the United States. Milbank Memorial Fund Quarterly 44:451–469.

Hickey, Tom. 1980. Health and Aging. Monterey, CA: Brooks/Cole.

Ishikawa, Akira. 1984. The 36th Abridged Life Tables: 1982–1983. Jinko Mondai Kenkyu (The Journal of Population Problems) 169: 64–71.

Jackson, Jacquelyne J. 1980. Minorities and Aging. Belmont, CA: Wadsworth Publishing Company.

Jain, S.P. 1980. Census Single Year Age Returns and Informant Bias. Demography India 9:286–296.

Johnston, Denis F., and Sally L. Hoover. 1982. Social Indicators of Aging. *In* Matilda White Riley, Ronald P. Abeles and Michael S. Teitelbaum (eds.), Aging from Birth to Death. Vol. II: Sociotemporal Perspectives. Boulder, CO: Westview, pp. 197–215.

Kane, Robert, and Rosalie A. Kane. 1980. Long-Term Care: Can Our Society Meet The Needs of Its Elderly? Annual Review of Public Health 1:227–253.

Keyfitz, Nathan. 1978. Improving Life Expectancy: An Uphill Road Ahead. American Journal of Public Health 68:954–956.

Keyfitz, Nathan, and Wilhelm Flieger. 1968. World Population: An Analysis of Vital Data. Chicago, IL: University of Chicago Press.

Kitagawa, Evelyn M., and Philip M. Hauser. 1973. Differential Mortality in the United States: A Study in Socioeconomic Epidemiology. Cambridge, MA: Harvard University Press.

Kleinman, J.C., J.J. Feldman, and M.A. Monk. 1979. The Effects of Changes in Smoking Habits on Coronary Heart Disease Mortality. American Journal of Public Health 69:795–802.

Laslett, Peter. 1976. The Societal Development and Aging. *In* Robert H. Binstock and Ethel Shanas (eds.), Handbook of Aging and the Social Sciences. New York: Van Nostrand Reinhold Company, pp. 87–116.

Lee, Everett S. 1980. Migration of the Aged. Research on Aging 2: 131–135.

Lewis, Myrna. 1982. Aging in the People's Republic of China. International Journal of Aging and Human Development 15:79–105.

Longino, Charles F., Jr. 1982. The Impact of Population Redistribution on Service Delivery. The Gerontologist 22:153–159.

Longino, Charles F., Jr., and Jeanne C. Biggar. 1981. The Impact of Retirement Migration on the South. The Gerontologist 21:283–290.

Lopez, Alan D., and Kyo Hanada. 1982. Mortality Patterns and Trends among the Elderly in Developed Countries. World Health Statistics Quarterly 35: 203–224.

Macfadyen, David M. 1982. Introduction to World Health Statistics Quarterly Special Issues on Public Health Implications of Aging. World Health Statistics Quarterly 35:120–123.

Maddox, George L. 1982. Challenges for Health Policy and Planning. In Robert H. Binstock, Wing-Sun Chow and James H. Schulz (eds.), International Perspectives on Aging: Population and Policy Challenges. New York: United Nations Fund for Population Activities, pp. 127–158.

Manton, Kenneth G. 1980. Sex and Race Specific Mortality Differentials in Multiple Cause of Death Data. The Gerontologist 20:480–493.

Manuel, Ron C. (ed.). 1982. Minority Aging. Westport, CT: Greenwood Press.

Markides, Kyriakos S. 1983. Minority Aging. In Matilda White Riley, Beth B. Hess and Kathleen Bond (eds.), Aging in Society: Selected Reviews of Recent Research. Hillsdale, NJ: Lawrence Erlbaum Associates, pp. 115–137.

Mathisen, R. W., and R. B. Mazess. 1981. A Revised Method for the Calculation of Life Expectancy Tables from Individual Death Records which Provides Increased Accuracy at Advanced Ages. Human Biology 53:35–45.

Mazess, R.B., and S.H. Forman. 1979. Longevity and Age Exaggeration in Vilcabamba, Ecuador. Journal of Gerontology 34:94–98.

Mazess, R.B., and R.W. Mathisen. 1982. Lack of Unusual Longevity in Vilcabamba, Ecuador. Human Biology 54:517–524.

Menzel, Paul T. 1983. Medical Costs, Moral Choices: A Philosophy of Health Care Economics in America. New Haven, CT: Yale University Press.

Meyers, Allan R. 1980. Ethnicity and Aging: Public Policy and Ethnic Differences in Aging and Old Age. In Elizabeth W. Markson and Gretchen R. Batra (eds.), Public Policies for an Aging Population. Lexington, MA: D. C. Heath, pp. 61–79.

Morris, Robert. 1980. Social Welfare Policy and Aging: Implications for the Future—Between the Good Earth and Pie in the Sky. In Elizabeth W. Markson and Gretchen R. Batra (eds.), Public Policies for an Aging Population. Lexington, MA: D.C. Heath, pp. 121–131.

Mossey, Jana M., and Evelyn Shapiro. 1982. Self-Rated Health: A Predictor of Mortality among the Elderly. American Journal of Public Health 72:800–808.

Myers, George C. 1978. Cross-National Trends in Mortality Rates among the Elderly. The Gerontologist 18:441–448.

———. 1982. The Aging of Populations. In Robert H. Binstock, Wing-Sun Chow and James H. Schulz (eds.), International Perspectives on Aging: Population and Policy Challenges. New York: United Nations Fund for Population Activities, pp. 1–40.

―――. 1983. Demographic and Socio-Economic Aspects of Population Aging. Paper presented at CICRED Conference, Montreal, Canada, October.

Myers, George C., and Constance A. Nathanson. 1982. Aging and the Family. World Health Statistics Quarterly 35:225–238.

Myers, Robert J. 1966. Validity of Centenarian Data in the 1960 Census. Demography 3:470–476.

Nam, Charles B., Norma L. Weatherby and Kathleen A. Ockay. 1978. Causes of Death Which Contribute to the Mortality Crossover Effect. Social Biology 25:306–314.

National Council on the Aging, Inc. 1981. Aging in the Eighties: America in Transition. (Survey conducted by Louis Harris & Associates, Inc.)

Neugarten, Bernice L. 1974. Age Groups in American Society and the Rise of the Young-Old. The Annals of the American Academy of Political and Social Science 415:187–198.

―――. 1978. The Future and the Young-Old. In Lissy F. Jarvik (ed.), Aging into the 21st Century: Middle-Agers Today. New York: Gardner Press, pp. 137–152.

―――. 1982. Policy for the 1980s: Age or Need Entitlement? In idem (ed.), Age or Need? Public Policies for Older People. Beverly Hills, CA: Sage Publications, pp. 19–32.

Omran, Abdel R. 1977. Epidemiological Transition in the U.S. Population Bulletin 32(2). Washington, D.C.: Population Reference Bureau.

Orbach, Harold L. 1983. Introduction to Symposium on Aging, Families, and Family Relations: Behavioral and Social Science Perspectives on Our Knowledge, Our Myths, and Our Research. The Gerontologist 23: 24–25.

Palmore, Erdman. 1982. Predictors of the Longevity Difference: A 25–Year Follow-Up. The Gerontologist 22:513–518.

Pampel, Fred C. 1981. Social Change and the Aged: Recent Trends in the United States. Lexington, MA: D.C. Heath.

Parant, Alain. 1978. Les Personnes Agées en 1975 et le Vieillissement Démographique en France (1931–1975). Population 33:381–412.

Petri, Peter A. 1982. Income, Employment, and Retirement Policies. In Robert H. Binstock, Wing-Sun Chow and James H. Schulz (eds.), International Perspectives on Aging: Population and Policy Challenges. New York: United Nations Fund for Population Activities, pp. 75–126.

Place, Linda Funk. 1981. The Ethnic Factor. In Forrest J. Berghorn, Donna E. Schafer and Associates (eds.), The Dynamics of Aging: Original Essays in the Processes and Experiences of Growing Old. Boulder, CO: Westview Press, pp. 195–228.

Preston, Samuel H. 1984. Children and the Elderly: Divergent Paths for America's Dependents. Demography 21:435–457.

Reimers, David M. 1981. Post-World War II Immigration to the United States: America's Latest Newcomers. The Annals of the American Academy of Political and Social Science 454:1–12.

Rice, Dorothy P., and Jacob J. Feldman. 1983. Living Longer in the United States: Demographic Changes and Health Needs of the Elderly. Milbank Memorial Fund Quarterly 61:362–396.

Rosenwaike, Ira. 1968. On Measuring the Extreme Aged in the Population. Journal of the American Statistical Association 62:29–40.

———. 1979. A New Evaluation of United States Census Data on the Extreme Aged. Demography 16:279–288.

Rosenwaike, Ira, Nurit Yaffe, and Philip C. Sagi. 1980. The Recent Decline in Mortality of the Extreme Aged: An Analysis of Statistical Data. American Journal of Public Health 70:1074–1080.

Rosenwaike, Ira, and Barbara Logue. 1983. Accuracy of Death Certificate Ages for the Extreme Aged. Demography 20:569–585.

Schulz, James H. 1980. The Economics of Aging (2nd ed.). Belmont, CA: Wadsworth Publishing Company.

Sclar, Elliott. 1980. Aging and Economic Development. In Elizabeth W. Markson and Gretchen R. Batra (eds.), Public Policies for an Aging Population. Lexington, MA: D.C. Heath, pp. 29–38.

Sheldon, Henry D. 1958. The Older Population of the United States. New York: John Wiley and Sons, Inc.

Shryock, Henry S., and Jacob S. Siegel. 1973. The Methods and Materials of Demography. U.S. Bureau of the Census. Washington, D.C.: U.S. Government Printing Office.

Siegel, Jacob S., and Jeffrey S. Passel. 1976. New Estimates of the Number of Centenarians in the United States. Journal of the American Statistical Association 71:559–566.

Siegel, Jacob S. 1980a. On the Demography of Aging. Demography 17:345–364.

———. 1980b. Recent and Prospective Demographic Trends for the Elderly Population and Some Implications for Health Care. In Susan H. Haynes and Manning Feinleib (eds.), Proceedings of the Second Conference on the Epidemiology of Aging. Washington, D.C.: National Heart, Lung, and Blood Institute and National Institute on Aging, pp. 289–315.

Siegel, Jacob S., and Sally L. Hoover. 1982. Demographic Aspects of the Health of the Elderly to the Year 2000 and Beyond. World Health Statistics Quarterly 35:133–202.

Soldo, Beth J. 1980. America's Elderly in the 1980s. Population Bulletin, Vol. 35, No. 4. Washington, D.C.: Population Reference Bureau.

Soltero, I., K. Liu, R. Cooper, et al. 1978. Trends in Mortality from Cerebrovascular Diseases in the United States, 1960 to 1975. Stroke 9:549–558.

Stamler, J. 1978. Lifestyles, Major Risk Factors, Proof and Public Policy. Circulation 58:3–19.

Stoto, Michael A. 1983. The Accuracy of Population Projections. Journal of the American Statistical Association 78:13–20.

Streib, Gordon F. 1983. The Frail Elderly: Research Dilemmas and Research Opportunities. The Gerontologist 23:40–44.

Stuart, Reginald. 1983. 'Old Old' Grow in Numbers and Impact. New York Times. June 20.

Stub, Holger R. 1982. The Social Consequences of Long Life. Springfield, IL: Charles C. Thomas.

Susser, Mervyn. 1969. Aging and the Field of Public Health. In Matilda White Riley, John W. Riley, Jr. and Marilyn E. Johnson (eds.), Aging and Society. Vol. II: Aging and the Professions. New York: Russell Sage Foundation, pp. 114–160.

Sweden Statistika Centralbyran. Various Years. Sveriges Officiella Statistik. Befolkningsförändringar. Stockholm: Government Publishing House.

Taeuber, Irene B., and Conrad Taeuber. 1971. People of the United States in the 20th Century (A Census Monograph). Washington, D.C.: U.S. Government Printing Office.

Tas, R.F.J. 1982. Living and Deceased Persons Aged One Hundred Years or Over in the Netherlands, 1830–1982. Maandstatistiek van de Bevolking 30(11):16–27.

Thatcher, A.R. 1982. Discussions of the Span of Life. Journal of the Institute of Actuaries 109:346–349.

Uhlenberg, Peter, and Mary Anne P. Meyers. 1981. Divorce and the Elderly. The Gerontologist 21:276–282.

United Kingdom Office of Population Censuses and Surveys. 1982. Census 1981: Historical Tables, 1801–1981: England and Wales. London: Her Majesty's Stationery Office.

———. 1983. Census 1981: Sex, Age and Marital Status: Great Britain. London: Her Majesty's Stationery Office.

United Nations. Various Years. Demographic Yearbook. New York: United Nations.

———. 1973. The Determinants and Consequences of Population Trends: New Summary of Findings on Interaction of Demographic, Economic and Social Factors (Vol. 1). New York: United Nations.

———. 1982. Levels and Trends of Mortality Since 1950. New York: United Nations.

United States Bureau of the Census. 1897. Compendium of the Eleventh Census: 1890. Part III. Washington, D.C.: U.S. Government Printing Office.

———. 1906. Twelfth Census of the United States: 1900. Special Reports. Supplementary Analysis and Derivative Tables. Washington, D.C.: U.S. Government Printing Office.

———. 1913.Thirteenth Census of the United States: 1910, Vol. I. Population 1910 General Report and Analysis. Washington, D.C.: U.S. Government Printing Office.

———. 1933. Fifteenth Census of the United States: 1930 Population, Vol. II. Washington, D.C.: U.S. Government Printing Office.

———. 1943. Sixteenth Census of the United States: 1940, Vol. II. Characteristics of the Population, Part 1, U.S. Summary. Washington, D.C.: U.S. Government Printing Office.

———. 1953a. U.S. Census of Population: 1950, Vol. II. Characteristics of the Population, Part 1, U.S. Summary. Washington, D.C.: U.S. Government Printing Office.

———. 1953b. U.S. Census of Population: 1950. Institutional Population. Special Report P-E (2C). Washington, D.C.: U.S. Government Printing Office.

———. 1963. U.S. Census of Population: 1960. Inmates of Institutions. Final Report PC(2)-8A. Washington, D.C.: U.S. Government Printing Office.

———. 1964. U.S. Census of Population: 1960, Vol. I. Characteristics of the Population, Part 1, U.S. Summary. Washington, D.C.: U.S. Government Printing Office.

———. 1965. U.S. Census of Population: 1960. Nativity and Parentage. Final Report PC (2)–1A. Washington, D.C.: U.S. Government Printing Office.

———. 1972a. Census of Population: 1970. General Population Characteristics, Final Report PC (1)-B1, U.S. Summary. Washington, D.C.: U.S. Government Printing Office.

———. 1972b. Public Use Samples of Basic Records From the 1970 Census: Description and Technical Documentation. Washington, D.C.: U.S. Government Printing Office.

———. 1973a. Census of Population: 1970. National Origin and Language. Final Report PC(2)–1A. Washington, D.C.: U.S. Government Printing Office.

———. 1973b. Census of Population: 1970. Persons of Spanish Origin. Subject Report, PC(2)–1C. Washington, D.C.: U.S. Government Printing Office.

———. 1973c. Census of Population and Housing, 1970. Evaluation and Research Program. The Medicare Record Check: An Evaluation of the Coverage of Persons 65 Years of Age and Over in the 1970 Census. PHC(E)–7. Washington, D.C.: U.S. Government Printing Office.

———. 1973d. Census of Population: 1970. Detailed Characteristics, Final Report PC (1)-D1, U.S. Summary. Washington, D.C.: U.S. Government Printing Office.

———. 1973e. Census of Population: 1970. Persons in Institutions and Other Group Quarters. Final Report PC (2)–4E. Washington, D.C.: U.S. Government Printing Office.

———. 1974. Estimates of the Population of the United States, by Age, Sex and Race: April 1, 1960 to July 1, 1973. Current Population Reports, Series P–25, No. 519. Washington, D.C.: U.S. Government Printing Office.

———. 1975. Projections of the Population of the United States: 1975 to 2050.

Current Population Reports, Series P–25, No. 601. Washington, D.C.: U.S. Government Printing Office.

———. 1977. Projections of the Population of the United States: 1977 to 2050. Current Population Reports, Series P–25, No. 704. Washington, D.C.: U.S. Government Printing Office.

———. 1979. Siegel, Jacob S. Prospective Trends in the Size and Structure of the Elderly Population, Impact of Mortality Trends and Some Implications. Current Population Reports, Series P–23, No. 78. Washington, D.C.: U.S. Government Printing Office.

———. 1981. Social and Economic Characteristics of Americans During Midlife. Current Population Reports, Series P–23, No. 111. Washington, D.C.: U.S. Government Printing Office.

———. 1982a. Preliminary Estimates of the Population of the United States, by Age, Sex, and Race: 1970 to 1981. Current Population Reports, Series P–25, No. 917. Washington, D.C.: U.S. Government Printing Office.

———. 1982b. Projections of the Population of the United States: 1982 to 2050 (Advance Report). Current Population Reports, Series P–25, No. 922. Washington, D.C.: U.S. Government Printing Office.

———. 1982c. Census of Population and Housing, 1980: Summary Tape File 2. Technical Documentation. Washington, D.C.: U.S. Government Printing Office.

———. 1983a. Census of the Population: 1980, Vol. I. Characteristics of the Population. Chapter B, General Population Characteristics, Part 1, U.S. Summary. Washington, D.C.: U.S. Government Printing Office.

———. 1983b. Census of the Population: 1980, Vol. I. Characteristics of the Population. Chapter C, General and Social Economic Characteristics, Part 1, U.S. Summary. Washington, D.C.: U.S. Government Printing Office.

———. 1983c. Census of Population and Housing: 1980, Public-Use Microdata Samples. Technical Documentation. Washington, D.C.: U.S. Government Printing Office.

———. 1984a. Census of the Population: 1980, Vol. I. Characteristics of the Population. Chapter D, Detailed Population Characteristics, Part 1, U.S. Summary. Washington, D.C.: U.S. Government Printing Office.

———. 1984b. Estimates of the Population of the United States, by Age, Sex, and Race: 1980 to 1982. Current Population Reports, Series P–25, No. 929. Washington, D.C.: U.S. Government Printing Office.

———. 1984c. Spencer, Gregory. Projections of the Population of the United States, by Age, Sex, and Race: 1983 to 2080. Current Population Reports, Series P–25, No. 952. Washington, D.C.: U.S. Government Printing Office.

———. 1984d. Siegel, Jacob S., and Maria Davidson. Demographic and Socioeconomic Aspects of Aging in the United States. Current Population Reports, Series P–23, No. 138. Washington, D.C.: U.S. Government Printing Office.

United States Department of Health, Education and Welfare. 1979. Health, United States, 1979. Chapter 1, "Health Status of Minority Groups." Washington, D.C.: U.S. Government Printing Office.

United States Health Care Financing Administration. Annual. Medicare: Health Insurance for the Aged and Disabled. Washington, D.C.: U.S. Government Printing Office.

————. Annual. Unpublished tabulations, various years. Job 5234, Actuarial Enrollment Data.

————. 1983. Annual Medicare Program Statistics: 1981. Washington, D.C.: U.S. Government Printing Office.

United States National Center for Health Statistics. Annual. Vital Statistics of the United States. Vol. II-Mortality. Washington, D.C.: U.S. Government Printing Office.

————. 1968. Comparability of Age on the Death Certificate and Matching Census Records, U.S., May-August 1960. Vital and Health Statistics, Series 2, No. 29. Washington, D.C.: U.S. Government Printing Office.

————. 1975. Klebba, A.J., and A.B. Dolman. Comparability of Mortality Statistics for the Seventh and Eighth Revisions of the International Classification of Diseases. Vital and Health Statistics, Series 2, No. 66. Washington, D.C.: U.S. Government Printing Office.

————. 1979. The National Nursing Home Survey: 1977 Summary for the United States. Vital and Health Statistics, Series 13, No. 43. Washington, D.C.: U.S. Government Printing Office.

————. 1981. Hing, Esther. Characteristics of Nursing Home Residents, Health Status, and Care Received: National Nursing Home Survey, U.S., May-December 1977. Vital and Health Statistics, Series 13, No. 51. Washington, D.C.: U.S. Government Printing Office.

————. 1982a. Advance Report of Final Mortality Statistics, 1979. Monthly Vital Statistics Report 31(6) Supplement. Washington, D.C.: U.S. Government Printing Office.

————. 1982b. Fingerhut, L. Changes in Mortality Among the Elderly: United States, 1940–78. Vital and Health Statistics, Series 3, No. 22. Washington, D.C.: U.S. Government Printing Office.

————. 1983a. Advance Report of Final Mortality Statistics, 1980. Monthly Vital Statistics Report 32(4) Supplement. Washington, D.C.: U.S. Government Printing Office.

————. 1983b. Feller, B. Americans Needing Help to Function at Home. Advance Data from Vital and Health Statistics, Series 3, No. 92. Washington, D.C.: U.S. Government Printing Office.

————. 1983c. Rice, D.P., H.M. Rosenberg, L.R. Curtin and T.A. Hodgson. Changing Mortality Patterns, Health Services Utilization, and Health Care Expenditures: United States, 1978–2003. Vital and Health Statistics, Series 3, No. 23. Washington, D.C.: U.S. Government Printing Office.

————. 1983d. Ries, Peter W. Americans Assess Their Health. Data from the National Health Survey, Series 10, No. 142. Washington, D.C.: U.S. Government Printing Office.

————. 1983e. Hing, E., M.G. Kovar, and D. Rice. Sex Differences in Health and Use of Medical Care, United States, 1979. Vital and Health Statistics, Series 3, No. 24. Washington, D.C.: U.S. Government Printing Office.

————. 1984a. Fingerhut, L. Changes in Mortality among the Elderly: United States, 1940–78: Supplement to 1980. Vital and Health Statistics, Series 3, No. 22a. Washington, D.C.: U.S. Government Printing Office.

————. 1984b. Graves, E.J. Utilization of Short-Stay Hospitals, United States, 1982, Annual Summary. Vital and Health Statistics, Series 13, No. 78. Washington, D.C.: U.S. Government Printing Office.

————. 1984c. Advance Report of Final Mortality Statistics, 1982. Monthly Vital Statistics Report 33(9) Supplement. Washington, D.C.: U.S. Government Printing Office.

————. 1984d. Vital Statistics of the United States, 1980. Vol. II—Life Tables. Washington, D.C.: U.S. Government Printing Office.

United States Senate, Special Committee on Aging. 1983. The World Assembly on Aging. *In* idem, Developments in Aging, Vol. I. Washington, D.C.: U.S. Government Printing Office, pp. 535–563.

United States Social Security Administration. Annual. Medicare: Health Insurance for the Aged and Disabled. Washington, D.C.: U.S. Government Printing Office.

————. Annual. Unpublished tabulations, various years. Job 5234, Actuarial Enrollment Data.

————. 1978. Bayo, F.R., H.W. Shiman, and B.R. Sobus. United States Population Projections for OASDHI Cost Estimates. Actuarial Study No. 77. Washington, D.C.: U.S. Government Printing Office.

————. 1983. Faber, Joseph F., and Alice H. Wade. Life Tables for the United States: 1900–2050. Actuarial Study No. 89. Washington, D.C.: U.S. Government Printing Office.

————. 1984. Wade, Alice H. Social Security Area Population Projections, 1984. Actuarial Study No. 92. Washington, D.C.: U.S. Government Printing Office.

Verbrugge, Lois M. 1983. Women and Men: Mortality and Health of Older People. *In* Matilda White Riley, Beth B. Hess and Kathleen Bond (eds.), Aging in Society: Selected Reviews of Recent Research. Hillsdale, NJ: Lawrence Erlbaum Associates, pp. 139–163.

————. 1984. Longer Life but Worsening Health? Trends in Health and Mortality of Middle-Aged and Older Persons. Milbank Memorial Fund Quarterly 62:474–519.

Warlick, Jennifer L. 1983. Aged Women in Poverty: A Problem without a

Solution? *In* William P. Browne and Laura Katz Olson (eds.), Aging and Public Policy: The Politics of Growing Old in America. Westport, CT. Greenwood Press, pp. 35–66.

Watson, Wilbur. 1982. Aging and Social Behavior: An Introduction to Social Gerontology. Monterey, CA: Wadsworth Publishing Company.

White House Conference on Aging. 1981. Chartbook on Aging in America. Washington, D.C.: U.S. Government Printing Office.

Wilkin, John C. 1981. Recent Trends in the Mortality of the Aged. Transactions of the Society of Actuaries 33:11–44.

Wilson, Ronald W. 1984. How Good Are Health Data from Health Surveys? Paper presented at Annual Meeting of American Statistical Association, Philadelphia, PA, September.

Wilson, Ronald W., and Thomas F. Drury. 1984. Interpreting Trends in Illness and Disability: Health Statistics and Health Status. Annual Review of Public Health 5:83–106.

Wiseman, Robert F. 1980. Why Older People Move: Theoretical Issues. Research on Aging 2:141–154.

Wiseman, Robert F., and Curtis C. Roseman. 1979. A Typology of Elderly Migration Based on the Decision-Making Process. Economic Geography 551:324–337.

World Health Organization. 1977. Manual of the International Statistical Classification of Diseases, Injuries and Causes of Death. Ninth Revision. Geneva: World Health Organization.

Yuzawa, Yasuhiko. 1977. The Aged and Family Life: The Trends of Supports for the Aged. Asian Medical Journal 20:753–761.

Index

About the Author

IRA ROSENWAIKE is a Research Specialist at the University of Pennsylvania. He is the author of *Population History of New York City* and numerous articles on demographic and public health topics which have been published in *Demography, American Journal of Public Health, American Journal of Epidemiology, American Journal of Sociology, Human Biology,* and *Journal of the American Statistical Association.*